MY HEROES

RANULPH
FIENNES
MY HEROES

HODDER &
STOUGHTON

First published in Great Britain in 2011 by Hodder & Stoughton
An Hachette UK company

1

Copyright © Ranulph Fiennes 2011

A CIP catalogue record for this title is available from the British Library

Hardback ISBN 978 1 444 72242 0
Trade Paperback ISBN 978 1 444 72243 7
eBook ISBN 978 1 444 72244 4

Typeset in Sabon MT 12.25/16 pt by
Palimpsest Book Production Limited, Falkirk, Stirlingshire

Printed and bound by Clays Ltd, St Ives plc

Hodder & Stoughton policy is to use papers that are natural,
renewable and recyclable products and made from wood grown in sustainable
forests. The logging and manufacturing processes are expected to conform to the
environmental regulations of the country of origin.

Hodder & Stoughton Ltd
338 Euston Road
London NW1 3BH

www.hodder.co.uk

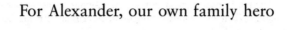

For Alexander, our own family hero

Contents

Introduction

A few days after becoming the oldest Briton to summit Mount Everest, and the first to do so with a bus pass, I was asked by my long-time publisher, Hodder, to write a book on the subject of heroes.

'Why,' I asked, 'choose me?' 'Because,' was the quick reply, 'you must meet a lot of heroes on your expeditions, and when you select your expedition teams, you must be on the lookout for brave individuals.'

My reaction was immediate disagreement, but I did like the idea of rereading my favourite war stories and selecting some valiant Victoria Cross winners. So I agreed to the Hodder offer and started my research, only to discover that I quickly became bored by tales of successive waves of brave men charging machine-guns and being bravely blown to bits. Although not a natural cynic, I also began to question the degree of heroism exhibited by a good many of these VC-winning machine-gun-chargers because I vaguely remembered having once, long ago, charged machine-guns myself, and I suspected that my motives for having done so were definitely not heroic ones.

Checking back through forty-year-old dusty files, I found a faded citation for the Sultan's Bravery Medal that the Queen had awarded me in 1969. It cited six occasions, with comments such as 'Captain Fiennes coolly rallied his men and conducted a skilful withdrawal (his only possible course), frequently exposing himself to aimed enemy fire and firing the .50 Browning himself.' And, 'a swift advance by Fiennes on to a dominating piece of ground forced the enemy to withdraw.' And, 'throughout this and other operations, Fiennes has set the highest example of dogged determination, tactical skill and physical courage. His independent operations have proved the ascendency of a small force over larger enemy groups on many occasions.'

A good many of the Victoria Cross citations I studied sounded very similar, so I checked back in my diary from the 1968–9 days which described my personal impressions of various contacts with the Marxist guerrilla forces, some of which did sound quite hairy. But one thing that stood out very clearly from my diary comments was that my greatest fear at the time was not that of injury or death so much as the fear of appearing to be a coward in front of the sixty brave men in my reconnaissance platoon. Their opinion of me was of paramount importance, almost an obsession, and this was abundantly obvious from the diaries.

So, if my own medal-winning, gung-ho advances on the enemy were based, as with hindsight I could clearly see was the case, entirely on fear of peer disdain, then surely the same may well have been true of a great many Victoria Cross recipients.

This line of thought made me check the CVs of VC winners, and this led to the discovery that quite a few were subsequent deserters, thieves and drunkards. When it was suggested in the 1920s that the medals of such characters be officially confiscated, the King (George V) declared that, even if a VC winner were to be hanged for murder, he should be allowed to wear his VC on the scaffold.

Another of my reasons for deciding not to concentrate on medal-winning heroes was the plethora of books that already existed on the topic, including a brace by the recently ousted prime minister, Gordon Brown.

So I thought about my personal heroes and realised that, if I had any, they are my late wife Ginny, who never flinched from making brave decisions in all the thirty-six years that we were together, and two male relatives, neither of whom I had ever met but about whose lives I had been told many a memorable story by my mother since I was little. They are my father and my grandfather, both dead just before I was born, whose lives fighting for God, King and Country in various parts of the world had so impressed me in my youth.

To help me decide on individuals whose heroism appealed to me most, I read a great many biographies and made many lists of possible nominees. The following chapter discusses some of these nominees and some of the generally accepted characteristics of heroism.

Your Heroes?

In July 2010 a nightclub bouncer, whose greatest pride was the size of his steroid-assisted biceps and whose domestic history included beating up women friends, was jilted by his twenty-two-year-old girlfriend, Sam. Raoul Moat, thirty-seven, reacted by shooting her and killing her reputed lover. Then, on the rampage with a brace of shotguns, he shot and blinded a policeman who happened to be parked in a nearby police car. Moat was hunted for a week before finally shooting himself when cornered by police marksmen after a six-hour stand-off.

A Facebook tribute page immediately appeared which set Moat up as a legend (popular-speak for 'hero'). This Internet site, 'RIP Raoul Moat You Legend', attracted 38,000 supporters, and was followed by the creation of a second similar fan-site glorifying the murderer which had over 12,000 subscribers and the stated aim 'so that the legend that is Moat lives on'. Weeping Moat disciples laid wreaths at his Gateshead home and in the village of his demise, for to them Moat was truly a hero and an updated, if distorted, version of Robin Hood.

A strong contender as a nominee for my hero collection was the Polish prisoner, Slavomir Rawicz, who with six fellow inmates escaped from one of Stalin's gulags and managed to trek thousands of hostile miles to freedom in India via

Siberian forests, Mongolian deserts and the high Himalayas. I had read his book, *The Long Walk*, as a teenager, and was saddened in 2004 to hear of his death, aged eighty-eight, in the Nottinghamshire village where he had lived for many years following his fabled escape. I was about to submit my chapter about the Slavomir Rawicz story to the publishers when I happened to pass a vast billboard advertising *The Way Back*, the Hollywood movie version of the heroic trek. Interested, I looked up the film critics' comments, only to discover that the whole Slavomir Rawicz story was almost certainly a fabrication which for fifty years had hoodwinked the world, including me.

You will not be surprised that neither Raoul Moat nor Slavomir Rawicz made it to hero status in this book, and after my Rawicz shock, I tightened up my hero selection process by extra carefully checking on the accuracy of their recorded histories.

Back at school in the 1950s my heroes were the, mostly British, commando raid leaders, clever detectives, daring explorers or pioneering ships' captains whose exciting deeds were described in the comics which constituted my entire source of learning (outside classroom hours). The only non-Brits whose imaginary exploits also thrilled me were the American super-heroes, Batman and Superman (who, along with Spider-Man, are currently all played in their ongoing Hollywood movies by British actors).

In the classroom studying Classics as a young teenager, I thrilled to the adventures of Jason and the Argonauts, the Spartan warriors of Thermopylae, and that greatest of all heroes – Odysseus (Ulysses) of Ithaca, as he battled exotic monsters such as the one-eyed Cyclops and the snake-haired Medusa.

As early as the mid-nineteenth century, Thomas Carlyle, the most eloquent of writers about heroism since the chroniclers of ancient Greece, wrote: 'In these days . . . the thing I call Hero-worship professes to have gone out, and finally ceased.' Today's hero-worship mostly involves the world of those celebrities whose talents and antics sell newspapers and excite bloggers. The pursuit of excellence in many sports can quickly elevate athletes to hero status, whether they be models of good behaviour such as Michael Jordan of basketball fame or foul-mouthed footballers like Wayne Rooney. Sexy singers who look and sound good, or at least different, can obtain heroic (aka superstar) status if not overnight then at least as quickly as their media-savvy agents can manage it. I suspect, and indeed hope, that a century from now Ulysses and Spartacus will be more readily remembered as deserving heroic status than the likes of Elvis Presley and Lady Gaga.

There are, of course, thousands of 'niche heroes' known to and admired by the groupies of their specific sport or art. Daredevil skiers, rock climbers, kayakers and other adrenalin-pumping, high-risk practitioners, as well as the breakers of speed records such as the late Donald Campbell who was killed on the job, often obtain a limited hero status.

I researched the experiences of many people whose heroism appeared to me to stem from different motives. Many fought for freedom or equality, such as Gandhi, Mandela, Solzhenitsyn, Aung San Suu Kyi, Wei Jingsheng, and those who protested in Tiananmen Square. A student from Qinghua University, one of 50,000 students and 100,000 citizens present at the Tiananmen massacre, wrote: 'I'd be lying if I said we weren't afraid but . . . we were imbued with a lofty sense of mission.

We were prepared to sacrifice ourselves for China's democracy and progress.'

In 2011 many countries experienced uprisings, aided by the Internet, against dictators. Some of these, as in Syria, the Yemen and Libya, were met with violence. This so-called Arab Spring involved considerable courage by many thousands of protesters, young and old.

Also in 2011 the governor of Punjab was murdered, as a few weeks later was the Minister for Minorities of Pakistan's ruling party. Both men were from their country's Christian community (5 million in a population of 180 million), and both had knowingly risked their lives by speaking out against Pakistan's blasphemy laws which impose the death penalty on anyone deemed to insult Islam. Both men were true heroes in their commitment to justice for all.

In 2011 it is estimated by the European Union that 42 per cent of women in Turkey are seriously abused within their families, despite laws in that country to prevent such abuse. Yet Turkey is far more advanced in the field of human rights issues than a great many of its neighbours. For a woman in many, mainly Islamic-ruled, countries, to fight for the rights of her sex requires great courage.

Afghani writer, Hirsi Ali, writes of one such heroic woman, Malalai Joya, who grew up under the sexist cruelties of the Taliban. 'To get a seat in [the Afghan] parliament and refuse to be silent in the face of the Taliban . . . shows true fiber. When Malalai Joya did this, her opponents responded in the usual way: expulsion from parliament, warnings, intimidation and attempts to cut her life short. She has survived all of it.' The Taliban has assassinated hundreds of women for daring to challenge their sexist laws, and the bravery of the likes of

Malalai Joya impresses me even more than the earlier efforts of Emmeline Pankhurst and her fellow suffragettes.

There are global heroes whose achievements have made life better for millions, such as Marie Curie through her research into cancer treatment, but I have chosen my subject matter more for their courage than for their knowledge, skills and dedication.

I have steered clear of individuals whose bravery and self-sacrifice, whilst deemed heroic by some, is considered merely fanatical by others. Suicide bombers and factional political martyrs come under this heading. Roger Casement, for instance, was a great hero to the Irish but not to the British who executed him. Equally, Jean McConville probably warrants a whole chapter, but I will only mention the bare outline of her single instinctive act of heroism and its outcome, since to many of her fellow countrymen she was misguided in her act of humanity.

At the height of the Northern Irish sectarian troubles in 1972, Roman Catholic widow Jean was observed giving aid to a wounded British soldier after a gun battle outside her Belfast door. As punishment for this treasonable behaviour, a masked IRA gang broke into her home at night and dragged her into a waiting car. She was never seen again by her ten orphaned children aged fourteen and under who were for many years themselves subjected to persecution. Jean's subsequent torture, including the cutting off of her fingers, was followed by her murder and burial at a secret site not to be discovered for the next thirty-one years. Even today some would brand Jean as a traitor to her own people. Others would say her single act of conscience stands for humanity over violence and hatred.

I have studied the lives of a disparate group of individuals whose courage gave them lasting fame, at least in their own countries, and who, in my opinion, were true heroes of conscience although their various background situations were very different. Under this heading I include the likes of William Wilberforce and John Brown (he of the soul which 'goes marching on') who fought for the freedom of slaves. And Mother Teresa, whose concern was poverty and disease; Dian Fossey who died to save gorillas in the Congo from death by poachers; and Mordechai Vanunu, the archetypal whistle-blower. Vanunu was a former Israeli nuclear technician who, citing his opposition to weapons of mass destruction, revealed details of Israel's secret nuclear weapons programme to the media in 1986. He has been imprisoned in Israel, on and off, ever since.

Helping Jews escape the gas chamber during and before the Second World War was hazardous in the extreme, and thousands of non-Jewish Poles were executed or died in concentration camps for doing just that. Of the many Jew-saving heroes, the most famous must be the Swedish diplomat Raoul Wallenberg, whose brazen daring, cunning and dedication saved some 100,000 Jews from a cruel death.

The most unlikely of all Jew-saviours was Albert, the brother of Hermann Goering, an anti-Nazi who saved dozens of Jews by trading on his brother's all-powerful position in the Nazi hierarchy. He once turned up with a big lorry at a German factory and, by using Hermann's name, ordered the factory owner to assemble fifty or so Jewish slave workers. He packed them into the truck, drove them to a wood near the border with Switzerland, and shepherded them across to safety. No one made him do it: he just thought he ought to.

He was a womaniser and a drunk, and he died soon after the war with his courage unrecognised.

Witold Pilecki was a Polish officer in his mid-forties who volunteered to get himself arrested by the Nazis in order to be imprisoned in a huge new camp called Auschwitz, with the specific aim of then sending reports back to Polish intelligence as to the goings-on inside this camp. He soon learnt about, and indeed witnessed, the horrors of the gas chamber and the details of Nazi genocide plans. Pilecki seized every chance between 1940 and 1943 to get news of the Holocaust out to the Allies, and it was hardly his fault that senior officers in London simply failed to believe that such inhumanity by man to man was possible, and so they did nothing. Pilecki eventually escaped from Auschwitz and survived the disastrous Warsaw uprising, but was executed as a Polish spy by the Soviets in 1948.

Giovanni Falcone, born in Mafia-infested Palermo in the 1930s, became an anti-Mafia judge, but in the 1970s was helpless due to lack of funds or support from the Italian government. Many of his associates were murdered, often in front of their families, and few judges were brave enough to take on anti-Mafia cases. Thanks to Falcone's dedication over ten years of meticulous investigation work, he and a dozen other Sicilian judges, many of whom were later murdered, managed to commit 350 Mafiosi, including top Godfathers, to trial and imprisonment. But Falcone was always aware that his days were numbered. In 1989 after a narrow escape from a poolside bomb, he wrote: 'My life is mapped out: it is my destiny to take a bullet by the Mafia some day.' In 1992 Falcone, his wife and three bodyguards were blown to bits by a half-ton bomb buried under a motorway. Thousands attended his funeral, for Sicilians appreciated full well the extent of his courage.

An Irish version of Falcone, although a journalist not a judge, was Veronica Guerin who wrote for the Dublin-based *Sunday Independent*. In 1994, investigating local drug dealers, she started to receive death threats, bullets were fired at her home and, on her doorstep, a caller shot a bullet through her leg. In 1995 a convicted criminal told her that he would rape her young son if she wrote about him. Guerin ignored this and many other threats, continuing to fight Irish criminals through the power of her pen. Some miles outside Dublin on 16 June 1996 a motorbike drew up beside her car, and she was shot six times through the head.

There are heroes like Falcone and Guerin all over the world and down through the ages.

Whilst I was in Afghanistan with John Simpson, the BBC's senior and longest-serving foreign correspondent, John observed:

Some of the greatest heroes I've come across are usually unimportant characters who can't any longer take the wrongdoing they see around them. For instance, there was a mayor of a horrible little drugs town in the Peruvian jungle whom I came across, who simply didn't want to be part of the general corruption linked to the cocaine trade.

Immediately after being elected he went to a meeting with the army and police commanders, where they offered him the usual mayoral fee for turning a blind eye to the drugs flights out of the town. He refused it. Everyone at the meeting laughed and thought he was looking for a bigger cut. When they realised he thought it was immoral, he started to have difficulties. Then he decided to go public about the murders the army were carrying out in the town, as well as the drug smuggling. He was lucky to survive, but he did. The army commander was later gaoled, and the mayor was a big local hero.

John Simpson was and is to my mind a hero in his own right who for thirty years and more has risked his skin to tell the world the truth about many injustices and horrors, often in countries from which he had previously been evicted but then re-entered in secret. One such country was Zimbabwe, whose murderous dictatorship has also blacklisted Peter Godwin, one of the heroes of this book.

Heroes of many an urban scenario all over the world are the have-a-go individuals who, knowing full well the danger to themselves, nonetheless intervene to stop gangsters and bullies beating up or raping innocent parties. One example from many happened on a Munich commuter train when two seventeen-year-olds with knives robbed four schoolchildren. All fellow train passengers did nothing except for a fifty-year-old businessman, Dominik Brunner, who asked the knife-wielders to leave the children alone. Brunner was knocked to the ground and kicked to death, as are the vast majority of have-a-go heroes.

The Australian *People Magazine* in 1999 commented: 'There is a special category [of hero] . . . made up of people whose heroism crystallizes in a single moment of selflessness – who tempt fate for the sake of others.' This aptly describes the small group of passengers aboard United Airlines Flight 93 who attacked their al-Qaeda hijackers and forced them to crash in Pennsylvania rather than on their probable intended target, the US Capitol in Washington DC.

Turning from have-a-go heroes of Germany and the USA to those of France, I think almost automatically of Joan of Arc, but the Frenchman I most admire is Émile Zola, not for his great novels but for his stubborn defence of Captain Dreyfus, the only Jew in the French War Office who, in 1895, was sent to prison on Devil's Island for passing French secrets to the German embassy. Anti-semitism was rife at the time, especially in the French Army, government and judiciary. The French media fanned the flames of Fascism and any man who dared attempt a defence of poor Dreyfus became instantly a figure of hate and a traitor to the nation. So the previously well-liked Zola who, convinced of Dreyfus's innocence, took up his cause in court, was threatened with his life, made intensely unpopular and impoverished, and was sentenced to imprisonment. Only after he had died was Dreyfus eventually pardoned and Zola's courage exonerated.

One chapter of this book is devoted to a hero of faith and belief, one to a great survivor and one to those who, loving a challenge for its own sake, pit themselves and their skills against great natural dangers. Another focuses on the courage fostered within close family groups caught in situations of unimaginable horror.

London police officer Dick Coombes, who I met many years after his life had been ruined by a single act of great bravery, behaved as he did out of inbuilt loyalty to his colleagues, which is a feature of many 'in the line of duty' stories. Under such a heading I considered a Welsh ship's officer who was a hero of the *Titanic* disaster, and Captain 'Sully' Sullenberger, who in January 2009 managed to ditch his passenger aircraft in New York's Hudson River after both engines were disabled by bird-strike soon after take-off from

LaGuardia Airport. In doing so he saved 155 lives, and described the moments before the crash as 'the worst sickening, pit-of-your-stomach, falling-through-the-floor feeling' he had ever experienced.

Bodyguards who shield presidents, popes and royalty have on several occasions proved their bravery by physically taking bullets meant for their bosses. Firefighters, such as those reacting to 9/11, and many a lifeboat crew have showed great courage and paid with their lives in saving others. Specialists in reacting to dangerous but rare technical problems may never test their mettle. Others, like the nuclear workers called in to make safe damaged reactors at Fukushima, following the earthquake and tsunami disaster there, knowingly exposed themselves day after day to ever-increasing levels of deadly radiation. Pioneering astronauts and test pilots share great danger whenever they take off on maiden flights. The slightest engineering error may well see them blown to bits, or even lost in space.

The above 'line of duty' heroes are all civilians, and I explained in the Introduction why I have avoided Victoria Cross winners. But there are, as I write this, daily stories of bravery emanating from Afghanistan. Bomb disposal stories have been told in many biographies, as nerve-racking today with Taliban Improvised Explosive Devices (IEDs) as during the Blitz of 1940 with unexploded bombs. Equally well documented are the heroics of fighter pilots in the Battle of Britain and of the crews of Bomber Command in their flying coffins packed with incendiaries, high-explosive bombs and thousands of gallons of high-octane fuel.

The fear felt by every bomber crew member prior to take-off for another mission must have been made far worse by the sheer statistics of death or at least of horrific burns injuries. Forty-four thousand out of 125,000 crew members involved were killed. On a night raid in April 1944, when one engine of his Lancaster bomber caught fire, crew member Norman Jackson climbed out along the wing with a fire extinguisher. This, despite an ongoing attack by a German fighter, an air temperature many degrees below zero, a speed of 200 mph and an altitude of 22,000 feet. I include this astonishing feat despite the fact that Jackson did receive a VC for his action.

War stories of great fortitude under Gestapo or Japanese torture have included those of the men and women of the Special Operations Executive (SOE) dropped into Gestapo territory, caught and tortured. One, Odette Hallowes, emerged from Ravensbrück concentration camp at the end of the war crippled and emaciated. Violette Szabo, who parachuted twice into occupied France, fared even worse. Also tortured, she gave away nothing and was shot through the head, aged twenty-three.

As research progresses into the psychological effects of wars on their protagonists, more is known of the lasting mental effects of great trauma, now termed Post-Traumatic Stress Disorder (PTSD). More British soldiers killed themselves *after* the Falklands War due to PTSD than died during the actual fighting. The charity Help for Heroes is doing great things for the hundreds of injured soldiers with mental and physical war wounds of varying degrees of severity, but the personal courage of these soldiers remains a very real ingredient in 'making the best of a bad deal', and Simon Weston, badly burnt during the Falklands War, is a fine example of just such inner spirit.

The heroes, or groups of heroes, whose actions, taken against a backdrop of terror, are described in this book make me feel truly proud to be a fellow human being, and I hope they will have the same effect on you.

I

Hunted

'Fortune favours the brave'
Terence, 190–159 BC

To hide and to survive in a hostile land whose inmates want to kill you requires certain specialist skills and the ability to react with speed, not haste, when things go wrong.

This is the art of the men and women of the Special Forces who, at short notice, can be inserted behind enemy lines, often hundreds of miles from possible assistance, in order to complete some specific assignment such as the assassination of a known top terrorist or the demolition of a key road bridge.

Rule number one for such squads is to do the job without being seen and to escape before your presence is even suspected.

But if things go wrong and you become the hunted, you may experience a very special sort of fear, the fear of the fox as the baying of hounds gets closer. To panic at such a time is all too easy and can lead to a wrong move, a faulty decision that will seal your fate. To keep your nerve as your enemy closes in and your options rapidly diminish, that is the true test of your mettle, and I know no finer example of a hunted man who saved his own life by keeping his nerve under conditions of extreme stress than the story of Marcus Luttrell.

Marcus was, in June 2005, one of a four-man squad of Navy SEALS, the most elite unit of all American Special Forces, heli-dropped into the epicentre of a Taliban-held mountain stronghold in Afghanistan's remote Hindu Kush region. Their mission was to locate and kill a notorious al-Qaeda leader named Ben Sharmak, then known to be active in or near a particular mountain village with his own armed group of some 200 mountain fighters.

Marcus, a six-foot-four-inch Texan, when later explaining the aim of that fateful June operation into the Hindu Kush, simply wrote: 'This was payback time for the World Trade Center. We were coming after the guys that did it. If not the actual guys, then their blood brothers, the lunatics who still wished us dead and might try it again.' And summarising his opinion of his own unit, the SEALS, he wrote of '. . . our unspoken invincibility . . . the silent code of the elite warriors of the US Armed Forces . . . Big, fast, highly trained guys . . . armed to the teeth, expert in unarmed combat and so stealthy no one ever hears us coming. Our SEALS philosophy runs, "I will never quit. I persevere and thrive on adversity. My Nation expects me to be physically harder and mentally stronger than my enemies. If knocked down, I will get back up, every time. I will draw on every remaining ounce of strength to protect my teammates and to accomplish our mission. I am never out of the fight."'

I once spent a year as an officer with the 22nd Special Air Service Regiment, and a year with their Reserve Squadron as a trooper. The former unit was considered by the rest of the British Army to be their most efficient Special Force, but I never saw a written version of their philosophy other than their motto 'Who Dares Wins'. And if the men of 22 SAS did consider themselves invincible, they were far too frightened to admit as much openly for fear of having the mickey taken by their colleagues. Whatever the outward differences in style between the Yank and the Brit Special Forces, both groups are made up of soldiers from various backgrounds who have passed extreme tests of endurance, both physical and mental, which have identified them as very special alpha males.

The reason why the Hindu Kush operation of Marcus Luttrell and his three SEAL teammates turned to tragedy was simply because, despite their macho, Robo-killer image, there are times when SEALS, to their own detriment, allow their hearts to rule their heads.

There were three other men of the elite, 'invincible' SEALS in Luttrell's squad who were trained to act individually or in ruthless harmony as a long-range reconnaissance group. Luttrell wrote of 'a strictly American brotherhood, mostly forged in blood. Hard-won, unbreakable . . . Built on a shared patriotism, shared courage and shared trust in one another . . . There is no fighting force in the world quite like us.'

All four men had beards in the bushy style of the Taliban. Luttrell's best friend, Lieutenant Mike Murphy, was thirty years old, a highly trained lawyer turned soldier. About the same age, Matt Axel Axelson was, like Luttrell, six-foot-four-inches and immensely strong. The fourth SEAL, Danny Dietz, was, at thirty-seven, the granddaddy of the squad who, back at his New Hampshire home, was a devoted husband and father to seven children. He spoke fluent Russian, not that this was of any help to the squad, since the only Russians in the area, and there were thousands of them, were the scattered skeletons of Soviet soldiers killed earlier by the same mountain Pashtun fighter bands as would soon begin their deadly hunt for Luttrell, Mike, Axel and Danny. Danny was a close friend of Luttrell's from his SEAL training days and an expert in martial arts.

After much nocturnal zigzagging and false landings, the Chinook dropped Luttrell's squad at their agreed drop-off point and disappeared noisily into the darkness to make several more dummy landings. For many minutes after their arrival, the squad froze to the ground without a movement, savouring the utter silence of the mountain escarpment.

They knew they were some four miles from the village and, although at least 10,000 feet above sea level on their wrist barometer gauges, they would have a considerable climb still to make over extremely steep mountainsides, knowing that they must be in position and invisible before daylight.

The squad headed silently in near darkness towards the village where Intel had pinpointed their target terrorist leader, Ben Sharmak. The date was 27 June 2005 and the squad knew exactly how vulnerable they would be at all times until their mission was completed or aborted. Ben Sharmak had with him a force of some 200 mountain fighters, all from the Pashtun tribe, who knew every hidden pathway and crag-top village in the region.

The squad had been fully briefed about the Pashtun and their unpredictable clannish ways. Blood feuds between neighbours, families and sub-tribes could last for generations. US Intelligence estimated that 42 per cent of all Afghans were Pashtuns – over 12 million of them, whilst in Britain there are 88,000, and 48,000 in the USA. Pashtunis form the backbone of the Taliban fighting force in the twenty-first century, just as they provided most of the mujahideen armies fighting the Soviet invaders in the twentieth century.

In their very own mountains, these men of the Taliban made for a highly capable enemy, but Luttrell stressed (in his account of the disastrous action to follow) that SEALS, and to some extent all modern soldiers who fight terrorists, live with an entirely different, but ever-present, fear on their minds. He expressed it thus: 'We have an extra element of fear and danger when we go into combat against the Taliban or al-Qaeda . . . the fear of the American media and their unfortunate effect on American politicians. We all detest them, partly for their lack of judgement, mostly because of their ignorance and their toe-curling opportunism . . . The first minute an armed combat turns into a media war, the news becomes someone's opinion, not hard truths. When the media gets involved in the United States, that's a war you've got a good chance of losing because the restrictions on us are immediately amplified, and that's sensationally good news for our enemy.'

Luttrell, after dwelling on the numerous restrictions placed on SEALS at war, pointed out that the Taliban have no media fears but simply get on with their standard methods of enforcement, torture, mutilation, beheading, live burials, stonings and lashings. Suicide and car bombings kill and maim mostly innocent women and children who are 99 per cent Muslim. Luttrell's summary was: 'The Taliban are right up there with the monsters of history.'

For all the verbal bravado about being 'invincible and unstoppable', Luttrell and his mates experienced the same basic emotions as any other human about to head into known hostile territory with a high chance of dying violently and soon. In one of his less gung-ho moments, Luttrell admitted: 'It was pretty damn creepy for us because this was the heartland of terror . . . the homeland of bin Laden's fighters . . . our enemy was brutal, implacable, with no discernible concern about time or life.'

As the four SEALS crept along faint mountain pathways, their specific aim was always at the forefront of their awareness. They had studied photos of Sharmak, their target, and of the village he had recently frequented. He and his men, the SEALS also knew, must never outstay their welcome in any one of the high, craggy hamlets where village elders held near-complete control over their population and, although Pashtun, they could, if riled, withdraw cooperation and render life a lot less comfortable for the local Taliban.

Sharmak, US Intel declared, had killed many US Marines by various means, usually bombs in cities. He was well-educated, spoke five languages, numbered among his close friends a certain Osama bin Laden, and was highly trained in military tactics.

Sharmak would clearly be more useful to the CIA and the FBI, both of whom wanted him badly, alive rather than dead. Luttrell's squad's orders were to 'just find this bastard, nail him down, his location and troop strength, then radio in for a direct action force to come in by air and take him down'.

After several false alarms, US Intel had determined that

Sharmak's band was definitely in residence in the mountains close to the target village on whose hospitality they were currently dependent.

So Luttrell, Axel, Mike and Danny, prior to leaving their base, had studied the layout of each of the thirty-two houses in the target village so that, although they did not know exactly which house Sharmak himself used as his headquarters, they knew that they must by daylight insert themselves somewhere on the steep mountainside with a very clear sniper's sight view of the village and its approaches.

When not away on missions of their own, the members of Sharmak's force were fully aware that US Intel was desperate to locate them, and they were adept at spotting any unusual movement in the mountains around their chosen stamping grounds. They would detect a 'normal' US Army unit approaching their host village in no time at all.

SEAL squads like Luttrell's, however, had spent weeks and months, first in training and later on many previous Afghanistan operations, perfecting the meticulous fieldcraft skills needed to move from A to B in all types of terrain, whilst remaining virtually invisible to hostile watchers with or without night vision facilities.

The four men carried M4 rifles, grenades, 350 rounds of ammunition each, emergency beacons, surveillance gear and four days of field rations.

The Chinook 47 helicopter that took the squad to their drop-off point, first dropped off two other SEAL patrols near an old Russian base, Asadabad, where in the late 1980s Afghan fighters had surrounded the Russian garrison, infiltrated the base and slaughtered all the enlisted men.

Rain clouds came from nowhere and the men were soon

soaked. And cold. They followed slippery mountain paths with nearly sheer drops below and cliffs above. They slid, caught at roots or rocks and cursed the mud. Gnarled trees with shoulder-high tangled branches caught at their heavy backpacks and their weapons, but they reached the ridgeline and came upon a well-used footpath, a likely Taliban route to the target village.

Moonlight between rain showers and fleeting banks of fog outlined their silhouettes from time to time, and this they dreaded. Whenever thick undergrowth or fields of high grass gave them cover, they relaxed. When they smelt goat dung they knew a hut or village was close by and moved to the flanks to avoid the risk of barking dogs. When confronted by a sudden cliff or big drop, Axel, the navigator, would use his NODS, night vision goggles, to scan the near horizon for a better route.

At some point, to avoid traversing a part of the summit plateau with no cover, Axel decided to descend to the valley floor between two forested spurs, then up the far side to regain the escarpment only an hour before dawn. Eventually they found a good hide below the ridgeline and overlooking the target village about one and a half miles away.

As successive banks of fog blocked their view, they realised that a further move was needed and, a thousand yards back along the ridge, they came to a rocky redoubt with enough undergrowth to burrow into cover. The sun rose, dried their clothes and it became, in Luttrell's words, 'hotter than hell'. The four men sat and waited, their binoculars scanning every movement in the village far below.

Without warning, a youth with a turban and an axe appeared immediately behind Luttrell and, a few minutes later, two other men with a hundred or so goats materialised as it seemed from nowhere.

This was a no-win situation and one about which Special Forces handbooks are specific, the accepted solution being to avoid compromise by silencing any local who has clearly spotted your presence. This may seem harsh, but let me give examples of reacting in a more humane way to such chance discovery by unarmed civilians.

In the 1960s, not long before I joined the SAS, one of their long-range patrols was operating, just like Luttrell's squad, deep inside enemy territory in the Radfan mountains of Southern Yemen. A shepherd boy happened to blunder into the SAS men's hide and a heated discussion followed with many of the patrol trying to persuade their captain to slit the shepherd's throat. The officer clearly found the thought of cold-bloodedly murdering an innocent teenager distasteful and let the lad go. Within hours the British patrol were surrounded by the Radfan's version of the Taliban and, in the ensuing battle, two of the SAS men were captured. The officer, Captain Robin Edwards, and Trooper John Warburton were badly beaten before their heads were cut off. Some time later the Radfanis proudly marched around the Yemeni capital with the SAS men's heads impaled on poles.

A couple of years later, on a two-year posting to the army of the Sultan of Oman, I led a patrol of sixteen Muslim soldiers, all volunteers, into a remote enemy-held region of the Dhofar mountains. I knew that if things went wrong there would be no friendly forces to come to our rescue, no helicopters to remove the wounded, no medics and no stretchers. My instructions were to meet up with a guide and then move overnight to observe a hidden village where, according to intelligence, two key Marxist commissars were likely to visit. I was to capture them and escape to the safety of the desert region north of the Marxist-held mountains.

Soon after sending me out on this mission, my commanding officer learnt that my force was less than half its normal size due to sickness and, unable to make radio contact, he sent the Sultan's supply aeroplane, a Beaver, to drop red flares as a warning for me to abort the operation. Failing to appreciate the meaning of the flares and desperate to reach cover above the village before daylight, I pressed on. As in Afghanistan, Dhofari villages are detectable from a distance, even on the darkest of nights, thanks to their noxious smell of goat dung, so I was careful to skirt all habitation and the inevitable village dogs.

Arriving just before dawn on a grassy knoll high above the designated village, I searched its perimeter by telescope and spotted groups of armed men digging defensive works on the far southern edge of the village. I checked that the rest of my men were well hidden among boulders and crept into a bushy thicket overlooking a steep path which climbed up our hillside from the village.

The key to survival when this deep into enemy-held mountains was to remain unseen. Our guide, supplied by the Sultan's intelligence officer, was a Dhofari mountain man from the Mahra tribe who said that he hated the Marxists. My men did not trust him. Like them, I could only speak Omani Arabic and not the *jebali* (mountain men) dialect of this Mahra. But he seemed to be saying that we must wait in our bushy hide because Marxist soldiers, including the wanted commissars, would soon, he was sure, pass by on their way to or from the village.

I suffered a bad attack of diarrhoea, which was embarrassing in the close confines of the bush beside my three
Omani soldier friends, and even more so when, unexpectedly,
there appeared on the footpath a few yards ahead of us two
jebalis with flintlock rifles and a small herd of goats.

One of my men, Said Salim, nineteen years old, ran his
fingers across his throat, his eyebrows raised with the silent
enquiry. Should he silence these men? Unable to make up my
mind but realising that we were already in serious trouble, I
merely aimed my semi-automatic FN rifle at the two men
and Said beckoned them into our bush hide with his index
finger on his lips. During the next two hours, as the heat
mounted steadily, seven more *jebalis*, including a woman and
two children, came by our thicket, saw us and the beckoning
black snout of Said's Bren gun and wisely joined us in our
cramped and stinking lair.

Even before the arrival of the woman and children, I had
already realised that I did not have the courage to order the
slitting of our interlopers' throats. This was despite the fact
that I knew very well the story of the SAS men's fate in the
Radfan and I had always promised myself and my men that,
given such a predicament, I would never risk all our lives by
failing to silence anyone or anything (like a goat) likely to
compromise us deep inside hostile territory.

A single shout in the *jebali* tongue from any one of our
hostages would be enough to alert the *adoo* (our name for
the Marxist forces), who would quickly cut us off with no
hope of rescue or reinforcement.

In my case (but sadly not in Luttrell's) Allah intervened
when the two commissars, easily identifiable by the hexagonal
red star badges on their forage hats, appeared without

warning on their way from the village and on the goat path some fifteen yards from our overcrowded thicket.

The first man stopped abruptly, seeming to sniff the air. His face was scarred, his hair close shaven. I watched fascinated as the Kalashnikov, its ugly round magazine cradled in his elbow, swung around slowly as the man turned to face us. A Kalashnikov is an unpleasant weapon; a touch of its trigger will squeeze off a long rip of hollow-nosed 7.62 bullets that rip bone apart and pass through a man's guts like papier mâché.

Inch by inch I lifted my rifle. The sun was in the east behind the man, outlining him. Only his shadow falling upon the thicket shielded my eyes, stinging with sweat, from direct glare. He peered directly at me now. I remember thinking, he has seen us. He is weighing his chances.

My voice seemed to come of its own volition. 'Drop your weapons or we kill you.'

The big man reacted with incredible speed, twisting at the knee and bringing the Kalashnikov to bear in a single fluid movement.

I squeezed the trigger automatically. The guerrilla was slammed back as though caught in the chest by a sledgehammer. His limbs spread like a puppet and he cartwheeled out of sight down the grassy slope.

Behind him, the other man paused for a minute, unsure what to do. I noticed his face beneath the jungle cap. He looked sad and faintly surprised. His rifle, a Mark 4 .303, was already pointed at my stomach when a flurry of shots rang out. Said Salim, forcing himself over our hostage bedu, fired at the *adoo*'s head.

The man's face crumpled into red horror; his nose and eyes

smashed back into his brains. Further bullets then tore through his ribs and a pretty flowering thorn bush caught his body at the top of the grassy slope.

Said Salim crawled on his belly from the thicket. There might be other *adoo* behind these two. Expertly he searched the nearest corpse, bringing back rifle, ammunition and a leather satchel stuffed with documents.

I glanced south; the bush was glinting with movement, dark forms scurrying towards us through scrub. There was little time for making decisions; my other sections would be awaiting orders. I flicked the transmit switch of my National walkie-talkie, no longer bothering to whisper. 'All stations 5. Withdraw now . . . over.'

Fatigue forgotten, the men needed no encouragement and broke from their hides to fan out in a long straggling line. Speed was our only hope and the men moved with the wings of fear. Shots sounded from behind, passing overhead like vengeful hornets. We literally fled north for our lives and with no regard to any military formation. But we moved too fast for the *adoo* to cut off our retreat and, exhausted but alive, we descended the northern cliffs and reached the safety of the desert and our hidden Land Rovers by midday.

Soon afterwards, on an operation in steep mountain country with the colonel of my regiment accompanying my men on an ambush, three goatherds with some 400 goats arrived slap in the middle of our ambush position. Again, I failed to have them killed, and five hours later, on our way down the mountain, we were ourselves caught in a well-prepared ambush which can only have been put in place on information from the goatherds.

My two experiences of exposure by nomadic goatherds

were like blueprints of what happened to Luttrell's SEALS squad. They too realised that a perilous but still workable mission had suddenly turned deadly, and the only way of possibly saving their own skins would be by killing the Afghan goatherds who had discovered their presence above the village.

The four Americans argued the case for and against executing the unarmed goatherds. They tried to contact their headquarters to ask for a direct command. But, for some reason, the radio was dead. Axel recommended execution. 'We're on active duty behind enemy lines, sent here by our senior commanders. We have a right to do everything we can to save our own lives. The military decision is obvious. To turn them loose would be wrong.'

Mike and Danny were ambivalent, so the casting vote went to Luttrell, who said, 'We gotta let them go.' So they did, and immediately they had done so they realised their chilling predicament. Luttrell recorded: 'It was the stupidest, lame-brained decision I had ever made in my life. I had cast a vote which I knew could sign our death warrant.'

The squad had not yet identified any sign of their specific target, Sharmak's Taliban force, and their position was easy to cut off, they had lost radio contact with the outside world and, therefore, any hope of help, and they had, through their own fault, almost certainly alerted Sharmak's forces as to their presence as an easily isolated prey.

'What now?' Danny broke into their gloomy reverie.

They had to move. So, in the midday glare, they followed their own outward trail back to a point on the upper flank of the mountain, still above the village but in the dense bush that covered the precipitous mountainside, an incline where, if you missed your footing, you would bounce rather than

fall free but still reach the village a thousand feet or more
down below. Jammed into tree roots and well hidden, the
four men lay in wait.

An hour passed by in silence but for an occasional sound
from the village.

Then Luttrell heard a soft 'Alert!' sound from Mike over to
his right. He followed the direction Mike's rifle was pointing,
straight up the mountain to the open ground above the treeline
at Taliban fighters, heavily armed with fully automatic AK-47
rifles and, many of them, with rocket-propelled grenades.
Other groups were out to the flanks and also descending.

Luttrell's immediate reaction was to curse to hell the three
goatherds and, equally, himself 'for not executing them when
every military codebook ever written had taught me otherwise'. The squad could definitely not escape uphill. Ever more
Taliban were appearing up there as he watched, and others
were already moving down both flanks into the bush and
trees to either side of their position. The four Americans kept
motionless, but then, hearing a twig crackle, Luttrell saw a
turbaned fighter not twenty yards away, his AK-47 pointed
directly at Luttrell's head, so he squeezed the trigger and, at
that range, literally blew the man's face away.

A huge volume of enemy fire responded in seconds, with
well over a hundred automatic weapons opening up, all aimed
into the brush where the Americans lay hidden. They fought
back with well-aimed shots. Each was a trained sniper, and
a dozen Taliban were quickly downed.

For a long five minutes the firefight continued without a
lull. The trees and rocks around the squad took a great
amount of the steel impact but, as the encirclement process
slowly progressed, the squad knew that they must move

elsewhere, and the only way to go was clearly down. That entailed an almost sheer drop. Luttrell and Mike, close together, tried to move with care, but they slipped and cartwheeled from bush to bush, legs flailing, backpacks crashing off tree trunks and rocks, until they arrived at a copse of trees on a sloping ledge with a slightly less severe gradient than elsewhere. They reached this copse and grabbed desperately at passing branches, but their downward velocity was such that they passed through it and, like skiers off a ramp, plummeted into the void below.

Soon afterwards Danny and Axel landed nearby, and the four men, all badly scratched and bruised, jammed themselves in the crux of two great fallen trees. Rockets exploded all about them. A bullet ripped right through Mike's stomach and blood seeped down his trousers. Much of Danny's right hand, including his thumb, was shot away, but, gritting his teeth, he slotted a new magazine into his rifle and joined the others in systematically killing successive Taliban as they crossed his ever-deadly sights. All his attempts to date, he confirmed to the others, had failed to make radio contact.

All Luttrell's gear in his backpack and belt-packs had been ripped away during his fall so, along with his food and his water bottles, his medical bag was gone. Through sheer good luck his ammunition magazine pouches and his rifle were still with him.

The Taliban, as they followed the squad down the mountainside, were hell-bent on outflanking and encircling them, so the Americans, fully aware of this, agreed to continue their hairy descent in stages. They estimated that they had to date killed fifty Talibanis and that, at most, some 150 remained. Maybe, just maybe, they could account for most of the remainder by the time they had climbed or dropped down the rest of the mountainside and reached the village.

Such optimistic, or at least positive, thinking, despite the dire circumstances, was the result, at least in part, of their Special Forces training. Never give up until you have breathed your last and your last man is down. A philosophy that encourages stubborn drop-dead heroism.

The enemy fighters soon began to outflank their new position, and shrapnel from rifle-fired grenades burst all about their tree trunk redoubt. Once the Taliban flanking group could fire uphill at the squad, the game would be up. Luttrell reckoned that a dozen SEALS could have held out with odds of ten to one. But the situation was, in fact, thirty-five to one, and so retreat was the only way to survive. He knew that given good cover and flat ground all around them, the four of them *could* still hold out, and both such requisites would be immediately available if they could but make it down to the village and a solid house with flat open spaces around it.

Mike gave the order. 'Jump, guys, for fuck's sake, JUMP!' And they did, leaping off the rock lip immediately below their legs and landing many feet down on the mossy slope below. Even before they could find new cover the Taliban were shooting down at them, and a bullet, passing through Danny's back, came out of his stomach. He kept on shooting, every shot counting, but blood poured out of his mouth. Then grenades like mortar bombs exploded all around the new position and Danny was hit yet again, right through his neck. Somehow he propped his back against a rock and kept firing and changing his magazines.

Once again, on Mike's order, they jumped to yet a lower

series of ledges, and again all four made it still alive. But there a fourth bullet struck Danny, this one in the base of his neck. Luttrell grabbed his dying friend and dragged him to a wall of boulders. A Taliban who had sneaked close unseen appeared, but yards away, and raised his rifle to kill Luttrell. Axel shot the Afghani between his eyes.

The three men, dragging Danny, made one last downhill move as a squad. Then Axel was shot through the chest and head and yet another bullet cracked into Danny, this time in the face. Luttrell, under ever more accurate fire, had no choice but to leave Danny's body and join his two badly wounded comrades on their ever downwards flight towards the village, now plainly visible a mile or so below. The three survivors, tucked below low rocks, agreed that they had accounted for nearly a hundred Taliban. Some sixty or so remained, as intent as ever to kill the Americans.

Sensing that success was imminent, the Taliban sent a shower of Russian-made RPG rocket grenades into the rock cleft protecting the SEALS. Then, when the explosions and the dust had died away, they began again to use their rifles, all the while closing in.

Mike was shot through the chest. Axel's head wound bubbled gobs of dark blood and, as Luttrell kept up the only steady return fire, a dying Mike Murphy, their squad commander, moved away from the rock wall into open ground where his personal mobile phone might send a signal and began to punch in emergency numbers. He neatly summarised the squad's position, their extreme situation and the enemy's strength. Then, hit again through the back and chest, he stumbled back to a spot some way below where Luttrell and Axel were crouched. Taliban then crept close to Mike's body and, out of sight themselves, fired repeatedly into his corpse. Axel's eyes were by then blood-black, the sockets full from where half his face had been shot away. Before he died, he bade Luttrell tell his wife Cindy that he loved her.

Luttrell, alone now, was blown right out of the rocks by a grenade blast and hurled down the slope. He landed upside down in a dank hollow covered by tangled undergrowth. For a while he lost consciousness but, coming to, saw that his trousers had literally been blown away and his left leg, impregnated with grenade shrapnel, was a bloody mess. His nose was broken, his back felt as though it must have multiple fractures and neither of his legs would move.

He clutched at his rifle, miraculously still with him, and counted his magazines. Only one and a half still left. He was now entirely alone, unable to move and surrounded by an enemy who were well aware that only three bodies out of the four they had chased at such a deadly cost to their force had, as yet, been found. Luttrell knew that they would hunt him down.

But, as he was later to admit, he did not feel alone. Brought up as a Christian, he told himself that he was clearly meant to survive, because otherwise why would his rifle have stayed beside him though falling free and out of his grasp during at least three of his long tumbles down the mountain, and even during this last blast from the grenade? Additionally, it was surely some sort of statistical miracle that, under intense fire from up to 200 weapons for over an hour, he had not been hit by a single bullet.

So, his legs paralysed, Luttrell belly-crawled from the undergrowth to a narrow rock cleft in the very face of the mountainside, and there he waited, his rifle at the ready, as the searchers combed the slopes all around, whilst firing their rifles to flush him from his cover. To staunch the flow of blood from his leg and a deep head cut, he packed the open wounds with mud. He stayed still for hours on end listening to the ongoing search all about his hide. Some feeling returned to his legs. He felt dizzy and knew that he had lost a lot of blood. His wounds throbbed, but he had no painkillers and no plasters.

Some eight hours after he first reached his hide, he caught glimpses of his hunters searching other nearby mountain flanks quite far away but within his narrow field of vision. And then, abruptly, he saw them in groups running fast in a single direction intent on some specific goal or target. For a long while Luttrell would be ignorant as to the cause of this reprieve.

Not long afterwards, American fighter aircraft and helicopters flew past Luttrell's rocky cleft and he did his best, with his strobe light, to attract them. But nobody paid attention. He fired off his emergency distress beacon on his pouch-radio, even though he knew that the Taliban could use this to pinpoint his position. He knew that this was working because he could hear the voices of aircrew talking in his earpiece. But he was quite unable to talk back, for his throat was gummed up with dirt and his tongue was stuck to the roof of his mouth. He was desperately thirsty, but had no water. He knew that the Taliban had captured radios like his before and made dummy distress calls which lured helicopters, in response to emergency calls, to their demise by shoulder-fired missiles.

That evening, desperately thirsty, Luttrell flashed his strobe light whenever he heard a helicopter clatter by. At dusk when no help came, he decided to risk a sortie to find water, but just before trying to stand, he spotted a lone armed Taliban dead ahead on an opposing mountainside goat path who was clearly searching for him. If this man carried on his current traverse, he would surely find Luttrell, so he shot him and watched the body plummet off the cliff. Two more Taliban then appeared, and Luttrell disposed of them too. Three bullets: three Taliban.

Luttrell tried to think clearly and positively. There were almost certainly other groups out searching different sectors of the mountainside and sooner or later, with their normal tenacity, they would almost certainly pick up his trail. But he had to drink soon or he would die, so after darkness cloaked the hillside, Luttrell limped out of his hide and began his painful search for water. Each time he brushed against a branch with his wounded leg, from which the ends of shrapnel shards protruded, he moaned with pain. He would have sworn but had no voice, and any noise would in any case be inadvisable.

He was not to know it just then, but he had cracked three vertebrae in his lower spine during one of his falls and had torn the rotator cuff in his right shoulder. His back and shoulder felt broken, but his immediate focused concerns were water and rescue. No helicopter could reach him halfway up the mountainside so, to reach flat ground where it could, he must either go up or down. The latter choice, the village which was doubtless full of Sharmak's Taliban, was a no-brainer, so much as the thought of climbing back up the cliffside appalled him, the dogged and dazed Luttrell climbed into the darkness, hoping on his way up to cross one of the streams he had noticed on his earlier precipitous descent.

Sometimes, when not grasping a branch, he slipped, never knowing whether his fall would be blocked by a nearby obstacle or end with a long drop over a cliff. Then he heard voices, excited voices, at first way down below but, later on, much closer. Since he could hardly move his wounded leg at all and only with maximum clumsy effort, there was no way he could climb in silence without cracking branches and setting off rockfalls.

He realised his chances of losing his nocturnal hunters were minimal. Making very little height with his zigzag course, he once fell a hundred feet, but the damaged leg and vertebrae somehow survived enough to allow him, on will-power alone, to keep going. Eventually a group of three Taliban caught up with him, but their first surprise shot merely ripped through the fleshy part of one thigh and, finding protection in low-lying rocks, he took out the leader with a single shot and the other two with a grenade from his belt-pouch. After that he heard no more voices from behind and soon came to a cliff-top from where he heard the longed for sound of water.

At that point Luttrell either blacked out or his bad leg buckled. Either way he fell and bounced his way down the rocky slope to just below a pool. Unable to walk at all, he clawed his way to the water. It was, he recorded, the sweetest water he had ever tasted. Focused entirely on assuaging his thirst, he failed to notice three men standing right behind him. But when he did, and to his utter astonishment, they proved to be friendly.

Luttrell's amazing survival story, in so far as it depended largely on his steel-like determination to keep going against desperate odds, ended at that point due to a remarkable slice of good luck. I will not go into the details of precisely what happened except to say that two or three extremely plucky villagers, led by their elderly chief and his policeman son, decided to place Luttrell under their *lokhay*, or traditional village hospitality, a bond which cannot with honour be broken under any threat, even that of the Taliban who were, of course, soon alerted as to Luttrell's presence in the village where, near dead for a while, he was cared for and from time to time smuggled into hides prior to Taliban visits to kidnap him. *Lokhay* in essence charged the entire village to defend their guest against the Taliban, or anyone else wishing to harm Luttrell until, if necessary, every villager was dead.

On one occasion when his *lokhay* protectors were away, a Taliban group did find Luttrell. He pretended to be an American doctor and non-combatant, but they beat him up and broke both his wrists. He was saved by the arrival of the village elder who, Luttrell assumed, held power over Sharmak's Taliban because they were dependent for supplies on the hospitality of these mountain villagers and their leaders.

For much of his time in the village and in temporary hides nearby, Luttrell's *lokhay* protectors dulled his pain with copious doses of opium of the type that al-Qaeda feed to young suicide bombers before their missions. Gulab, the policeman son of the elder, soon received and showed Luttrell a missive sent to him from the chief of the Taliban Army of the north-east which demanded that the village elders hand over the American immediately.

Gulab's response, as he repeated it to Luttrell, had been along the lines of he was not frightened, his village was well armed with its own laws and rights and that they, the Taliban, needed the villagers' support more than the village needed the Taliban's. Nonetheless it was clear that Gulab and everybody in the village were increasingly apprehensive and, one night, the elder himself set out to walk to the nearest American base some forty miles away over the mountains to arrange for Luttrell to be picked up at a pre-agreed spot outside the confines of the village.

Whilst the old man was still on his way, American efforts to reach the squad included heavy bombing of the mountain slopes above the village, a parachute supply drop and the helicopter drop-off of a US Ranger platoon to find and rescue the squad.

Luttrell grew desperate lest the elder had failed to reach the US base and lest his friends in the village would soon suffer the full wrath of the Taliban. So, once his leg had recovered to the point where he could hobble when helped by two strong villagers, he agreed a plan with Gulab whereby they would creep by night through the Taliban watchers' lines and attempt to reach an American base.

On the fifth day of Luttrell's stay in and near the village the Taliban came back in force, firing volleys into the air and raiding the house where, until a short while before, Luttrell had been kept. They bullied the villagers, but nobody betrayed Luttrell's new whereabouts.

Gulab took Luttrell by night to a nearby field, a place ideal for a helicopter pick-up, but Sharmak himself, easily identified by Luttrell who had studied many photos of the Taliban chief, and his armed group lay in wait. With Gulab and his villagers protecting Luttrell, it was a stand-off.

Sharmak personally gave Gulab a Taliban missive, an official order and warning: 'Either you hand over the American or every member of your family will be killed.'

Then the Taliban melted away into the bush, leaving only armed groups of Gulab's men alert and defensive on the farmed outskirts of their village. Two of them took Luttrell's arms around their shoulders and set out on what he assumed was either his removal to a new *lokhay* hide or an attempt to reach the US base, somehow evading Taliban capture en route.

They had limped their way only a few hundred yards from the open field and along a forest path when, with no warning, they ran into the search patrol of twenty heavily armed US Rangers. Knowing Sharmak's men lay in wait on the slopes above the village, the Rangers called in the Air Force who strafed the entire mountainside with bombs and rockets before a Chinook arrived in the village opium field to evacuate all the Americans and Luttrell's saviour, Gulab.

On that flight out of hell, Luttrell learnt that, as soon as SEAL headquarters had picked up Mike's mobile phone emergency message, they had rushed an eight-man quick reaction SEAL team out by helicopter to land close to the point from which Luttrell's squad had originally begun their fatal mission.

By sheer bad luck, a nearby Taliban patrol witnessed the helicopter's arrival and fired a rocket-propelled grenade into its fuselage just as the rear ramp was being lowered. The fuel tanks exploded and all the occupants, including many of Luttrell's friends, were killed. It was the worst loss ever sustained by the SEALS in any conflict in the five decades of their existence.

Marcus Luttrell recovered well from his wounds, and a year or so later, in the fall of 2006, he was back in action as part of SEAL Team 5, who were to operate from Ar Ramadi, a notorious trouble spot some sixty miles west of Baghdad.

Soldiers from many nations have fought, and still fight, in Afghanistan, and many stories of great bravery, of iron resistance and of determination to survive could be told. In Marcus Luttrell's amazing escape I have picked just one.

Training plays a great part in self-confidence. Trainees for dangerous missions show a reduction in fear and an increase in confidence, and this is especially true of such Special Forces units as the SEALS, as it is of mine clearance engineers. People tend to be more courageous in groups than when alone. This also heightens their fear of not achieving their part of a mission, of endangering others in the group or of appearing cowardly.

*   *   *

'There's nothing like it, nothing in the world,' Steiner, a gunner in Second Platoon, told me about combat. 'If it's minus 20°F outside, you're sweating. If it's 120°F, you're ice cold. It's an adrenalin rush like you can't imagine.'

Sebastian Junger, War, 2010

2

Going Back into Hell

'No words can adequately describe the
horror of that night'
Police Commissioner Peter Imbert, 1988

'I learned that courage was not the absence of fear,
but the triumph over it. The brave man is not he who
does not feel afraid, but he who conquers that fear'
Nelson Mandela

In 1994 I spent time researching events involving some
London-based Asians then living in an apartment on a
Tottenham estate known as Broadwater Farm. I talked to
local drug dealers, police and many estate-dwellers, which is
how I came to know about and meet a very brave Scotsman
named Dick Coombes. His story and that of his small band
of colleagues is also the story of the Farm, as the Broadwater
Estate was locally known.

I learnt from a young Indian girl that, by the mid eighties,
life for an Asian on the huge estate was hell-like. In September
1985 her two Indian cousins, who ran a post office in
Birmingham, had been burnt to death in riots there which

had destroyed £42 million of property, most of it owned by small Asian family businesses, so my informant's family had moved down to London. This proved to be a mistake, for her family had suffered constant threats and harassment ever since their arrival on the Farm, from bad elements, black and white, who hated Asians.

'Black drug dealers,' she told me, 'ruled the estate and the police daren't touch them. Most of the time there were only four policemen on the entire estate, and they were as scared as us.'

Broadwater's construction began in 1967 and ended in 1973, a twenty-one-acre estate of ten five- or six-storey blocks and two eighteen-storey monsters. Most of these units were built on stilts because the River Moselle, which flowed across the estate, was prone to flooding. The Department of the Environment gave the estate an award for 'good housing', and the Planning Committee's chairman, Roy Limb, told the press, 'Broadwater Farm will be an everlasting memorial to my Committee.' A memorial it would certainly be; to one of the worst breakdowns of law and order ever to occur in Britain.

For a short while the first tenants of the Farm were content, but as rain and gales battered the monstrous blocks, deterioration quickly set in with katabatic winds roaring through the stilted concrete tunnels and passageways.

No thought had been given to the weak and elderly, nor to police access to catch rapists, muggers and thieves preying on the tenants. Cars were vandalised and stolen, their drivers often beaten up in the dark carports of the basements. Flat roofs and burst pipes in upper storeys flooded flats, lifts and heating systems broke down and were not repaired, window frames rotted, and doors hung off their hinges.

Ventilation systems gave easy access to the flats for germs, cockroaches, rats and exotic forms of flea. Lighting was poor and broken bulbs were seldom, if ever, replaced. Condensation and fungal slime skeined concrete walls that never dried out. Privacy was non-existent, and the corridors amplified noise so that the sound of footfalls on the walkways, neighbours snoring, screaming and playing radios was magnified and transmitted day and night into the apartments.

Refuse chutes were too narrow to take full rubbish bags, so they jammed and the stench filled the passageways. Fearful of entering the lifts and corridors below, tenants threw bulging garbage bags off balconies to the rats at ground level, or left them outside their doors to rot. Invalid cars were smashed. Urine puddles, excrement and used needles were everywhere. Old folk had been killed by motor-cyclist boy racers along the high walkways. Waste areas between blocks were heaped with litter, glass and the faeces of dogs kept by tenants for company and protection.

The safest place for the lonely and the sick was to stay double-locked in their prison-like flats, but this was often not possible, since local vandals terrorised postmen and milkmen. Nothing was delivered and nobody would come to do repairs, thanks to the Farm's fearful reputation and its air of alien menace. Anything left outside a door would soon be smashed or stolen. To buy milk or bread, to collect a newspaper or post a letter meant a long journey through the corridors of fear.

Many Asians, including the old and ill, lived in a state of constant apprehension, awaiting the next sudden hammering on their door, dog mess or flaming newspapers through their letterbox, and scrawled messages of hate. Life in an assassin district of Bangladesh might well have been less fearful.

No minicab driver would risk a visit. Nor, after their first bad experience, would most friends or relatives. Shopkeepers gave no credit to 'Broadwater people', such was the stigma of the place as a sink estate. Nobody wanted to live there, so the Council increasingly used it as a dumping ground for drug addicts, the mentally and physically ill, alcoholics and 'ethnics'. The bullies reigned supreme.

Neighbourliness, at first a strong point among Farm people, fell away as individuals grew wary of one another. At any one time, eight unarmed policemen, in four pairs, were meant to patrol the nightmare labyrinth of the Farm. Many were assaulted and some badly injured. They could not protect themselves, let alone the tenants.

By the late summer of 1985, my informant added to her litany of gloom, many of the decent whites and mixed and Asian families who had lived on the Farm for fifteen years were finally moving out. The Tenants' Association was by then controlled by a few West Indians who ignored the Asian and white minority. Fifty-five per cent of the 3,000 tenants were Jamaican. Gangs ruled by day and by night, their hate-filled graffiti daubed all over the estate. To attempt to wash the messages from the outer wall of your flat was to invite retribution.

The police had, over the years, tried to find solutions, but the main troubles always stemmed from a small knot of powerful leaders of black groups. Police reactions were immediately labelled as racist aggression, which resulted in slow, reluctant police responses to cries for help from tenants.

A black social worker, Dolly Kiffin, had gradually built up a social centre and youth association in the estate block called Tangmere, which by October 1985 boasted a number of facilities, shops and a central venue where the youth of the Farm could come together.

Throughout the damp and dismal summer of 1985 tensions had run high on the Farm, but Dolly Kiffin's influence had kept the worst elements in check. However, towards the summer's end, she and many of her best youth leaders had gone on an official visit to Jamaica, whereupon drug dealers from outside areas had moved into the estate and incited the youth. Roving groups terrorised the estate, attacking inmates, firemen and refuse collectors. Life for the old, the weak and the infirm became even more hellish than usual. Police patrols were cut off and beaten up.

The law of the Farm was truly the law of the jungle.

It was at that time especially important for the drug-dealing Farm leaders to keep their egos and reputations to the fore, as a number of unsavoury characters from outside Tottenham, including 'heroes' fresh from riots in Birmingham, Liverpool, Brixton and Peckham, were inflaming the Broadwater locals.

On Friday, 4 October rumours spread through the concrete corridors of the Farm that big trouble was being planned and the brothers must be ready with petrol bombs, missiles and hand weapons. The very next day the storm burst, following a police drugs search of an ex-Broadwater family, the Jarretts, during which the housewife, Cynthia, died of a heart attack.

The chief superintendent of the Tottenham police division had quickly summoned local community leaders in an attempt to calm things down, especially on the Farm. But crowds of demonstrators, including known riot leaders from Birmingham, blocked the road outside the Tottenham Police Centre, screaming, 'Pigs and murderers.'

The scene was set for big trouble. Knives were sharpened all over the Farm.

At 2 p.m. on Sunday, 6 October a Half-Serial of beat bobbies, a bunch of local constables about as far as you could get from what could be described as riot police, was assembled at Hornsey Police Station under a genial sergeant named Dave Pengelly from Merseyside.

One of the older men, at thirty-five, was Dick Coombes, whom I mentioned at the beginning of this chapter. He was born in Scotland, and his first job as an orthopaedic theatre technician had bored him rigid. 'It was at the height of the protest era,' he remembers. 'Everyone was smoking pot, and joining the police was really not the done thing in my peer group. But it was right for me, an active life and one in which I could give something to the community.'

So he joined up in 1970, aged twenty, and was attached to the Hornsey division of the Met. He loved his work, married and had two children. He kept fit by jogging, and was captain of the Met cross-country team for two years. His various running trophies were proudly displayed in his sitting room, where I met him and his family some ten years after the fatal night that wrecked his life.

Alongside his running cups were various commendations, including one from the Royal Humane Society for rescuing the occupants of a blazing off-licence. In 1981 he had confronted an aggressive crowd of football hooligans and had been badly beaten. Dick's hobbies were folk music, guitar playing and DIY. His driving interest, prompted by his religious convictions, was to help the local community as a home beat officer, at which he proved a great success, and he was much respected by his colleagues for his personal bravery.

Another of Dave Pengelly's group on that Sunday afternoon was Constable Keith Blakelock, a long-time personal friend of Dick Coombes and a home beat bobby from nearby Muswell Hill. Both men were aware that the riots in other English cities and other parts of London were liable to erupt in Tottenham. They had heard the rumours in the canteen.

Senior police officers, fearful of doing anything that might spark off a new riot, had laid down softly, softly policies, which were much appreciated by the criminal fraternity. Gang rape on the Tottenham estate was widespread. Dealers were doing business in the main street, openly ignoring 'high-profile' Special Patrol Group vans out in the community, well aware that current police policy and prevailing inner-city tensions made it highly unlikely that the patrol would leave their van for anything short of murder perpetrated right under their noses.

Women went shopping, when they had to, wearing shapeless coats and thick headscarves to make themselves as unattractive as possible, carried no handbags and kept minimal cash in their shoes.

Police canteen lore ascribed the ongoing riots to general inner-city 'have-nots' who were keen to knock authority in general, that stratum of society motivated, according to the Hendon Police Training Centre's psychology course, by inequality-driven frustration. But mostly, and police informants were all agreed on this, the root cause of the riots was big drug dealers orchestrating trouble on their patches in the knowledge that the best way to keep police off their territory was to make the top brass scared of provoking mayhem.

Apart from Pengelly, Coombes and Blakelock, the other men included a mixed bag of constables, mostly in their twenties. Two were from Scotland, a British Jamaican from Greenwich, a Cumbrian, a Yorkshireman, a Gloucestershire lad, and two Londoners. They had never trained or worked together as a single unit.

Late that afternoon, as they took their canteen break, Dave Pengelly was summoned to the Control Room of Wood Green Police Station. 'It was pretty hectic up there, but a decision was eventually made that I would outfit my unit with riot gear and head for Seven Sisters Underground station, where large numbers of youths were arriving from other parts of London.'

Pengelly gathered together his eleven men and, at the back of the station, they collected the standard riot gear of flame-proof overalls and riot helmets. The key items were riot shields, and Pengelly decided to take three long ones which could only be used with efficiency after a specific training course. Two men without shields would move behind the long shield bearers to bind them together. The rest of the unit drew short, round, plastic, see-through shields. Standard police batons, unchanged in their design since the early 1900s, were their only weapons, and just two of the group had hand-held radios.

Dick Coombes was sent off for transport and came back with a prisoner-type Sherpa van with no rear windows, in which they set off for Seven Sisters. Pengelly recalled, 'Dick, luckily, knew the way, as I didn't.'

By the time they reached the tube station, everything was quiet and a new order was received. They were to head for the Broadwater Estate. Everyone in the van knew what that meant.

They came to the edge of a major confrontation between hundreds of hooligans and lines of police. Cars were ablaze, bricks and bottles smashed against shields. 'The noise of the crowds,' Constable Miles Barton recalled, 'was the constant, aggressive roar of a football stadium. As we drove along Mount Pleasant Road, overturned and blazing cars were piled across the pavements and petrol bombs rained down.'

After some minutes, Pengelly's men were given a specific task along a road that bordered the Tangmere block at Broadwater Farm. Two police shield units were already there under a chief superintendent, and a fire engine's crew was busy extinguishing flames along a barricade of wrecked cars.

The superintendent soon redeployed all police other than Pengelly's group, codenamed Serial 502, who remained alone with five firemen on the edge of the Farm. At first all was quiet but for the distant roar of the rioting.

A few hundred yards away more than 500 youths, many high on drugs, prepared for action. Their plans included, as became clear at later trials, the chopping off of a policeman's head to impale on a pole, with which to taunt police at ongoing riots. A careful trap was being prepared to ensnare and surround 'some pigs' on the Tangmere block.

Pengelly's men lined up along the road beside Tangmere, separated by a short downhill stretch of grass from the looming estate block. The occasional street light still worked, and the night sky was clear. Pengelly and the superintendent conversed with the firemen when the last car blaze had been doused.

Dick Coombes recalled: 'The visibility was good and we saw a group of men on a high balcony of the Tangmere block. They shouted at us that the supermarket on the mezzanine floor of their block was on fire. This, to me, smelled like a trap. They had probably lit the fire to lure us in. I heard the superintendent on the van radio saying, "Whatever you do, do not go into the Farm." But within minutes that policy was reversed, because the fire officers feared innocent folk on the floors above the blaze might be trapped. So we were to escort and protect the firemen. That was that. I recall thinking, this could be dangerous, could be iffy.'

Pengelly added: 'The superintendent assured me that he would request back-up resources, but nonetheless this did not seem to me like a great assignment.

'Off we went, single file over the grass, looking for a way up to the shop-level of the block. We moved as quietly as possible, the firemen dragging their hose, into the dark stilted parking zone under the ground floor and then up a series of concrete stairways. By now, I was pretty scared. I assigned Keith and Ricky Pandya to guard a walkway which could be used to cut off our exit route. The rest of us continued upwards, with the long shields unit up front, then our firemen, then Tappy and Barton with small shields.

'When we reached the open area with the shops, you could look down over a balcony at the ground thirty feet below. I thought I saw moving shadows down there. But all was quiet.'

Smoke belched from the smashed windows of the supermarket, food tins and scattered debris littered the concrete deck and, above the entrance, black graffiti announced, "TANDOORI SHIT GET OUT. NIGGERS RULE."'

The firemen began to hose down the source of the smoke. Pengelly, on his squad radio, heard that 400 yards away on the far side of the Tangmere block, four police had been shot and more than 200 injured. He wondered how long before he and his little squad were spotted *inside* Tangmere.

From a distant part of the block, Dick Coombes heard the

clang of a handbell. He felt the hair rise on the back of his neck for the first time in sixteen years with the force, as he glanced over the balcony. A mass of youths in balaclava masks streamed towards the base of the stairs where Keith and Ricky were stationed. From the silence of one moment erupted, as though on signal, the baying of the mob. 'They were yelling, waving knives, blowing whistles and ringing bells. I knew in that moment that we were in deep trouble.'

Within minutes and from various dark corridors and stairways, there appeared groups of armed youths, all masked, and they surrounded Pengelly's group, who retreated in a bunch around the firemen. Pengelly stepped in front of his men, raised his hand at the mob and shouted, 'All we are doing is protecting the firemen. When they're finished, we will all go.'

'This,' Pengelly recalled, 'was clearly not the right password for, with howls of anger, they rushed forward to cut us off from the stairs.'

Over a hundred rioters, most, but not all, black, closed in for the kill. Coombes heard yells of 'Fuck off, pigs', 'This is the Farm!', 'No pigs here' and 'You'll never get out alive'. The individual chants soon merged into a steady booming chant of, 'Kill, kill the pigs'.

Petrol bombs exploded, chunks of torn paving smashed against helmets, sharpened machete blades sliced into the shields, and Pengelly screamed out orders for a group retreat down the stairs. The mob above was the main threat, so the squad, the firemen in their midst, slowly fought their way backwards down the stairway, their three long shields locked as they retreated, tripping over the fat hosepipe of the firemen.

'Burn the bacon' suddenly became the new theme chant,

and Coombes froze as he saw through the scarred plastic of his visor one of his assailants trying to light a flame-thrower. The police were soaked in fuel from unlit petrol bombs thrown at them. Now he knew why. Luckily the apparatus would not ignite.

By then the superintendent back on the road had summoned a reserve police unit, but their way to Tangmere was currently blocked. Dick Coombes recalled: 'The staircase seemed much narrower on our way back down – the fire hose had been flat on our way up, but it now bulged with water and we kept tripping on it. Every man held the belt of the man in front. We had to keep together. The noise was deafening. They screamed in our ears, 'Kill them. Kill. Kill.' In the dim light I could barely see, for the Perspex visor of my helmet was old and scratched. I had a tiny, short truncheon. Crazy. We were woefully under-equipped.'

Somehow the men of 502, some already bloody from stab wounds but with all the firemen still safe in their midst, eventually reached the concrete carport at the base of the stairs. There they were met by an ever-growing crowd of rioters, later reckoned to be more than 500, intent on cutting them off from the road a hundred yards away and above the grassy slope.

Once the squad, by now in separate groups, was beyond the transitory protection of the staircase, their three long shields became worse than useless. It was every man for himself. To his flank, Dick Coombes saw Keith Blakelock stumble and fall. Thirty masked men literally dropped onto the struggling body, hacking at it with their knives and screaming, 'Kill, brothers, kill. We've got a beast.'

Fireman Alan Briars recalled: 'All hell was let loose. I was one of the lucky ones. I managed to get away. I ran like mad, frightened out of my life.'

Another fireman saw Blakelock go down: 'He was totally engulfed. The last I saw of him was his head and his hand above his head trying to fend off blows. I didn't stop running. You can imagine the fear we were experiencing.'

The mob tore away Blakelock's shield, truncheon and helmet. His arms were slashed, his fingers half-chopped off, stakes and knives were plunged into his chest and neck, but he did not die.

The natural and sensible instinct for self-preservation at such a moment of terror after the escape from within the Tangmere trap was all-consuming. And yet, in what to me was a defining moment of true courage, some of the men of 502, seeing Blakelock's plight, gave up their own slim chance of survival from an equally horrific fate by turning back into the heart of that screaming mob of killers in order to save Keith.

Dick Coombes saw the crowd 'like a flock of murderous birds in a feeding frenzy, hacking and jabbing'. Fire Officer Stratford and nineteen-year-old Constable Maxwell Roberts grabbed at the wounded Blakelock, but both were themselves under lethal attack. Stratford's spine was smashed with a brick, and Roberts was stabbed.

Coombes, running back to help Blakelock, was blocked by a large group. A vicious blow floored him and he was set upon with the dedication of hatred. They tore off his visor and slit his neck open with knives. His jawbone was shattered by a machete and he lost consciousness. The killers then continued to set about his inert body with knives and clubs.

Dave Pengelly, on his own, was hunted by a separate group.

At some point he clearly saw a body of rioters, their arms rising and falling about a dark mass he knew must be one of his squad. Without hesitation he charged over with truncheon and short shield flailing, to join Stratford, Roberts and Tappy dragging the inert body of Blakelock back up the slope, their free arms raised against clubs and knives. Two others, Milne and Shepherd, also under furious attack, had hauled Dick Coombes, blood pumping from his face and neck, back to the Sherpa.

With the wounded ringing their van against marauders, the firemen tried to revive Blakelock. His face was a bloody mess, the handle of a serrated knife driven four inches into his neck stuck out from beneath one ear, and a gaping wound ran from his lips to the back of his shoulder. They counted forty-two stab wounds on his chest, back and limbs. He died in their arms not long before some sixty fresh constables arrived to extricate Serial 502.

Pengelly's men sat in their van in silence. Their driver, Dick Coombes, had been taken away by ambulance before anyone realised that he had the van keys.

'We just sat there,' Dave Pengelly wrote to me in 2010, 'numb with shock, and life was never the same again for any of us.'

The riots elsewhere in Tottenham set records that night. For the first time ever in mainland Britain, firearms were used by rioters against the police. By the time the mobs dispersed, 250 policemen had been injured. Only seven complaints of injuries to civilians were made.

Dick Coombes later told me: 'That night not only ruined the lives of Keith's family, but many, many others. All of us have been affected. It will never be over for us.'

To this day, more than twenty-five years after Dick's brave rush into that murderous mob, he still cannot work, drive or read a book. He suffers daily blackouts and several serious epileptic fits each month. He cannot enter crowded rooms and flinches on seeing a knife. In his dreams he sees again and again the man with the machete raised over Keith Blakelock's bloodied body.

Dave Pengelly and Miles Barton wrote to me in 2010 and confirmed that, down the long years since Broadwater, they have both suffered badly from post-traumatic stress, but that given the choice of a replay, they would again go back for a fallen comrade.

Interdependence, social identity, cohesion and informational influence can promote courageous behaviour. They could have gone the other way and looked after themselves but they chose not to.

3

Endurance in the Face of Terror

To watch friends of many years sliced up into piles of body parts, to listen to their screams and to know that their butchers are also your friends and long-time neighbours, such a nightmare will never, you must pray, happen to you. But it happened to Paul Rusesabagina in Rwanda, a hero among heroes, during the genocidal frenzy of April 1994 when he was forty years old.

Paul is a businessman in Brussels these days. Back then he was the manager of Rwanda's most luxurious hotel in the capital city of Kigali. For two fear-ridden months he risked the most horrific of deaths for no reason other than to save the lives of other humans; most of them mere strangers to whom he owed nothing. To fully appreciate the utter madness of the killing days in Rwanda is to shake your head in disbelief at the depths to which human folly can plunge.

The hate-spurred cruelties committed by one 'normal' Rwandan citizen to another in April 1994 resulted from a series of unfortunate twists in the nation's history, or, if you prefer, to the cynical vagaries of Sod's Law. Go to Rwanda today and the countryside is little changed from those fatal days of mass murder, when every hilltop, every valley, every nook offering potential concealment exuded the fear of the soon-to-be-killed and echoed to the shouts of the hunter bands high on bloodlust.

In reality, there was no safe hiding place that the hunted could hope to reach, save maybe for the Kigali hotel of Paul Rusesabagina. For Rwanda is a small country, densely populated and aggressively farmed. The inhabitants call it 'the land of a thousand green hills'. Not far south of the Equator, the surface soil is always warm and generously fertile. Bananas are the bountiful national crop. The average altitude of these highlands acts to keep at bay those deadly scourges of Africa, the tsetse fly and the mosquito. Much mild rain makes for lovely river vales and flower-filled meadows grazed by fat cattle. The most beautiful land in all Africa, many European writers have decided.

Lucky Paul Rusesabagina was born the son of a banana farmer on one of the 'thousand hills'. His father was from the Hutu caste, traditionally farmers, and his mother a Tutsi. In Rwanda bloodlines are deemed to pass through the father, so Paul was officially a Hutu.

There is no scientific proof that the Hutu and the Tutsi groups of Rwanda and Burundi are of different ethnic origins, although this is a popular misconception worldwide. The two have lived together and inter-married in all the hill villages of Rwanda for over 500 years. They share a single language and most cannot be told apart by their outward appearance, clothes, habits or religion.

During the French Revolution in Paris, the men, women and children whose heads were cut off were as French as those who denounced them. Their crime was one of class and, since aristocratic families were less inclined to live off stodgy bread and cheap beer, they may well have exhibited higher cheekbones and longer, thinner fingers than those of the proletariat. And so with the Tutsi, who for hundreds of years were those Rwandans who rose to the top of society and lorded it over the majority rabble.

No region of Rwanda was ever predominantly Hutu or Tutsi. For centuries the kings, or *mwarni*, kept powerful courts of nobles with a long tradition that all royal courtiers should be taller than the masses. Thus, in all probability, evolved the two groupings who, at some point unrecorded by written history, became divided into separate groups called the Tutsi and the Hutu, the upper or ruling and the lower or subservient classes of the same people. These two groups had lived together cheek by jowl for 400 years by the time, in 1863, when the British explorer John Hanning Speke claimed to be the first white man to locate Lake Victoria, the apparent source of the Nile.

Speke maintained, in a popular description of his African travels, that the ruling people of Rwanda, the Tutsi tribe, were a noble Christian race from North Africa with fine bearing and features who ruled over the snub-nosed Hutu, who Speke wrote off as an exiled and servile Hamitic tribe.

By the late nineteenth century, when Africa was carved up into colonies, the Germans were titular lords of Rwanda but, uninterested in its paltry natural resources, they left the tiny country to the Tutsi ruling group and to their dynastic king.

After the First World War, the United Nations awarded Rwanda to the Belgians, who already owned the neighbouring Congo and were zealous at profiting wherever possible from their African colonies. Using the existing command relationship between the Tutsi elite and the Hutu farmers, Belgian administrators gave top jobs only to Tutsis and stressed the

Tutsi *Übermensch* superiority at every turn. In 1933 they forced every Rwandan to carry an identity card proclaiming their ethnic 'race'.

Until that point, there were many ways by which any Hutu who became wealthy (for instance, by obtaining more cattle) could become a Tutsi. The Belgians, by enforcing Tutsi superiority, turned what was merely a class-based hierarchy into tribal hatred. Hutu chain gangs, forced to harvest timber for Belgian profit, were policed by Tutsi foremen charged by the Belgians to dole out harsh treatment to slackers.

In the 1930s Belgian attempts to convert Rwandans to Christianity were blocked by the then Tutsi king, so they deposed and replaced him with a fanatical Roman Catholic. Catholicism caught on like wildfire with Hutu and Tutsi alike, and droves of Belgian priests, many of them with Flemish inferiority complexes, arrived to guide these eager new Rwandan flocks. They soon found themselves sympathetic to the lot of the Hutu underdog and persuaded the authorities to redress the long-standing imbalance of power between the two groups, which swung through 180 degrees from the elite Tutsi minority to the brutish Hutu masses, one of whom, though his mother was Tutsi, was Paul, the five-year-old son of a banana-farming Hutu. Paul's parents made sure that he and his siblings remained good friends with all their fellow hill-villagers, whether Hutu or Tutsi, rich or poor.

Throughout the late 1950s relations between the Hutu, with their new-found power, and the increasingly disenfranchised Tutsi worsened until, in 1959, the see-saw favouritism of the Belgians caused the start of a killing spree by Hutu in certain parts of Rwanda. In the early sixties Belgium declared Rwanda to be a self-governing republic and left their

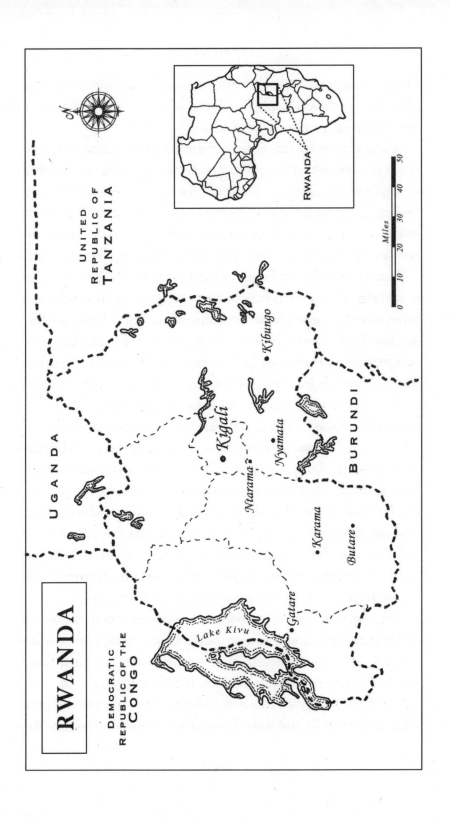

former colony on its own with soon-to-be murderous consequences, not dissimilar to those that followed Britain's
precipitous departure from India.

In 1959 slaughtered Tutsi numbered less than 500, but by
late 1961, their homes looted and burnt, over 20,000 had fled
to Uganda. In early 1964 10,000 Tutsis were murdered, and
those left behind lived in terror of their lives. This latest
massacre was sparked by an attempt of Tutsi refugees to
return home in what amounted to an armed invasion.

There are today in England many urban families who live
in a state of perpetual fear of their local gang: their lives are
miserable and filled with apprehension. Yet the worst they
are likely to suffer is a beating, verbal bullying in the street
or a broken window. Compare their fate with that of a million
Tutsis, surrounded on all sides, day and night, by potential
killers. There was nobody to appeal to for help since the
police, the army and the law were all Hutu controlled.

The 1959–64 massacres were vicious, but did not reach
every part of Rwanda. Paul remembered only a night when
a group of bedraggled strangers came to his home. His father
uttered words which have stayed with Paul over the years.

'Don't worry,' he'd told the strangers, 'you're safe here.'

They had all spent that night outside and away from the
house. When this also happened the next night, Paul asked
his father why. And again he would never forget his response.

'Because, my son, if somebody comes to burn our house
down, we will not cook to death inside it. These people who
we help are called Tutsis, and other people who hate them
are out there right now searching for them.'

What Paul's father did not tell him was that those Hutu
who tried to help and hide Tutsi fugitives were themselves to

be tortured and sliced to death, for the new Hutu authorities made it clear that there was no room for moderation in post-colonial Rwanda. And no room for sympathisers. Since Paul's Hutu and Tutsi village friends had always played the same games together, spoke like each other and mostly looked like each other, he was confused. But his father's attitude and policy was crystal clear and stayed with him: 'Always offer shelter to the distressed, no matter what the circumstances.'

In 1972 neighbouring Burundi suffered a military coup, following which 200,000 Hutu there were wiped out by the Tutsi-led Burundi Army, and Hutu refugees fled to Rwanda where local Tutsis were killed by way of tit-for-tat reprisals.

Because Paul's village was well away from the worst trouble spots, his school years had been relatively free from inter-group tensions and atrocities. But soon after the Burundi troubles, ripples of hatred pulsed through all Rwanda, and Paul, in his late teens and last days at school, watched his best friend and soul-mate from childhood expelled alongside all other Tutsi students.

A few years later Paul married a local Hutu girl and, gaining a scholarship in theology, studied to become a pastor. For the very first time, he moved away from his home village to the world beyond banana trees. In the capital of Kigali he became, in his own words, 'enchanted with the world of airplanes, elevators and azure swimming pools'.

He noted that on a clear night you could, from Mount Kigali, view the verdant land all about, and he recalled the local proverb: 'God wanders all the world by day and returns home to Rwanda by night.'

Realising that the life of a village curate would bore him rigid, Paul gave up his religious studies and became a desk clerk in Kigali's luxury hotel Les Milles Collines, where he quickly picked up French and English and the knowledge of how to handle awkward guests with charm and diplomacy. The hotel's Belgian manager, recognising Paul's potential, sent him to Switzerland on a course.

This caused a rift in his marriage, and when his wife left him, their three children stayed with him in Kigali. He threw himself into hotel work and, in 1987, married again. This time to a Tutsi nurse. They had two children, and by 1992 Paul was promoted to general manager of the Milles Collines's nearby sister hotel, the Diplomates, as the first black general manager in the Sabena Hotel Group's history. Not bad for the son of a village banana farmer.

His father had died the previous year, and when Paul had sat beside his deathbed, he had muttered his last words of paternal advice. 'Listen, my son. You might meet hyenas on their way to hunt. Be careful.' Paul was to meet more than his fair share of hyenas in the very near future.

In the 1980s, whilst Paul had slowly climbed the promotional ladder in Kigali, the post-colonial Hutu government under President Habyarimana had developed a single-party system which increasingly tolerated no opposition. Nonetheless, for a while the ethnic killings had lessened, Tutsis could survive, and even thrive, providing they kept their heads well down and never interfered in politics.

In 1990, under the leadership of one Paul Kagame (who, as a three-year-old on his mother's back, had fled Hutu persecution way back in 1959), a well-disciplined Tutsi force crossed the Rwandan border from Uganda and advanced some way towards Kigali before they were defeated by Habyarimana's army.

The scene was set for a three-way struggle between the autocratic president, the growing army of Tutsi exiles, and various internal Hutu political groups striving to change the government. Habyarimana decided to trumpet the external threat of a Tutsi invasion to quell his Hutu rivals and to get rid of all Tutsis in Rwanda by stirring up Hutu fear of a fifth column waiting to exterminate them just as soon as the exile army managed to invade.

At some point either then in 1990 or over the next two years, Habyarimana or the *akazu*, the aggressive power group that clustered around the president's powerful wife, decided that the only answer to maintain ultimate power was to rid Rwanda of every last Tutsi. The name of their game was genocide.

For two years the *akazu* secretly trained and armed killer groups with help, both practical and financial, from Egypt and South Africa, but mainly from France. French army and intelligence specialist groups trained the 1,500-strong Presidential Guard, who in turn trained various Hutu militias. The enemy to be wiped out were quite simply all Tutsi and any Hutu who opposed any aspect of the *akazu* rule.

Habyarimana's trump card was his long-term friendship with the French in general and President Mitter and in person. France, he knew, would support him, even in genocide, for although they had no particular commercial interest in Rwanda, it was, due to the Belgian colonial period, French-speaking, and that was enough to ensure French loyalty.

Unlike the other old colonial powers in Africa, France alone had retained the political will and the zeal to hold on to close ties, the right to military intervention and, above all, to stop the francophone countries falling into the hands or language of the Anglo-Saxons. And that, France knew, was exactly what would happen, should the Tutsi exiles from anglo-Uganda take over in Rwanda. So the French helped the president, as he knew they would, and just as they always had in Chad, the Central African Republic, Togo, the Ivory Coast, Senegal, Djibouti and Gabon.

France's nationalised bank, Crédit Lyonnaise, extended sufficient credit to provide every Hutu male over twelve years of age with a killing weapon in the shape of a Chinese-made machete, or panga, to use the African name.

After the failure of the 1990 incursions, Paul Kagame's exile army, the RPF (Rwanda Patriotic Front), moved into Rwanda in cautious, but well-executed, bounds. The *akazu* decided that there could be no acceptable compromise treaty and, realising that the RPF were highly likely to win all Rwanda sooner or later, they decided to murder every Tutsi in the land along with all Hutus who opposed them in any way.

The masterminds of the genocide plan included two of the brothers of the president's wife, one of whom was believed to be involved with illegal trading in endangered species and with the murder of the American gorilla zoologist, Dian Fossey. At one point, doing business in Canada, he made death threats against Rwandan expatriates there, and was deported. After the genocide, he was convicted but then cleared on appeal, few accept his innocence.

His colleague in planning the Tutsi extermination stated in public: 'Why are we waiting to get rid of the families? Our mistake in 1959 was to let them escape. They belong in Ethiopia and this time we will send their bodies there by way of the Nyabarongo River. We have to act. Wipe them all out.'

At first the *akazu* group master-minding the genocide plans called themselves Network Zero. They often met in the luxury rooms of the Milles Collines and the Diplomates hotels, and Paul, blessed with a photographic memory and a silver tongue, kept a secret book in which he noted who was who in the corridors of evil. But he also observed many of his other wealthy visitors and, alongside comments on their positions, their ambitions and their spheres of influence, he kept their phone numbers 'for a rainy day'.

The Zero killers, in plotting the death of over a million Tutsis of all ages, were aware that not all the Hutu would willingly give a hand. So they would need coercion by fear; fear of the imminent RPF invasion and fear that non-compliance with a kill-your-Tutsi-neighbours edict would mean that you would yourself be killed.

From 1990 onwards the *akazu* stockpiled arms for the Presidential Guard and the regional militias, mostly from France and Egypt, including Kalashnikov rifles with 3 million bullets, mortars and shells, rocket-propelled grenades, machine-guns, long-range artillery and anti-personnel mines.

Part of the Zero policy was to turn all Hutu into murderers so that all would then be complicit and so more pliant. But to arm every Hutu citizen would be to invite long-term trouble for the *akazu* leadership after the Tutsis were all gone. The answer was clearly to use traditional rural tools, such as the bush-cutter or machete. So these were ordered in hundreds of thousands to be cached until D-Day. By the end of 1992 Paul and many other alert urban Hutu were painfully aware of at least the general gist of the genocide plan, but not when it might take place.

The conditions necessary to create a genocidal mind-set within any given population include a depressed economy (due largely, in Rwanda, to a global drop in coffee prices), uneven distribution of wealth, the existence of an identifiable minority, the strong political ambition of an oppressor group, and impunity. On top of all that, the genocidal leadership needs a base of social deprivation and tension which it can exploit to its own ends. It must excite a sense of unjust suffering among the masses, and focus the resultant anger against a specific group. Preparing a population to commit genocide against lifelong neighbours is a complex job that takes time. Natural feelings of revulsion and guilt must be overcome. Hitler took at least six years to achieve this; the Rwandan *akazu* had so far taken three.

Since a great many moderate Hutu across Rwanda were also openly hostile to the government, they too were marked for assassination.

The *akazu* evolved a mass killing system shaped to create maximum psychological terror and planned to the finest detail. The entire Hutu population was to be mobilised to kill their Tutsi friends and neighbours as a civic duty. Anybody who refused to become an executioner would themselves be murdered.

All moderate Hutu leaders or people attempting to shield Tutsis were to be killed. The resulting cleansed Rwanda would be pure Hutu, and all citizens would be bound together through their communal involvement in genocide. Network Zero and the other members of the extremist clique which planned all this were lucky in that the Belgians had already created a country where citizens could be easily disciplined through the introduction of ID cards, and had established a simple chain of government where regional parish bosses reported to provincial ones, who in turn reported to Kigali.

The slaughter was meticulously organised, using the army,

the police, the local mayors and, above all, regional groups of thugs called the Interahamwe, meaning 'those who work together', who were recruited from every village in the land. Each new border incursion by the RPF gave the clique a new excuse for a dress rehearsal of their killing system. Between 1990 and 1993 they had assassinated several hundred Hutu moderates and thousands of Tutsis in small regional massacres.

To achieve genocide anywhere the level of education of the relevant population probably defines the level of sophistication required to mobilise them as killers. Remember that most such killers are average, gentle, decent people like you or me, not brutal psychotics. It is no more natural to murder a neighbour than it is to bungee jump. We have to be mentally trained to kill, to be taught why it is right and then be motivated to act at a certain time. Normally it needs the justification of a war to convince us to join bands of killers (called armies) and accept training in how best to shoot, bomb, bayonet and effectively kill or maim the citizens of those very countries in which we may have been taking annual holidays for years.

In Rwanda, the government was indoctrinating the masses at national and local levels into believing that they were indeed at war. The government-controlled radio stations, newspapers and television were ceaselessly preparing their audiences for action. Militias were being trained to kill in every district. The Tutsis, the designated enemy, were painfully, fearfully aware of the impending Armageddon, yet they could do nothing but wait and hope. The army and the police, indeed every armed authority in Rwanda, was Hutu controlled. There was no escape for a Tutsi.

Of course, the ruling Hutu needed its killers to be well trained and armed for the massive task ahead, since the Tutsis could not be expected to lie down meekly and be slaughtered. As with the Nazi policy of *Nacht und Nebel*, or darkness and fog, a policy of deception should hopefully confuse the victims, with a rash of intermittent mini-massacres before the big one.

As with the many secretive groups planning Hitler's genocidal programme, so the Rwandan *akazu*'s Network Zero was complemented by the *Amasasu* (the Bullets) secret society formed in 1992 by extremist army officers. The end aim of this devil's mix was absolute power through absolute terror.

In February 1993 General Paul Kagame's RPF army managed to push back the Rwandan army to the very outskirts of Kigali, at which point Habyarimana called in French support, and the UN entered the equation to negotiate a cease-fire. In order to stop the RPF advance Habyarimana would need to sign the UN plan, the Arusha Peace Accords, agreeing to a truce with the RPF and to share power in Rwanda with them. But he knew the *akazu* extremists would never agree to such a coalition with Tutsis, so he bought time by indicating that he would sign the Accords when in due course they were ready.

The *akazu*, worried lest Habyarimana were actually to sign the Accords, realised that their genocide plans should begin as soon as possible. But they would need a major event to occur to spark mass hysteria among the Hutu citizenry. Towards the end of 1993 they put their heads together, and all over Rwanda their local cells were instructed to make lists of each and every Tutsi in every house in the land. These would become Death Lists. Lists were also drawn up of many thousands of opposing Hutu politicals and of Hutus married to Tutsis. Like Paul.

For many years Paul, as manager of the most salubrious meeting place in Kigali, had assiduously befriended the many powerful hotel guests. A free drink, a special table by the pool, or extra attention at the right moment. Such little things, Paul knew, usually made their mark. Yet at the very time when the *akazu* were drawing up their Death Lists of all who in any way fell from their favour, Paul stood on his principles in a manner likely to sign his own death warrant.

The RPF leadership, prior to their involvement in the pending Arusha Peace Accords, were looking for a suitable Kigali venue in which to hold a press conference. Scared rigid, the managers of every public venue in the city turned them down. But Paul agreed to host their event at a standard cost because he firmly believed in fairness and equal access to his hotel for everybody, no matter their race or ideology. He survived, but was told in no uncertain terms how he had angered the government.

And that was not the only occasion when his principles were his near-undoing, for he heartily disliked President Habyarimana and, though he normally kept this dangerous sentiment to himself, he drew the line at wearing the presidential likeness as a badge on his suit jacket. Habyarimana's fat smirking face already leered from billboards and shops all over town, but in 1993 he decided that all those in positions of public responsibility should wear his portrait badge whenever doing their professional duties. The Archbishop of Kigali happily led the way by wearing the badge on his cassock whilst saying Mass.

On the twenty-fifth anniversary of Rwanda's independence, a major dinner function was held at the Milles Collines. Everyone who was anyone in Kigali was there, including the

Belgian king and prime minister. So too was Paul, in an impressive white suit notable for the missing Habyarimana badge. A presidential thug hauled Paul out of the receiving line, but the Belgian chairman of Sabena Hotel Group had him reinstated in time for him to shake the president's hand, his lapel still unadorned. Next day a bagful of badges arrived with instructions that they were to be worn henceforward by *all* hotel staff. What followed is in Paul's own words:

The next morning I showed up to work without wearing a medal. A black car arrived at the front door roundabout and I was escorted over. They told me I now had earned 'an appointment' at the office of the president. I followed them there . . . and was screamed at for several hours.

'You do not respect the boss, our father!' they [yelled].

'What did I do wrong?' I asked.

'You stupid man, you did not wear your medals! Why not?'

'I don't see the benefit in doing that,' I said.

It went around and around like this before they kicked me out of the office [with the] command to be back the next morning. And the next day, they screamed at me for hours and gave me another kick in the butt before they let me go.

It went on like this every day for a month. I was no longer working at the hotel, just reporting to the office of the president. His thugs became my daily escorts. We started to get used to each other and exchanged morning pleasantries before the daily screaming began. And I would always tell them the same thing: 'I really don't see why I should wear the medal.'

The irony of this show of muscle was that the president was not really in control of his own power base. Everybody who was well informed in Rwanda knew that he was essentially a hollow man, largely the pawn of his own advisers. He had risen up through the defence ministry and was put in charge of the purge against the Tutsis in 1973 that had been responsible for the deaths of dozens and wasted the futures of thousands more, including my [school] friend Gerard.

So when I decided not to wear the president's portrait on my lapel I was putting my thumb in the eye of a very insecure man. My friends told me later that I had been taking a stupid chance. I should have just worn the stupid thing to make the flunkies happy and not risked my job or my family's welfare on a symbolic matter. I knew Habyarimana and the *akazu* didn't much care for me, anyway. It would have cost me a huge amount of self-respect to have worn that dictator's face on my jacket. If this was a risk, it was a calculated one.

Paul's two stands against the ruling bullies were made against a background where any Hutu with any sort of public profile was liable to be found dead and no questions would be asked. The fact that his European boss clearly favoured Paul may well have saved him, but he could surely thereafter count himself as a marked man. Which made his subsequent survival even more miraculous.

In August 1993 a new radio station went on air and crackled over millions of ancient battery-powered radios in hovels, on banana farms, in urban shacks and on remote river fishing boats all over Rwanda. Called RTLM, it was an overnight success, being, it seemed, an independent station in competition with its boring state rival, Radio Rwanda.

With merry Congolese music and reporters with American-style emphasis, people really trusted and believed in its news reports, simply because it was non-government and even dealt out light criticism of the president himself from time to time.

The KGB would have been proud of RTLM. The main shareholder, though nobody knew it, *was* the president, and other owners included most of the *akazu*. RTLM had an emergency power source in case of blackouts, which led back to the official residence of the president.

Just as riots the world over are today organised and advertised on the Internet and often spread like wildfire, so Hutu peasants were incited to kill their Tutsi neighbours by way of their ever-present transistor radios and the few government-controlled newspapers that were passed around the villages and read aloud at gatherings. Their content was treated as fact, not propaganda, and as the new year of 1994 approached, there were but two sides to all reported discussions and themes: the extremist and the slightly less extremist.

Tutsis and Hutus like Paul, married to a Tutsi, were increasingly mesmerised with fear, for in most cases there was no way for a family to find a place of safety. The borders were officially closed to Tutsi would-be emigrants. They lived like mice among snakes.

Paul said: 'I wanted to stop listening to RTLM but I couldn't. It was like one of those movies where you watch a car speeding in slow motion towards a child. You wince, you want to scream but you cannot look away. It seems impossible we could not know what was coming. How could the Tutsis and those of us Hutu who loved them not have

74

made a protest as we heard the irrational anger grow ever stronger.'

As the Arusha talks with the RPF dragged on and on, RTLM agitprop increased; the word 'cockroach' came to be used as the sole description of a Tutsi, with the same intent to denigrate as a white racist chanting 'nigger'. Hutu sympathisers such as Paul were lumped together under the same badge-of-the-scum. A popular Hutu rock star's latest ballad was repeatedly played on RTLM.

> I hate these Hutus, these arrogant Hutus,
> braggarts who scorn other Hutu – dear comrades
> I hate these Hutus, these de-Hutuized Hutu
> who have disowned their identities – dear comrades

In village markets and on Kigali street stalls in the spring of 1994 you could buy a hand-grenade for the price of two beers if you could prove that you were a Hutu. Machetes were the price of a mango. That February the Kigali journal *Kangura* printed a large cartoon of a machete above the text, 'We know where the cockroaches are . . . What weapons shall we use to conquer them once and for all?' 'For all' clearly included children, for the text continued, 'A cockroach cannot give birth to a butterfly.'

As the Arusha talks began to creak to fruition, a battalion of 600 RPF Tutsi soldiers was allowed to occupy the Kigali parliament grounds in preparation for the establishment of the transitional government.

The *Kangura* editors went berserk, but one article struck an especially weird note with the prediction that President Habyarimana would soon be assassinated by a Tutsi death squad, whereupon, unless revenge was instantly taken by every true Hutu in the land, the RPF would kill *them*. The message was, given such an event, kill or be killed.

For many months, opposition politicians, dissenting journalists and openly moderate Hutu business leaders had been murdered by *akazu* agents. Paul used to enjoy a drink with friends in a bar after work, but one evening he broke this routine for some reason and was glad that he did, for a man on a motorbike tossed a grenade into the bar and destroyed it. A taxi driver friend of Paul's witnessed the assassination of the Minister of Public Works and was willing to describe the killing. But she was herself shot the following day.

Paul, his Tutsi wife Tatiana and their five children were frightened. But then so were hundreds of thousands of others in all Rwanda, for a feeling of great dread at that time was later to be recalled by many a survivor of the hell that followed. Many a Tutsi with life savings available tried too late to flee, but the borders were closed. Ongoing and increasing killings were no longer partially designed to frighten Tutsis out of Rwanda. Now the policy was total extermination, and the trap was set, the cage doors closed.

The brotherhood of nations, the United Nations, set up with admirable aims which included intervention should another Holocaust look likely anywhere, had plenty of warning that Rwanda was on the brink of internal mass murder. So why, after sending 2,500 troops into Rwanda, did the UN not prevent what was to follow? Who controls the UN?

The members of the controlling Security Council are Russia, France, Germany, UK, USA and China, most of whom were previous colonisers of Africa. France was acting head of the Council and was herself the most loyal of Hutu supporters who had both trained and armed many of their killer squads. The UK never interferes in francophone countries, the USA had recent bad memories of armed intervention in Somalia, and neither Russia nor China made a fuss about human rights due to their own ongoing abuses of them.

The commander of the UN Force in Rwanda, General Roméo Dallaire, a Canadian, was a good friend of Paul's after many a business function held at the Milles Collines, and Paul both liked and respected him. Early in January 1994 the *akazu*'s paid ex-army instructor, hired to train Hutu militias to defend their villages against the RPF, discovered that the real aim of the *akazu* was to use his militia to make lists of every Tutsi in every village in readiness for murdering them. He made a secret visit to brief Dallaire with a summary that his militia were ready, in Kigali alone, to kill over a thousand top-level Tutsis within twenty minutes of receiving the order to do so. Dallaire immediately warned his UN boss, Kofi Annan, who forbade him to take any action other than to reveal the plot to the Rwandan president, who was, to all intents, a puppet of the *akazu*.

In Kigali *akazu*-ordered killings of the least favoured citizens continued daily through March, and Paul's wife was forced off the road by a man in an army jeep when driving their son to school.

'Do you know me?' he asked.

'No.' Paul's wife was terrified.

'Madame,' he went on, 'we know your home and your gate guards and your dogs. Soon youths will kidnap you to get ransom from your husband. I am warning you.'

Paul took the warning and moved his family from their house to a bungalow in the hotel grounds.

On 6 April the hotel's Belgian manager called Paul with the news that President Habyarimana's private jet had been shot down at Kigali airport. Nobody knew for sure who was responsible, but one thing Paul did know was that this meant major trouble. As he said, 'Murders at the top in Rwanda are usually followed by the slaughter of everyday people.' And since he was such a political moderate and Tatiana was a Tutsi, they were both in deep trouble. Soon, he feared, there would be a knock on his door.

Habyarimana had been president for twenty years with, latterly, the *akazu* ever more at his elbow. Many people believed, and still believe, that the *akazu*, including his wife, organised the hit squad whose shoulder-fired rocket hit his plane. With his death, an army man, Colonel Bagosora, emerged as the Hitler-figure and Hutu extremist at the nerve centre of the *akazu*, the man who coordinated the 'final solution'.

The prime minister at the time was a moderate Hutu named Agathe Uwilingiyimana, and General Dallaire tried to arrange that she address and calm down the nation by radio. The station manager would not allow this, for fear that his family would die. Dallaire sent a squad to protect the prime minister, but their vehicles' tyres were shot away and their engines shredded outside her home. She tried to flee and hid in a neighbour's bathroom. Soldiers dragged her out and a policeman shot her, the bullet removing half her face. She bled to death on her verandah. The UN soldiers sent to protect Agathe Uwilingiyimana were disarmed and five were clubbed to death. Ten escaped with one rifle and survived for an hour before they ran out of bullets. Surrounded, their Achilles tendons were cut to prevent escape. Slowly they were then tortured and mutilated.

Roadblocks were set up all over Kigali. Each car was searched and ID cards were scrutinised. All Tutsis were killed with machete blows and their bodies used to wall off the checkpoints. The Presidential Guard visited addresses on their Lists. Several thousand people were killed on the first day after the air crash.

Over the next week, Paul and Tatiana could see from their window many of their Hutu friends walking the streets grasping machetes that dripped with blood. A well-respected banker, who Paul knew well, was one of them, and he wore an army jacket.

'I didn't know you were a soldier,' Paul greeted him from his gate.

'The enemy,' replied the bespectacled banker, as though by rote, 'is amongst us. Many of those who we have long known are in fact traitors.'

What the banker did not know was that many 'traitors' were even then holed up inside Paul's home. Thirty-two terrified refugees, knowing Paul's moderate stance, had fled there before the killer squads had reached their listed addresses. Paul had squeezed them into his living room and kitchen, where they hid. He remembered a much-used saying of his late father: 'If a man can keep a fierce lion under his roof, why can he not shelter a fellow human being?'

After the fatal crash, Paul and Tatiana had warned their five children, aged between sixteen and two, not to leave the house, but Roger, fifteen, had climbed the wall to see the neighbour's son, his best friend. He returned home in shock, for his friend was dead, lying among the slashed bodies of his mother, six sisters and two neighbours. Some of them were still moving a little.

Next day Paul heard a commotion at the house of another neighbour, an elderly Tutsi lady. Paul rushed to fetch a friend, a soldier but a moderate, but they were too late, the mob had come and gone and the woman lay dead.

Not long afterwards they came for Paul in army vehicles. A captain marched up and poked Paul in the face. 'You, hotel manager, come with us. We need you to open up the hotel.'

Paul *wanted* to go to the hotel, probably safer than his home, but said he would only go if his family could go too. The thirty-two refugees in his house thus became his 'uncles, aunts, nephews and nieces'. The convoy stopped at a road-block formed by human torsos with side walls of legs and arms topped with heads. There the captain came up to Paul with a rifle.

'Do you know that all the managers in Rwanda are dead? You, traitor, are so far lucky. We are now going to kill all the people from your house and everyone at the hotel. *You* are going to help us.' He handed Paul the rifle. He was being offered to earn his right to survive by killing his family and the others. A moment of momentous decision with a terrible backdrop. A moment when, in my opinion, many men who might well have earned the Victoria Cross with gallant charges against machine-guns would at best have asked to be shot then and there.

But Paul, somehow sensing that there was yet room for manoeuvre, began to talk. 'Captain, I've no idea how to use a gun.' Paul pointed at a baby. 'Is this baby your enemy? You are yet young. Do you want blood on your hands all your life?' As his words faded, Paul instantly saw that such moral arguments would not work on this man. Next he tried his old 'hotel' trick. 'I have keys to the hotel. We have beer and whisky there.' Then he added his last card and offered cash. The captain suggested an outrageous sum, and Paul agreed. 'Only I,' he said, 'can open the safe. Take us all there.'

At the hotel, Paul paid off the captain with a million Rwandan francs, and the death squad drove away.

Within two hours of the president's death, organised killer squads were at work all over Rwanda, and RTLM Radio was instructing its listeners to kill their Tutsi neighbours. General Dallaire, horrified by what he saw all around him and with his 2,500 men unable to use force by UN mandate, cabled the UN in New York for permission for his men to use their weapons. This was not granted, and today's analysts concur that, if it had been, close on a million lives could have been saved.

Outside Kigali, militias went from village to village with their Lists and their machetes. No Tutsi was spared. Where there was a hint of resistance to the slaughter, the killers radioed for soldiers to help. Huge pits were bulldozed for the bodies. Villages were ticked off one by one as being free of cockroaches. No matter how well individuals might manage to hide, Hutu neighbours would direct the mob to find them.

Since Hutu and Tutsi are social groups, not tribes, and share both language and culture, living side by side in most villages, Tutsi families were therefore surrounded by Hutu. The individuals you had been to school with for years, prayed with in the same village church and gossiped with over a glass of banana beer, were likely to be the same people who would lead the mob to you or even help cut you up to show that they were not Tutsi sympathisers.

Any form of sympathy by a Hutu for a Tutsi was grounds

for death. African Rights Report *Rwanda: Death, Despair and Defiance* quotes the case of a Hutu pastor who was jailed because he visited his Tutsi in-laws after their house was burnt and some were killed. He was thereafter abandoned by all his own Hutu relatives. That testimony, from one Antoine Mupenzi, told of pregnant women cut open and, their babies removed, left to die. Others in the same village were cooked alive in vats of oil.

In Kibungu, on the border with Burundi, there had been sporadic Tutsi pogroms since 1992. One survivor of those days told the post-genocide judiciary, 'My father and my sister were buried alive in a latrine pit, and we know who did it. Knowing who in the village had killed your family made you more scared because you knew when the killings started again, you'd be their immediate target.'

The Rwandan bishop, John Rucyahana, deeply saddened, wrote: 'We have often been called Africa's most Christian country, with 90 per cent of the people identifying themselves as Christians. Yet people who had dutifully attended church on Sunday were slaughtering their neighbours by the end of the week. How did those who supposedly followed Jesus pick up machetes and chop children to death?'

How did a Hutu know who to kill, since not everybody was listed and many had lost their ID cards? The majority of Rwandans look alike, after all. How do Shia killers identify Sunni victims in a crowd? A former killer said: 'It was like madness, a frenzy. It was very exciting too, because the authorities were cheering you on, supporting you. But when I look back now, I see there was no reason for much of what we did. I killed babies with a machete, tiny babies. Why would I do that?'

Here is the testimony of one survivor: 'My husband and my brother were given massive machete blows on the shoulders. I started running with my two-year-old in my arms. She fell and I saw them cutting her up. I ran with all my strength, but everywhere people were screaming as I passed, "Here she is. Here she is." These were neighbours I had always considered friends, people I had always been kind to.'

For seven days she found shelter with many others in a nearby church, but: 'On the seventh day the white priest drove away and on the eighth they came for us. With nothing to fight with, our young men broke up the seats and threw them. But they were shot by a soldier. The mob, including many of my neighbours, then closed in. They macheted and macheted and macheted. Never can I forget the screaming.'

It was different in the towns like Kigali where people did not know each other. Quite a few people were murdered entirely due to their social class, because they owned a car, dressed well, or spoke good French. The same rationale often used for victim-choice in the Cambodian genocide.

In towns the militia had recruited a majority of poor people whose ranks, once the killing began, swelled with homeless street boys, car-washers and urchins who realised that the genocide was a great chance to loot and to get back at people who had what they didn't. In the words of one survivor, 'The people whose children had to walk barefoot to school killed people who could buy shoes for theirs.'

After a week or two in hiding, for those lucky folk on the killer lists who were not found at first, it was, of course, necessary to shop. But there were roadblocks on almost every street and guards at many shop doors checking ID cards. A Tutsi card meant instant death, or a slow one if the guards

wanted fun. To have lost your card, whatever your true identity, was also a death warrant.

Yet to have a genuine Hutu ID was not a guarantee of
safety. Many southern Hutu from areas known to favour
non-*akazu* parties were killed. So were Hutu cursed by birth
with longer-than-average noses or slightly taller than the
norm. Journalists, doctors or professionals like Paul were
high on local lists. Many thousands of Hutu died because
they were moderate or known to sympathise with Tutsis.
Those who, knowing the awful nature of the penalty, still
helped Tutsis were brave indeed. And none were braver than
Paul.

Tatiana's own family lived in a town which, RTLM Radio
daily assured listeners, was about to be cleansed. She knew
exactly what that would entail and could picture the horrible
deaths of her parents and siblings. But she knew that any
attempt to reach them would result in her own death at the
first roadblock.

Even greater was her immediate fear of the local mob all
around the Milles Collines awaiting a simple nod from their
militia leaders to exterminate every living soul in the hotel,
the refugees and their protectors alike. She knew the drill
from reports brought in by survivors. 'They often kill the
children first and force the parents to watch.'

Paul kept a diary. He wrote: 'We are terribly exposed here.
With Sabena management help I could probably get an escort
out with the family, but that would be a sign to the killers
that Milles Collines was no longer under special *akazu* protection.' Quite why he and everyone else in the hotel had not yet
been wiped out was as much a mystery to Paul as to anyone
else. He assumed that all the brownie points he had

A US special forces commando in Afghanistan.

The Taliban fighters' intimate knowledge of this hostile terrain makes them a formidable enemy, as Marcus Luttrell and his comrades discovered to their cost.

US Navy SEALs photographed in June 2005 at their base in Afghanistan a few days before the fatal reconnaissance mission in the remote Hindu Kush region. Matthew 'Axel' Axelson, left, Michael Murphy, right. Marcus Luttrell third from right, was the only survivor.

Paul Rusesabagina, the manager of the Hotel Milles Collines in Kigali, Rwanda. More than a thousand people took refuge there in 1994.

Government soldiers stand by as Tutsi refugees are evacuated by UN soldiers the day after Hutu militia surrounded the hotel.

The bodies of 400 Tutsis murdered by Hutu militia were found in the church at Ntarama.

More than three million people fled the genocide in Rwanda, and at least one million were massacred.

Weapons left behind at the border with Tanzania by Hutus fleeing Rwanda. The machete was the most dreaded killing-machine of the genocide.

PC Dick Coombes (left) the bravest man I've ever met, and Sergeant Dave Pengelly

PC Coombes recovering in hospital after the night of 5 October 198

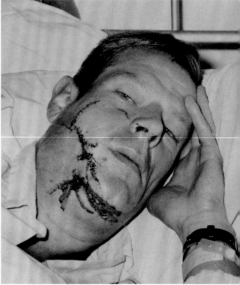

The back of PC Keith Blakelock's blood-stained uniform, with tape marking the wounds inflicted on him. The handle of a serrated knife driven four inches into his neck stuck out from beneath one ear.

Broadwater Farm estate in north London, the day after the riots.

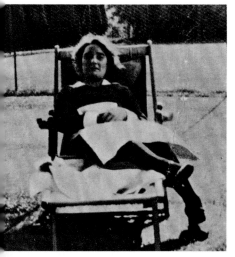

Gladys Aylward left school at 14, and took a job at the local Marks & Spencer before becoming a parlourmaid.

Gladys Aylward in Yangcheng, China 1936.

ladys with Jeannie Lawson's coffin, rrounded by some of her converts cluding the muleteers (back row) the Inn of Eighth Happinesses.

Pol Pot, left, with Cambodian Khmer Rouge supporters in 1975. For sheer murderous insanity and gratuitous brutality his regime left Hitler and Stalin way down the global roll-call of irrational psychopaths.

Khmer Rouge child soldiers holding M16 rifles. Children like these were taken from their families and indoctrinated into Pol Pot's manic regime.

The killing fields of Cambodia. Nearly two million people died during the brutal five-year rule of Angka.

Survivor Dith Pran at the site of a schoolhouse in Siem Reap, Cambodia in 1989.

With his family, while recovering from severe injuries received in North Africa in 1943, including the loss of an eye. The loss of some of his fingers made secretive bomb priming doubly difficult.

Klaus von Stauffenberg.

Adolf Hitler at the Wolf's Lair, Klaus von Stauffenberg stands on the left. This photograph was taken shortly before the attempt to assassinate the Führer.

Goering and Bormann are shown the devastation caused by the bomb explosion in the briefing room at the Wolf's Lair.

accumulated over the years with just about everyone of wealth, power and connections in Kigali, both good and evil, must be behind the miracle of inexplicable survival in the very eye of the storm. Paul knew that there were those among his Hutu staff who were spies for the militia, who listed each refugee under his care, and that included a fair number of Hutu moderates who had escaped the very first cull after the crash.

From the corridor windows of the hotel's west wing you could see through the rickety bamboo fence that surrounded the hotel grounds, and at all hours of the day and night the would-be killers, machetes at hand, patrolled the fence, stopping to peer into the hotel windows on spotting movement. Like ravening vultures awaiting their turn to tear up carrion prey, but temporarily held back, not by fear of a lion in this case, but by the daring and effrontery of a moderate Hutu with a Tutsi wife who had for many years been the charming representative of Kigali's most luxurious corridor of power. The Milles Collines, at least for a while, gave its ever-increasing number of desperate inmates an illusion of a safe haven from death. Paul charged no money because he knew that to take a man's cash was to strip him of money that could soon serve as a vital bribe.

Paul resolved, 'Nobody who makes it here will be turned away.'

The rumour had spread among Kigali's hunted and desperate that the Milles Collines was a safe haven, and the guest list soon approached a thousand in a hotel designed for three hundred. Paul noted that 'human beings are born with an extraordinary ability to fight evil with decency'. He had Hutu and Tutsi sleeping alongside each other on the floors, close up for comfort, for many had witnessed unimaginable horror. There was little privacy, although every now and again people would leave a room so that a husband and wife could make love.

Every day Paul phoned his bosses in Brussels, and they assured him that they were in constant touch with every known contact of *akazu* top men, especially their friends the French. They could promise nothing but hope, but the killer mobs often acted on impulse, uncontrollable even by the *akazu* or the army.

As the dread days and nights ticked by at the hotel and the militias still held off from an overt massacre, they tried to use other means to force the refugees out. In mid-April, they cut off the electricity and water supplies. Paul's emergency generator soon broke down, adding to the misery, low morale and fear.

Each room held an average of eight frightened people, at night reliving horror in dreams and screaming or weeping at the memory of their slaughtered loved ones. And each room was, they all knew, merely a death-row cell. Militia spies with knowing grins and belt-hung machetes came in and out of the hotel when they wished; cats and mice in the same cage.

Paul was worried as the level of his reserve water tanks slowly lowered. With a few days left, he decided to use the swimming pool with its 78,000 gallons. He reckoned that if each person used one and a half gallons per day, they could last out two months. Plastic waste bins were used to drink, wash and flush toilets. Through luck, Sabena and Air France had stored 2,000 prepared meal-trays at the hotel, and when these ran low, Paul sent a Hutu-driven truck with cash to a local market for corn and beans, which were then cooked in huge pots on a fire on the lawn.

Paul remembered elegant parties of Kigali glitterati in dark suits and long silk dresses, holding cocktail glasses, all chatting under fairy lights. Now the lawn was a cookhouse, the pool a discoloured well, and the guests scared refugees in dirty clothes, some with their gaping wounds seeping pus through bandages and many who had seen friends become killers and families cut to pieces. The stress on Paul, in whose sole hands a thousand lives continued to survive another hour, another day, was unremitting, and all about the hotel and throughout Rwanda the violence escalated.

A topic of conversation Paul heard discussed more than once, always in hushed tones, was the mobs' killing methods. What was the worst death? The *masu*, the pits or the machete? Hundreds of corpses were found with their nails torn from scrabbling at the walls of the Rwandan latrine pits into which they had been thrown. Or one could die of pain and poison from the deep puncture wounds of the *masu*, a wooden club spiked with nails. The nails are long and go through your skin into your bones. Might that be preferable to dying in faecal slime? Or the machete? Survivors of machete attacks had reached the Milles Collines with hideous wounds to their arms and faces.

Following frostbite damage to all the fingers on one of my hands, I once spent three months with severed nerve ends, and grew so desperate to stop the pain that I put the fingers one by one in a Black and Decker vice and cut away the dead ends with a fretsaw. The thumb took two days to remove, but the result was worth it. So I can well imagine the agony of whole limbs being macheted, and the utter terror of those who awaited such a fate. Including Paul.

There were those wounded in the hotel who told of death

squad killers who would select a wealthy-looking target, cut off one hand, then stand over the victim casually sharpening their machete with a whetstone and ask for money 'to avoid further treatment'. Others told Paul that they feared they would develop AIDS because of their wounds, since their attackers' machetes had dripped with the blood of previous kills.

There were also those who made jokes through it all: 'God does really love Rwanda, but right now he's busy elsewhere.'

One in every eight of the 8 million citizens of Rwanda was murdered in one hundred days, which, by simple mathematics, indicates a degree of commitment and efficiency comparable to that of Nazi Germany. The latter exterminated seven and a half million people, including five and a half million Jews, in four years with little protest from the populace, and at times with their active support. Their killer system was high-tech and efficient. Rwanda's was low-tech but brimful of eager commitment by a large section of the populace. Why was this?

Firstly, the *akazu* took advantage of the indoctrination of the mass of Rwandan peasants over five centuries to obey at all times those in authority, whether it be the monarch, the Germans, the Belgians, their initial favourite the Tutsi or, later, the Hutu Habyarimana regime. That which the government's representatives command must be right and must be obeyed. When the time came that the local mayor was ordered from on high to kill all Tutsis and their Hutu sympathisers, then you seize your machete without asking questions – unless you are a very brave individual.

Secondly, Rwanda had too many people for too little fertile land. In 1990 there were eight times more people crammed into the villages than in 1900. The peasants were well aware that, following the genocide, there would, with governmental approval, be land, cows, banana trees, and many other spoils up for grabs. Meanwhile, under cover of the killing times, one could steal, settle old scores, rape long-coveted neighbours' daughters, and get drunk. So groups of hitherto harmless villagers coalesced into monstrous killer mobs who learnt to enjoy what they were doing, as cats learn to play with mice.

As survivors of the original Death Lists in Kigali were picked off or managed to reach the Milles Collines, so the hotel was increasingly at risk lest Paul's anonymous protectors be overruled by other *akazu*, or merely by the predators outside the picket fence losing patience with any authority blocking their desire to rub out this last remaining nest of cockroaches.

Paul fended off each new danger by way of his office phone and his little black phone book, his fragile route to the nebulous and ever-shifting corridors of power. So when one day in April the *akazu* hardliners located and cut all the hotel phone lines, Paul felt utterly naked and helpless. Then he remembered. There was, from seven years before, an old fax machine plugged directly into the Kigali town switchboard, not the hotel's. Snatching up its handset he heard the best music of his life, the hum of a dial tone. That phone became the lifeline for a thousand people.

Late in April a local reporter, Thomas Kamalindi, who had been on the Death Lists but escaped to the hotel, gave an interview to Radio France describing the state of things in Kigali, the ongoing genocide and the slow advance of the RPF. Within an hour of the interview's transmission, RTLM announced a new and urgent Death Order on

Kamalindi. An army colonel was sent to arrest him. Paul persuaded this officer to have a drink in his office. And then another. He flattered, he charmed, he bribed, he tried moral Christian ethics. And at length the colonel, his jeep loaded with crates of red wine, agreed to go away and think about the killing of such a 'low priority scum' of a journalist. Paul had saved another life at further risk of fatally infuriating some unseen *akazu* top brass. Over ninety days Paul stuck his neck out in such a way many times in order to save members of his precious 'family' of terrified people, Hutu and Tutsi alike.

Every day brought new refugees and new tales of the evil at large everywhere, except within Paul's precarious haven.

Rwandans have always been brought up especially to respect and protect old folk, children and women. Yet the current reign of terror spared nobody. In fact, it often seemed that the more defenceless and innocent a person, the more likely they would be made to suffer terribly. Post-genocide court cases include children as young as ten being given machetes and told to murder their former playmates. In one village the schoolchildren were given the head of a Tutsi classmate to use as a soccer ball.

Rwanda: Death, Despair and Defiance, the African Rights Report cites many sickening first-hand accounts. One quotes a thirteen-year-old orphan girl from Nyamata, south of Kigali. 'I was very weak from the cuts. A few children among the bodies moved about. I called to one to help me, a girl of about nine. She replied that she couldn't because they had cut off her arms.'

One report involved the old and the young. 'The mob picked out the mothers and gave them *masus* to kill their sons. Some did, hoping to protect themselves. The majority, including me, refused. I had spent too many nights pregnant and waiting for my sons to be the one to kill them. And as I was then heavily pregnant, the idea of killing my own children seemed even more mad.' This woman managed to escape with her children, and later, in the bush near her village, she gave birth to a baby boy.

> I stayed there all day with my sons, afraid that the baby's cries would alert attackers. In the evening an old woman, a neighbour, passed by to fetch water. As I knew her, I greeted her. I hoped that, as a grandmother, she would understand my predicament. She asked about the delivery. She asked me about the child with a lot of sympathy in her voice, and she wanted to see it. I was afraid, but what could I do? When she saw it was a boy, she cried, 'Aha, so you have another cockroach.' She picked up a stick and hit my little boy. He was dead at once at ten hours old. She said, 'The other ones you have will do you. I hear they do well at school.'
>
> But she went back and fetched her sons. They dug a hole, then they put a sword through my Emmanuel, and while he was still groaning threw him in it. One of them hit me with a *masu* and macheted my last son Theo. I saw his brains spill out, but they hit me on the head and I passed out.

The African Rights Report contains detailed testimonies of specific crimes to women and bears out the stories told to Paul by traumatised survivors. Killers known to be HIV-positive were often 'assigned the task' of raping Tutsi women. Girls were gang-raped in front of their parents, women in front of their husbands and children, then raped to death with tree branches, knives or poles. Many women became mistresses to death squad leaders as a way to survive, and a high proportion of all Tutsi survivors were, indeed, women in their late teens and twenties with children whose fathers were killers and rapists.

By the end of May, Paul had 1,268 people crammed into a space designed for 300 maximum. Forty were in Paul's family's own room. Folk slept in corridors, bathrooms, pantries and the ballroom. A common sight as these survivors looked out at the street beyond the adjacent bamboo fence were the lines of construction work lorries en route to the mass grave pits, each one stacked high with bodies, and, Paul recorded, 'many with stumps where their arms and legs had been'.

Despite the urging of Tatiana and the ease with which he could have obtained one, Paul never bought a gun, for he knew his most powerful weapons were his phone and his brain. One severe test of these weapons came early one morning when he was fast asleep after an exhausting night spent working late, and the phone rang. It was an army lieutenant.

'The Ministry of Defence has ordered that you evacuate your hotel within thirty minutes.'

Paul tried to argue, but the officer was blunt.

'Do it now or I will do it for you.'

Paul raced to a window and his heart sank. The hotel was surrounded by hundreds of militia with spears, machetes and rifles. Paul knew that only he could save a mass murder within the hour. Half-dressed, he ran to his office. Too early, he realised, to call friends in Europe. Too late to call the USA. His only chance was to locate an army top brass who was senior to the lieutenant with the evacuation order. 'I pulled out my black binder,' Paul recorded, 'and started calling all my generals. Many knew what was going on and made no comment.' He was still phoning desperately when a clerk told him that he must go to reception *at once*. Half-dressed and realising this was it, Paul went to meet his fate.

Instead of the expected lieutenant, a senior police colonel greeted him with the simple words, 'The plan has been changed.'

An angry howl from the mob outside as they were told to disperse confirmed to Paul that one of his phone calls had worked. His key argument had been that a massacre outside the by now famous Milles Collines would shock the conscience of the world community, with terrible repercussions for the Rwandan government. The police colonel had outranked the army lieutenant who, Paul later learnt, was merely the extremist nephew of a top *akazu* killer.

The RPF advance on Kigali had meanwhile reached the stage where the *akazu* were forced to make a deal, and the UN were told that they could evacuate certain refugees from the Milles Collines. They would be escorted to the airport and flown to safety. But only individuals with letters from abroad agreeing to receive them could go.

Paul forged many letters for people with no overseas contacts. He and his own family qualified without a problem. He made his decision. 'Out! What a seductive concept! No more knives and blood and fear in our dark rooms with their stench of faeces and sweat. Away from the power-drunk fools with their empty smiles and machetes. No more worry. I could have all this. I can have it tomorrow!'

But, in his heart, he knew he could not go. 'If I leave, nobody will be left to save all those who have to stay. No one else has all those years of favours and free drinks to cash in. I could donate my black binder and the secret of the fax line to somebody else, but to them it would be useless. If I leave, there will be a killing and it will be as if I am the murderer.'

Some refugees came to Paul seeking confirmation of his intentions. 'If you are leaving,' they said, 'we have time to jump from the roof to avoid the pain of the machetes.'

Paul did, however, arrange with Sabena to evacuate all his family. 'If my wife or children are murdered when I could have seen them to safety, my life will be ruined. This is the most painful decision of my life, but I must stay and face whatever will come.'

The next day he waved off the UN convoy, but even as it pulled away, RTLM Radio announced a complete list of every 'cockroach' evacuated, and ordered roadblock groups to stop and kill them all. The UN move had turned from hope to doom.

A mile from the hotel the convoy was stopped and the seventy refugees beaten up. Tatiana was beaten and her back badly bruised. Luckily, an argument between the army and the militia, who began to open fire on each other, allowed the UN escort to save the refugees and rush back to the hotel, the entire mission aborted.

A few days later Paul received a secret warning that a mass attack on the hotel was planned in a few hours' time. Back to the fax line and calls to every number in the black binder. By dusk the attack had not materialised. At 10 p.m. a grenade smashed against a second-floor wall. Then silence. Paul phoned General Dallaire to say, 'The hotel is under attack,' and, amazingly, the general arrived with a small UN squad, and there was no follow-up to the grenade. 'Nearly delirious with fatigue,' Paul wrote, 'after one of the longest days of my life, I crawled into bed beside my wounded wife.'

Paul was near to the end of his tether. The endless stress and the daily diet of ever-new tales of terror were wearing him down. He wrote: 'I knew I was going to die. I have done far too much to cross the architects of the genocide. The only question is when and the method of my death and that of Tatiana and our children. I dread the machetes. It rages on, all around the hotel, on the capital's streets, in the communes, in the hills and in every little valley. It has become killing for killing's sake, killing for sport, killing for nothing.' He added that he held a stash of cash for his final bribe, for his family to be shot not macheted.

Swamps were favourite places for machete attack survivors where, often up to their necks and mosquito-mad, they tried to hide from their zealous hunters and their dogs. In many areas bush was cleared and trees felled to prevent concealment opportunities. River banks were seldom useful hides, for the rivers of Rwanda are usually swift. Indeed, corpse removal in many areas was simply to dump truck-loads of bodies in the local watershed. The Ugandans, alerted by sickness in lakeside villages, found Lake Victoria to be seriously polluted, and eventually fished a total of 40,000 putrefied corpses from the lake.

In Kigali itself, nine weeks after the presidential air crash, the city was rife with sickness, especially malaria. Disease-ridden rats and dogs, glutted from the ready supply of rotting human flesh, roamed the streets. The stench from the body piles on every corner filled the air and, according to a rare visitor (Jean-Paul Mari writing in *Le Nouvel Observateur*), it 'took several days to get rid of the feeling that it was sticking to my skin'.

As the RPF closed in on Kigali, the *akazu*'s city killers became obsessive in their drive to locate the nests of those cockroaches clever or lucky enough to still be alive. So the last known havens of the hunted were, by mid-June, under imminent threat. Aware of this, the UN managed to stage a second attempt to extract several hundred of the Milles Collines refugees, and this time succeeded. Once again Paul, with much mental anguish, gave up his chance to escape the death trap which his hotel had become. This time he kept his family with him.

One of the other rare refugee havens in the city, St Paul's church, which had managed to protect a specific group of Tutsi schoolchildren, was attacked by a local mob on 14 June, and forty of the children were hacked to death on the church steps. Three days later, a mere 500 yards from the Milles Collines, the Sainte Famille church was attacked. From the hotel roof Paul was able to observe the killings and knew who would be next. Going downstairs he met the mayor of Kigali, who was also an army colonel. Paul begged him to provide the hotel with at least a token defensive force, but the mayor refused. Risking all, Paul drove to the Diplomates hotel, five potentially lethal minutes away, where he knew he would find General Bizimungu, a very senior army man for whom he had done many hotel favours over many years. This was the first time in seventy days that Paul had risked leaving his hotel, and he only did so in the certain knowledge that time had finally run out for the Milles Collines.

He unlocked the wine cellars of the Diplomates, to which he still held a key, and invited the general to 'sample fine Bordeaux' with him. They were discussing the RPF advance and inevitable victory when a soldier arrived and reported to the general that 'the militia have entered the Milles Collines.' Paul's worst nightmare had happened. His wife and his children were even now either dead or being mutilated.

The general agreed at once to accompany Paul back to the Milles Collines, and when they arrived there, to Paul's amazement, Bizimungu shouted at his sergeant, 'You go up there and tell those boys that if one person kills anyone, I will kill them. If they do not leave the hotel in five minutes, I will kill all of them.'

The militia had by then searched every room and herded every living soul down to the bare ground all around the swimming pool. With his heart in his mouth, Paul rushed to his family's room, Number 126. The door was smashed but, the best moment in his life, he brushed aside the shower curtain in the dark washing cubicle, and there, clustered in his wife's arms, were his five children. He left them there and ran down to the pool, where his 'guests' were huddled in their hundreds and kneeling as in prayer to the screams and curses of the mob. The killing order, Paul sensed, was imminent. But Bizimungu, his camouflage uniform neatly ironed and his pistol drawn, strode out and roared at the militia, 'You go *now*. In five minutes you are gone or *you* are dead.'

The militia could easily have ignored him. They knew the general was powerful, but there had been many mutinies when the mob's bloodlust was up, and was this not the very last cockroach hide? If God had indeed gone AWOL from Rwanda in that spring of 1994, he must have glanced back at the right moment on that fateful day, for the militia slowly lowered their machetes and, muttering oaths at the general, trooped out of the hotel grounds.

Quite why Bizimungu, previously responsible for mass murders, acted as he did at the Milles Collines that day is not clear. As I write, he is locked up for war crimes in a Tanzanian jail, and likely to stay there for life. But whatever his role in the Rwandan genocide, he fell under Paul's charm for long enough to save the day and hundreds of lives.

Elsewhere in Rwanda the mobs were halted by no Bizimungu and stormed the last remaining redoubts where brave men like Paul had, until then, found a way of saving souls. Churches that had been havens were attacked. In the Catholic church of Ntarama, 5,000 people were massacred. In Chahinda parish over 20,000, and in Karama over 25,000 met their deaths. Hospitals were visited and cleansed, as in Butari where patients were clubbed and slashed in their beds and doctors and nurses murdered. At the Don Bosco School 2,000 students were killed, many with great brutality.

General Dallaire recalled: 'Right in front of our eyes the army men came into the hospital, lined up the wounded and machine-gunned them. All our Tutsi medics, doctors and nurses were killed.' Dallaire also witnessed the immediate aftermath of a church massacre. 'In the aisles and pews were bodies of hundreds of men, women and children; at least fifteen still alive. A baby tried to feed from its dead mother.'

Dallaire, the RPF and the Rwandan Army leaders, hearing of the near-miss at the Milles Collines, finally agreed to complete a full evacuation, and within forty-eight hours, under heavy guard, the last of the 1,268 souls whose lives Paul had saved were taken to safety. Paul and his family remained behind with a UN guard for protection.

The RPF finally took over Kigali on 4 July and, after much

scrubbing, fumigation and whitewashing, Paul reopened the Milles Collines on 15 July. He stayed there for two years, but he knew too many secrets about too many top people, and the new regime became for Paul and his family almost as dangerous as the last, so he took his family to a new life in Brussels.

He took a job as a taxi driver in the city, worked hard and started a small business which thrived to the point where he founded a charity for genocide orphans.

In 1999 the Academy Award-winning film *Hotel Rwanda*, based on Paul's story, was released to worldwide acclaim. That was twelve years ago but the very week that I decided to write about Paul and the genocide, he was declared by Rwandan President Paul Kagame, ex-RPF commander and saviour of the Rwandan Tutsis, to be an official enemy of the state. Paul's ongoing criticism in the Belgian media of Kagame's increasingly despotic regime had clearly hit home. Despite living in suburban Brussels, he and Tatiana are living in fear of their lives. Their home has twice been ransacked and documents have been seized. Their nightmare continues. The price of true and enduring courage.

So many heroes have died without the chance to give their personal views on their own bravery. Paul is the exception, giving me the opportunity to quote his thoughts where they may help define the elusive word *Hero*.

Remember that Paul's every action took place against the background of a hurricane of murder which eliminated 80 per cent of its targets in six short weeks in April/May 1994. Since 800,000 to one million were killed, the daily kill-rate was at least five times that of the worst Nazi death camps.

Paul wrote:

It was very strange for me to be called a 'hero' the way that I was when the movie, *Hotel Rwanda*, was released in Europe and America. Over and over people kept telling me that what I did at the hotel was heroic, but I never saw it that way. I said No to outrageous actions the way I thought that anybody would, and it still mystifies me that so many others could and did say Yes.

However, I was not the only one who said No. Individual acts of courage happened every single day of the genocide. It is true that Rwanda was full of killers, but it was also full of ordinary heroes.

We are all born with a powerful herd instinct which can force otherwise rational people to act in inexplicable ways. I have seen my own neighbours; gentle, humorous, seemingly normal people, turn into killers in the space of two days. They were bullied and cajoled into doing things they would never have dreamt possible without the eyes of the mob upon them.

When your individuality is dissolved into the will of the pack, you act in whatever way the pack directs, and the thought of acting otherwise becomes abhorrent, if not terrifying. The mass of men will thus easily commit atrocities for the sake of keeping up appearances. The lone man who dares cut himself away from the pack is ridiculed and despised, but he is the only one who can stand between humanity and the abyss.

There will be other genocides and the question will again be if uninvolved people will have the courage to save strangers.

I remember as a young man reading in the Bible, 'What

is your life? You are a mist that appears for a little while and then vanishes.' Our time here on our Earth is short and our chance to make a difference is tiny.

In this chapter I have attempted to describe one of the darkest chapters in human history. In such circumstances anybody who resisted the killings were men and women of great decency and extraordinary courage. None more so than Paul Rusesabagina.

* * *

It is often said that courage is an expendable quality which can easily become exhausted through over-use. To continue to hoodwink the Rwandan terror machine day after day, week after week, was a constant drain on courage, a cause of unimaginable ever-present stress in an atmosphere of the utmost menace. Rusesabagina's courage was truly rock-like.

4

Small But Great

'Where is the man who has the power and skill to
stem the torrent of a woman's will? For if she will,
she will, you may depend on't'
Canterbury Examiner, 1829

Gladys Aylward was born in 1902 in a suburb of north
London where her father was a postman. She left school
at fourteen, having failed all exams, and took a job as a shop
girl at the local Marks & Spencer. She then became a parlourmaid to an upper-class family but nurtured a secret desire to
be an actress. She was neither pretty nor clever, and she was
noticeably small in stature. So her dream of treading the
boards remained just a dream. The best somebody of her
background could hope for was to progress from parlourmaid
to head of the household's downstairs females and to marry
someone kind.

In her early twenties Gladys went one evening to a local
Protestant church meeting and, in due course, became involved
in religious activities. A missionary magazine sparked her
interest in the state of the people of China, where one quarter
of the world's population lived in dreadful poverty and most

had never heard of the Christian faith. Surely, Gladys thought, something should be done about those poor Chinese. So she suggested to her brother that he go there and tell them about the Bible.

'Not me,' was the reply. 'Why don't you go yourself?'

So Gladys decided that she would do missionary work in China, and, aged twenty-six, she took a three-month course with a missionary society. Due to her lack of education, the mission's committee decided that she was not up to the job and turned down her application on the basis that the Chinese language would be too difficult for her to learn. But they suggested that she could go to Bristol and help out a retired couple of old China missionaries. So she did, and loved to listen to their stories of that magic land on the far side of the world. Restless, she took a job in the Swansea docks as a Christian Rescue Sister trying to reform the prostitutes and save young local girls from joining that profession. Sailors off ships from all over the world enjoyed the girls' services and objected to anyone getting in the way of their immediate passion. Gladys felt that she was doing her, rather hazardous, bit for Jesus, but it was a far cry from evangelising in China, which had for her become an obsessive goal. Since no official mission would take her on, she decided that she would go there on her own. In order to save enough money to buy a ticket, she went back to work as a housemaid.

The local travel agent told Gladys that the cheapest sea passage to China would be £90, but to travel by train across Siberia was only £47 and ten shillings. Gladys had managed to amass life savings of £2 and ten shillings, so she had a long way to go. Nonetheless she took on evening work and part-time maid jobs in her time off, and she poured every penny into her ticket fund.

The travel booking clerk to whom she gave the money as she saved it told her one day that a war had broken out between the Japanese and the Russians and he could no longer guarantee that her booked train journey would not end somewhere in the middle of a Siberian nowhere. Gladys shrugged and carried on saving. Meanwhile, news of a seventy-three-year-old Scottish missionary lady who needed help in the Shansi province of north China reached Gladys, so she wrote to apply and eventually received the enigmatic response, 'I will meet you at Tientsin if you can find your way out.'

Gladys eventually saved the £47 and ten shillings. Another housemaid lent her an old suitcase and a scraggy fur coat, for the Russian weather could apparently get colder even than Swansea. Her mother sewed a secret pocket into her corset in which she hid her Bible, the magic passport obtained at length from the Ministry, and her journey money consisting of £2 in traveller's cheques. Nobody would look in her corset, not even Russians.

Evangelism meant letting as many people as possible know about the contents of the Bible and the advantages, especially to the soul, of becoming a Christian. Gladys knew that she needed to practise this, so in her rare spare time she went to Speakers' Corner in Hyde Park and, joining other soapbox speakers there, applied her rather weak voice to spreading the Word to whoever cared to listen. She learned to ignore hecklers and those who liked to jeer or merely leer. After many sessions at the Corner or, when rushed with her maid-work, merely on local street pavements, Gladys had made no converts but she felt a touch more confident that she could take on the Chinese.

When the great day of the journey approached, Gladys packed the suitcase with biscuits, corned beef, baked beans and meat cubes. In an army blanket she wrapped up her bedroll, spare clothes, a tiny spirit cooker, a kettle and a pan so that she could get to China, and maybe the place called Tientsin, without needing to spend money. Her family waved Gladys off to China (which they had found on a map) from Liverpool Street Station. They knew that she would be gone for quite a while. It would, in fact, be seventeen years before they saw her again.

The train passed through Holland, Germany and Poland. Gladys ate sparingly from her suitcase larder and slept on her bedroll. After seven days they reached the Siberian border and Gladys recorded, 'It's very very cold at night and hard to keep even slightly warm.'

Somewhere near the Manchurian border the other passengers, mostly soldiers, all left the train and marched off into the gloom. A railway official tried to shift Gladys but was unintelligible, so she stayed put because, though the carriage grew ever colder, the night outside looked even less inviting. There were no lights on the train or on the platform and, without warning, the staccato crackle of gunfire sounded in the darkness. At this point Gladys did leave the train, realising that it might be a target of the, as yet, invisible enemy. She sat on her luggage for a while on the deserted platform, but soon began to shiver uncontrollably.

Huddled round a fire in a small hut, Gladys found the engine driver and station porter who, with many signs, made Gladys realise that she was at the very end of the line and her only chance of going anywhere was to walk back down the line several miles to Chita Station, where she just might find a train heading towards somewhere useful to her.

So Gladys tramped down the railway line in the freezing

darkness, snow-laden forest on either side and the sound of gunfire alternating with the howls of hunting wolf packs. At midnight, exhausted from carrying her heavy suitcase and bedroll, she could go no further so, wrapped in the old fur coat, she slept in her suitcase on the railway line. Throughout the next day she forced herself on down the line and, reaching Chita at nightfall utterly exhausted, she was arrested.

The Russians were clearly suspicious. Her passport was British, but she had appeared down the line from the forest, and her ticket destination was China. Clearly she was a spy. However, she was saved by an interpreter's basic error, for he misread the word 'missionary' in her passport as 'machinery', and he told her in front of the interrogating soldiers that Russia was in dire need of machinery experts at that time. Gladys was also helped by an old photograph she carried of her brother in his best army uniform as a regimental drummer. To the Russians he was dressed like a senior general, and this suggested that Gladys moved in influential circles. So they decided to help her on her way and placed her on a train to Nicolshissur, to change at Pogranilchnai, and thence to Harbin and China.

At the second of these stations she learnt that the Japanese had advanced and closed the rail to Harbin. Sitting on her suitcase, cold and hungry, she watched a chained line of screaming men and women being driven along by guards. 'From that moment,' she wrote, 'I hated Communism with all my being.' In the morning she found a man who explained in English that her only chance was to take the next train to the most eastern town in Siberia, Vladivostok. She caught it. Standing room only for a very long way.

In Vladivostok an Intourist official who spoke English

confiscated her passport and took her to a cheap hotel. He even showed her round the town. At first he seemed friendly, but when he, unlike the Chita soldiers, discovered that missionary did not after all imply expertise in machinery, he showed his true colours and matters came to a head when he pushed into her bedroom waving her passport and clearly intimating that if she did not let him have his way with her, then she would not get it back.

Angry, she flew at the man and successfully grabbed her passport, then fled to the harbour where a kindly Japanese ship's captain agreed to take her to Japan. Not exactly China but by now, to Gladys, anywhere was better than Russia.

The British Consulate, amazed at the journey Gladys had already made, helped her to reach a Christian mission in Kobe, where the staff eventually arranged her passage by steamer to China and the port of Tientsin. Twenty-four days after leaving London she reached Tientsin, having never previously ventured further than Swansea and Bristol.

The Scottish lady's mission was, it now appeared, many miles north of Tientsin in the distant mountains of Shansi province. By this time Gladys had learnt that conditions all over China were not what might have been expected in a land of truly ancient culture and wisdom where the wheel was invented whilst her own ancestors were still wearing woad. Extreme poverty was the rule not the exception. There were no hospitals, shops or schools, and, in the great northern Shansi province where she was bound, no means of travel but by mule, camel or donkey; nothing on wheels, for there were no roads, only narrow trails. And, in all that arid region no wheat or rice was grown; only buckwheat and maize. Shoes were made from cloth with soles of tree-bark, and seldom lasted more than a month. Hard labour was needed to survive, so sons were valuable and daughters all but worthless.

So Gladys took a train to Peking, a rickety bus to Tsechow, and for two days and nights rode the back of a mule over three mountain ranges and numerous river fords to the walled town of Yangcheng, at the gateway of which she was met by the redoubtable Scottish missionary, the seventy-three-year-old Jeannie Lawson, who asked, 'And who are you?'

'I am Gladys Aylward who wrote to you from London.'

'Oh, yes . . . Well, are you coming in?'

Over a cup of hot liquid which Gladys found all but undrinkable, her new boss explained that the mission, a huge empty courtyard edged by a few derelict and windowless cubicles, was ideal as its rent was only two shillings and four pence a year because it was haunted.

Gladys slept fully dressed on her bedroll in one of the cubicles and woke to the goggle- but slant-eyed stares of a great many giggling children, all of whom were raggedy and unwashed. Word had got out that a new foreign devil had arrived in town.

Mrs Lawson put Gladys to work at once, with the specific job of turning the courtyard into a muleteers' hostel, or rather a spider's web in which passers-by, once ensnared, would have to listen to the Christian Gospel as described by Mrs Lawson in her fluent Shansi-dialect-Mandarin whilst they ate their dinner and later their breakfast. The winding, rock-strewn tracks of Shansi were trodden every day of the year by long mule trains led, usually from behind, by muleteers. There were already plenty of muleteer inns in Yangcheng but none where you could get bed, breakfast *and* free stories from one, possibly two, foreign devils.

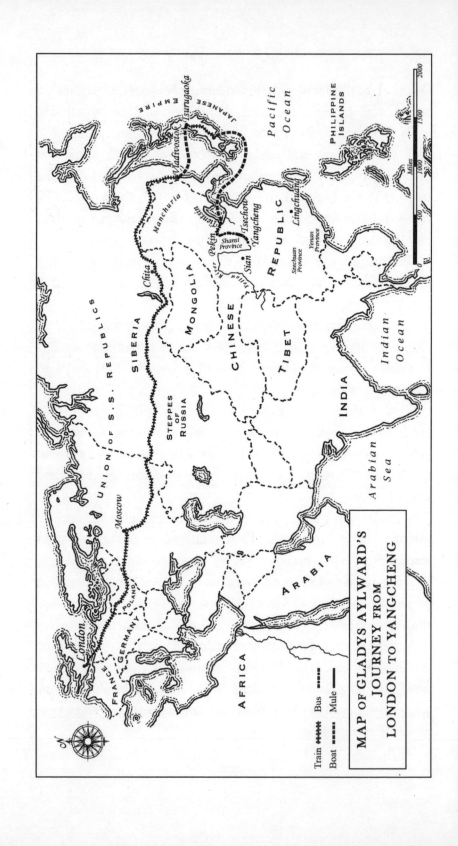

Pacific
Ocean

PHILIPPINE
ISLANDS

Miles

Vladivostok Tsuruyaoka

JAPANESE EMPIRE

Tsientin

Tsechow
Yangcheng

Pekin

Lingchuang

Manchuria

River

*Shansi
Province*

Yellow

Sian

CHINESE

REPUBLIC

*Yenan
Province*

*Szechuan
Province*

Chita

SIBERIA

MONGOLIA

TIBET

Indian
Ocean

UNION OF S.S. REPUBLICS

STEPPES
OF
RUSSIA

INDIA

Arabian
Sea

Moscow

London

FRANCE

POLAND

GERMANY

ARABIA

AFRICA

MAP OF GLADYS AYLWARD'S
JOURNEY FROM
LONDON TO YANGCHENG

Train ┼┼┼┼┼ Bus ▬▬▬▬
Boat ▬▬▬▬ Mule ▬▬▬▬

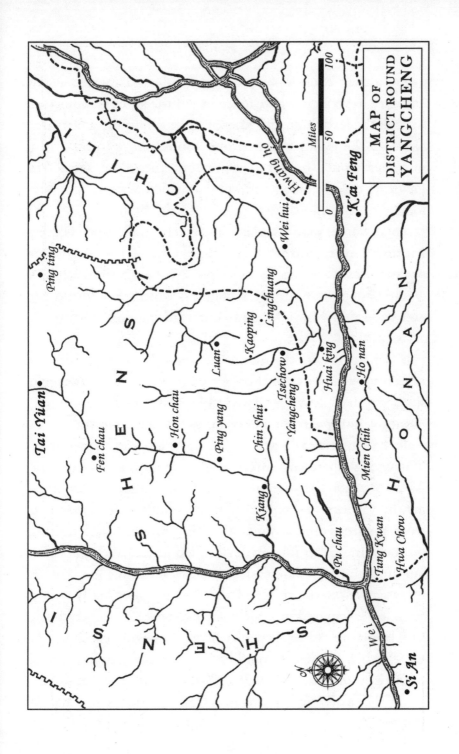

MAP OF
DISTRICT ROUND
YANGCHENG

Miles

0   50   100

CHIHLI

Ping ting

Wei hui

Hwang ho

K'ai Feng

Lingchuang

Kaoping

Luan

Tsechow

Yangcheng

Huai king

Ho nan

HONAN

Tai Yüan

Fen chau

Hon chau

Ping wang

Chin Shui

Kiang

Mien Chih

Pu chau

Tung Kwan

Hwa Chow

Wei

Si An

SHENSI

SHENSI

An ancient cook was hired, and Gladys was posted at the entrance to the newly christened Inn of the Eight Happinesses to grab the lead mule and forcibly steer it into the courtyard. Since all the mules followed one another nose to tail, their muleteer would have no option but to follow suit. Mrs Lawson's only retainer, an old man named Mr Lu, had mule fodder ready and waiting. Game, set and match.

This whole plan worked extremely well, and Gladys swotted hard to learn the language. One of her first fluent phrases was 'Good food. No bugs. No fleas.' Since China's gossip-system was run by muleteers, word soon spread far and wide that Mrs Lawson's courtyard inn was well worth a visit.

In a year or two, the old lady grew sick and, though well cared for by Gladys, for there were no doctors in Yangcheng, she soon died, leaving Gladys sole mistress of the inn and the only European for many miles around. She started to walk to isolated villages in the high mountains north of Yangcheng where she spread the Gospel on street corners. As at Speakers' Corner in Hyde Park, nobody listened to her, but at least the villagers stared, children screamed and women threw mud-balls at this tiny foreign devil ranting on about this other foreign devil called Jesus. Mud-spattered, but undaunted, Gladys slept in caves during her village forays and, on returning to the inn, would usually find a circle of fascinated mule-men being served their very basic supper by the old cook whilst listening goggle-eared to Mr Lu, by then a keen, if muddled, evangelist, regaling them with tales of how Noah (his favourite biblical character) saved the world in various ways and could even walk on water.

Slowly but surely a nucleus of Christian converts loyal to Gladys formed in Yangcheng and the surrounding mountain valleys, and Gladys was one day surprised by an official visit from the de facto ruler of all Yangcheng, the local Mandarin. Mr Lu feared for their lives, but the Mandarin had not, on this occasion, come to sever heads with his great curved sword. Faraway Peking, the Mandarin explained, had just issued a proclamation that, throughout all China, the ancient tradition of binding young girls' feet to make them attractive to men would henceforth cease.

The Mandarin was personally responsible in his area for ensuring that this ruling was carried out. He then announced to the astonished Gladys his decision that she was to become his official foot-inspector.

Men, he pointed out, could not inspect young girls' feet, and the only woman in all his district of Shansi province with unbound feet was Gladys, who by then was to all intents and purposes Chinese in dress, language and day-to-day behaviour. The Mandarin even favoured her religion, which he had heard did not encourage foot-binding, on top of which she was already well known in his region through her Gospel-spreading travels. She was the perfect choice.

And so Gladys, supplied with an official mule, a ration quota and two of the Mandarin's soldiers, became the local government foot-inspector. She took the job seriously and loved to watch the faces of hundreds of happy little girls as the often excruciating pain of their bindings was relieved under her watchful eye. Many of the old folk took badly against this interference with tradition, but Mandarin orders were not to be trifled with, even when transmitted by as surprising a creature as the diminutive Gladys.

She used her new job to spread her Gospel stories to the most remote corners of the mountains, and she soon became known to all as the Storyteller, or Ai-weh-deh (the Good Woman).

At school and as a parlourmaid Gladys had always had a circle of good friends and, at home, her own loving family. In Yangcheng, close to nobody, she often felt lonely until one day she came upon a woman by the roadside with a starved and filthy little girl for sale to any passer-by who could afford two shillings. Gladys only had nine pence, but she bought the child, named her Ninepence and brought her up at the inn as her own loving daughter. Ninepence later brought in other orphans, and before long Gladys had a little family of two dozen wastrels to love and to care for. She never felt lonely again.

Gladys had a great way with her Bible stories, her enthusiasm was infectious and, once her Shansi dialect became fluent, her visits to her mountain parishes became events much anticipated and enjoyed by the villagers, including many an erstwhile mud-slinger. She, in turn, found great satisfaction and happiness through those early years of the 1930s. Her horizons were limited by the mountains of Shansi, and outside news never reached her. The first she would learn of the Second World War was in 1941, two years after its declaration. The conflicts that would soon engulf her own little world had nothing to do with Adolf Hitler.

In 1936, with the help of the Mandarin who gradually became her friend and eventually a Christian, Gladys applied for and was granted Chinese citizenship.

There was no school in Yangcheng, but the governor of the local prison had three sons who joined her own crowd of adopted urchins to form the nucleus of a school, with Christian converts as volunteer teachers, located in the courtyard at the inn. Gladys first met the prison governor due to a major riot in his jail, in which an assortment of murderers, bandits, rapists and thieves were locked up for life in conditions of appalling degradation. The governor had sent in his paltry force of local militia to quell the riot, but such was the fury of the inmates, several of whom had already butchered their cell-mates, that the militia had fled. The governor, at his wits' end, remembered hearing from mule-men that Gladys preached about the living God who protects Christians from harm. So he sent for her and begged her to stop the riot before more of his charges murdered each other.

Gladys listened to the nightmare din from within the prison walls, the groans of the dying and the cries of anger or terror from those still alive. She knew she would die if she went into such a hellhole and she knew she would be laughed out of Yangcheng if she didn't. Not only would she lose face, but so would all her many hard-won converts and, indeed, the Christian faith itself. So, shaking with fear, she bade the guards let her into the prison. Alone, she crept inside and the gates clanged shut behind her.

A short dark tunnel led to a courtyard. The stench there was worse than any she could have imagined. Bloody bodies lay about the flagstones and separate battles raged inside the various locked cages that edged the courtyard. The main body of prisoners was grouped in front of a single ragged convict wielding a blood-wet machete and, as Gladys moved into the courtyard, he made a sudden dash forward that scattered the crowd in all directions. Then he focused on one individual who, terrified, sprinted straight at Gladys. The machete man, chasing him, came to a halt a few yards away, having noticed Gladys for the first time, and looked at her through eyes glazed, as she later remembered, with the pent-up pain and fury of many days and many years in such a place.

'Give me that weapon,' Gladys screamed. 'Give it to me at once.'

Confounded perhaps by the sudden appearance of this small foreign devil, the axeman meekly handed the offending item to Gladys. She felt her terror lessen and knew that she must maintain her moment of advantage. The governor, she shouted, had sent her in there to give the rioters the chance to avoid severe punishment. They must 'clean up the mess at once' and their spokesman must explain why the trouble had started. She would then do her best to see that they were fairly treated.

Quite why Gladys was not killed at once did not, at least to her, remain a mystery because her belief in God's protection was sufficient explanation. However, the governor, who had watched the whole event from the tunnel, was definitely impressed. As were the Mandarin and the inmates of all Yangcheng when the story was relayed to every corner of town.

The riot had come about, Gladys was sure, as an inevitable result of the desperate plight of the prisoners who lived in conditions of misery without hope and, since their only food came from friends or relatives, they never knew when their personal supplies would cease to arrive and they would starve. Watching other men eat when they had little or nothing caused jealousies which had come to a head that day when a guard has passed somebody the axe to chop up his food.

Additionally, they lived in permanent fear of unpredictable executions when one of their number would be beheaded without explanation in the centre of their courtyard.

Over the next few years, using her post-riot influence with the governor, Gladys hugely improved the lot of the Yangcheng prisoners for, at her suggestion, they were from time to time allowed out of the prison to attend church services or to carry out local public works. She also introduced a work programme into their hitherto wholly non-productive existence, in the form of looms with which to weave clothes, a miller's wheel to grind grain, and hutches in which to breed rabbits. She also visited them every week and read them her Bible stories. Many became Christians.

All the while the distant storm cloud of Communism spread over certain Chinese provinces, and the all-powerful Japanese Army, having taken control of Manchuria, was already planning their invasion of China by way of the northern mountain routes which passed through Yangcheng and neighbouring Tsechow, two days to the north, where a sister mission had been set up manned by Welshman David Davies and his Scottish wife Jean. Both Yangcheng and Tsechow stood in the path of the twin Communist and Nipponese tsunamis which would soon destroy the way of life of the Shansi region that had existed for over forty centuries. The Mandarin and the ways of old China were soon to be wiped off the face of the earth.

Somewhere to the south of the mountains there flowed the Yellow River, over a mile wide in places, and one year Gladys witnessed the desperate plight of refugees when this great river burst its banks, drowned hundreds and made thousands homeless. And again, when the entire river froze solid one bitter winter, the hated Communist troops from the neighbouring Yenan province headed south and even infiltrated briefly as far as Yangcheng which, for three terrible token days, they took over.

Gladys continued her frequent journeys, usually alone and for days at a time, into remote mountain villages to encourage the fledgling Christian groups that she had founded there. These forays were dangerous, a fact brought home to her when David Davies, on one of his own Gospel-spreading trips from the Tsechow mission, was attacked in the mountains by a dozen bandits who, covering him and his muleteers with a revolver, stole all his belongings and openly argued between themselves whether or not to kill Davies. On that occasion he was lucky.

One orphan who Gladys adopted and nicknamed Less was to stay close by her for ten years. He had been orphaned when bandits had raided his village, killed all the men and marched Less off with the women, including his heavily pregnant mother who collapsed on the forced march and died as little Less clung to her body.

Gladys heard vague rumours of Japanese advances in northern Shansi, but the muleteers who brought such news were all of the opinion that Yangcheng and Tsechow would not be involved, since neither had riches worth plundering. They were, of course, ignorant of both towns' tactical importance along the likely Japanese invasion route to the south, a harsh reality which first struck Yangcheng in the spring of 1938, six years after Gladys arrived there, when a squadron of Japanese dive-bombers arrived over the nearest range of mountains. Gladys was at the time in an upstairs room of the inn praying with converts.

Out in the fields people who had never before seen an aircraft pointed upwards in awe and shouted to their family to come and look as a thousand dark canisters whistled down to the houses below. Surprise switched to horror as the bombs exploded, masonry crumbled and bodies were blown to bits.

One direct hit on the inn shifted the boards from under Gladys and her friends and they dropped to the ground floor amidst falling timber and bricks. Gladys, pinned under a rubble pile by a floor joist, lost consciousness for a while but was pulled clear, bruised and cut, but uninjured.

Outside, the town was all but flattened. The dead, the dying and those with limbs torn off or stomachs peeled open lay about like the pieces of a devil's jigsaw. Gladys found the mission's medicine chest and removed the entire contents of boracic powder, permanganate and bundles of cotton wool.

The ex-parlourmaid spent the next frantic hours of daylight, right through the long night and well into the following day, organising dazed onlookers into gangs of rubble-clearers, searchers for survivors, water-carriers and grave-pit diggers, whilst she attended the endless lines of wounded and mutilated townsfolk, including many children and people who were her friends and converts. She noted that, without her prompting, the prison governor had let all his charges out on temporary release to help with the search for survivors under the rubble.

Six years after she had received only mud-balls from the natives of Yangcheng, Ai-weh-deh was now sought out by the Mandarin to make up a four-person committee to plan how best to alleviate suffering following the raid. The other three functionaries were the top merchant of Yangcheng, the prison governor and the Mandarin himself.

To add confusion and danger to the situation, news came by muleteer that the Japanese Army was about to invade Tsechow and could reach Yangcheng any time soon. The committee agreed to evacuate all survivors to the comparative safety of high mountain villages so that when, five days later, the Japanese did arrive they found only their own bomb damage and a ghost town.

Gladys, with a group of forty converts, trekked to a remote village of eight houses on the flank of a high mountain peak. A week later news came that the Japanese had moved on from Yangcheng, so many of the refugees returned to the town. Gladys, cautious by instinct, slipped back by herself, only to find that the Japanese had indeed left, but only briefly, and were already back in the town. She had a narrow escape and, back in the mountain village, she delayed her group's return until some days later she received definite assurances that the Japanese really had retreated back to Tsechow.

This time she approached the town with a sense of dread, for no noise and no movement came from within and, on reaching the main gates, her worst fears were confirmed. All those refugees who had returned too early had been surprised by the sudden return of the enemy. A few Chinese militia had fought back, but that had only served to infuriate the Japanese who soon beat them off and proceeded to butcher every human being in the town. Corpses lay everywhere, most of them bayoneted to death, many with their innards oozing from slashed bellies. Packs of pariah dogs grumbled and feasted, and Gladys found more bodies in the courtyard of the inn. That night she returned to the mountain village and opened a field station to nurse the sick and the wounded from ongoing air raids and guerrilla fighting patrols.

The very first muleteer that Gladys had inveigled into the inn, Hsi-Lien, long since a Christian convert, came to see her in a state of hopeless grief. Captured in his village home by a passing Japanese patrol, he had refused some order they had given which went against his Christian beliefs. He had been lashed to a post outside his house and forced to watch as his wife and three children were burnt to death. For a year Gladys did her best to comfort him.

In the following spring of 1939 the Japanese again advanced, and once more panic gripped the townsfolk all along the standard invasion route. The Yangcheng prisoners had, during the previous three invasions, been marched off in chain gangs to hide in the hills like everyone else. But now food was scarce, and the prison governor knew that his prisoners would all die of hunger. So they must, he told Gladys, either be released or executed. The consensus in town, since some were murderers, was to shoot them.

Gladys by now knew most of the convicts by name and persuaded the governor to let them go with her group until they could trace relatives who would guarantee their future good behaviour. This was agreed, so when Gladys left for her fourth exodus from Yangcheng, her band of Christians was augmented by a rabble of thieves, rapists and murderers, a couple of pretty slave girls from the Mandarin's disbanded geisha quarters, and her own family of unruly orphans.

They all spent the summer in the high peak villages just out of reach of the enemy patrols from Yangcheng, and when summer ended the Japanese retreated to Tsechow where, for once, they behaved with reasonable restraint for much, but not all, of the time.

In February 1940 when the snow between Yangcheng and

Tsechow began to melt, Gladys heard that David and Jean Davies at her sister mission in Tsechow needed help, so she went there by night. David would soon have to trek for weeks through war-riven lands to escort two old European missionaries to the coast, so Gladys agreed to take charge of the 200 orphans in his mission.

Hearing screams in the courtyard one night, she rushed out to find thirty Japanese soldiers assaulting a group of young girls and ripping their clothes off. Trying to stop this intended orgy, Gladys was clubbed across the head with a rifle butt. David, who had not yet left for the coast, was also beaten but, gushing with blood, managed to scream at the girls to kneel and to pray. This they immediately did, leaving their would-be rapists bemused and definitely less aroused by their half-undressed, but now kneeling, not struggling, victims.

Soon after this, a new Nationalist offensive forced the Japanese out of Tsechow, and Gladys met a handsome young Chinese intelligence officer who worked directly for the Nationalist Army's General Chiang Kai-shek. His name was Linnan and, whether out of her love for him or for China, Gladys agreed to use her frequent travels into the mountains to spy out any Japanese troop movements and report them to Linnan's men. Certainly she knew the intricate mountain trails in the region far better than most people who lived there for, unlike them, she had travelled far and wide between her fledgling Christian groups in the South Shansi Mountains.

Some months after they had first met, Gladys and Linnan agreed to discuss marriage once the war was ended. She was happy and excited.

Early that summer Gladys trekked to a conference of Christians from many outlying villages meeting in the town of Lingchuang. In between bombing raids the meetings and hymn sessions went happily on, but in the morning after the sessions ended and Gladys left the city with two of her children in tow, Japanese fighter bombers flew low over the crowded town streets and the road beyond, killing and maiming hundreds. Gladys turned back and spent the day tending the wounded.

The main trails between Lingchuang and Tsechow were now too dangerous, so Gladys, her children and others spent six weeks in a deep cave high above Lingchuang. At night Gladys and other adults kept watch at the cave mouth to fend off packs of prowling wolves.

Throughout that summer major battles raged in Shansi, but the Chinese managed to retain Tsechow and Gladys was eventually able to return to the mission there. The war raged on and on, but the following spring saw heavy Japanese armies ready themselves for a major offensive and Linnan warned Gladys to leave Tsechow sooner not later. They would this time, he assured her, kill all the inhabitants.

For a while Gladys refused to leave her friend David Davies, who had evacuated his family but intended to risk staying on himself. But, with the Japanese front line a mere mile from Tsechow, Gladys was shown a printed handbill being sent around all villages already taken by the Japanese. This notice offered a reward of 100 dollars for the capture, dead or alive, of three Tsechow inhabitants: the Mandarin, a named senior merchant, and 'the Small Woman known as Ai-weh-deh'. Somebody had clearly betrayed her spying activities to the enemy, and she knew she must leave Tsechow at once. But the Japanese advance troops arrived on the very night that she planned to leave, and they entered the main gates as Gladys scuttled out of the back gates. The soldiers spotted her and opened fire as she dodged between gravestones in the cemetery beyond the town walls. Bullets kicked up dust all about her and one zipped past her back, leaving a bloody runnel along the skin between her shoulder blades. She kept running and was soon out of range.

Her aim was to reach the group of children lodged at the Yangcheng inn, which had been free of the enemy since the previous summer. Two days later she arrived there to an ecstatic greeting from at least a hundred orphan children and their Christian guardians. 'Ai-weh-deh,' they cried, 'Ai-weh-deh has come back for us.'

Knowing that, after Tsechow, the Japanese would, as in the past, advance to Yangcheng, Gladys bade the children sleep well, for the very next morning they would all be going on 'a very long journey to safety.' She walked down the well-known pavements to the house of her old friend, the Yangcheng Mandarin. He was hard to recognise, for whenever the Japanese or the Communists had come to his town, he had fled to the hills, his life in danger from both armies. Even his long Mandarin pigtail had gone, for the Japanese found it funny to hang Mandarins from trees by their hair. The two old friends, their backgrounds so different, bowed low to each other and parted, never to meet again. That was, for Gladys, her last night in the Inn of the Eight Happinesses for, at dawn, she led her long column of excited children out to the mountain trails that she knew so well.

Her goal was the city of Sian, far away over many mountain ranges, across the Yellow River and then several days further west. She had corresponded with the wife of General Chiang Kai-shek who had organised and funded a refugee centre in Sian where, she assured Gladys, her orphans would be safe, if only she could get them there.

Gladys counted twenty big girls, all of whom she had looked after for many years, aged from thirteen to fifteen, including her very first orphan, Ninepence. There were seven boys of similar age and seventy or so aged from four to eight. Thanks to the Mandarin, they carried a small supply of millet in baskets, and they all reached an ancient Buddhist temple by nightfall where they slept to the scuttle and twitter of rats.

Some of the girls whose feet had once been bound soon found the walking painful. Smaller children had to be constantly encouraged. On the second night there was less millet to boil and nowhere to shelter. Children whimpered and shivered in the thick damp mist. Gladys knew that the Yellow River was twelve long days ahead; and more if Japanese patrols caused detours up side valleys. She prayed hard.

Seven nights later, the children were cold, dirty and exhausted. So was Gladys, but she kept up her air of optimism. Many children's feet, shoeless, were cut and blistered. There was no food. They were saved by running into a patrol of Nationalist soldiers who gave all their rations to the children. Japanese fighters circled menacingly overhead, but did nothing.

Some girls could only hobble slowly on their disfigured feet and needed to rest every few hundred yards. On the twelfth day they saw the great shining snake of the Yellow River, seemingly an impossible distance ahead. By then, some children with badly cut feet were being carried by others, and all were desperately hungry. Gladys kept repeating, 'Not far now.'

They came at last to the banks of the river, but no boats and no people could be seen. So they lay in the sun and wondered how near were the Japanese. Three dreadful days and nights passed, and Gladys worried that some of the children would soon die. On the morning of the fourth day, desperate but trying to keep up their group spirits, Gladys led the children in their favourite hymns.

Ninepence said to Gladys, 'Why does our God not open the water like he did for Moses?' Gladys could think of no adequate response. But, a mile away on the far bank, the young Nationalist officer of a small patrol heard the singing, focused his binoculars on the source and, although he knew the Japanese or their bombers could arrive at any time, launched his one little ferry boat.

The Japanese stayed away, and three ferry trips took all the children over to the southern bank where, three miles inland, Gladys found friendly villagers who fed the desperately hungry children. Gladys, normally robust, felt dizzy and weak. The village Mandarin directed them to the nearby railway and, in due course, a slow and very ancient train took them for four long days towards Sian. Gladys dozed a lot and felt increasingly sick.

Then the train stopped because a bridge up ahead had been bombed and destroyed. They must again trek over a great range of mountains. Gladys felt that she could not walk another step, but the following dawn she roused her children and slowly, very slowly, they dragged their swollen feet, aching limbs and gaunt frames ever upwards to the high horizons between them and Sian. The next three days and nights were a long dark nightmare, especially in the knowledge that, in these new mountains unknown even to Gladys and with no guide, it would be all too easy to lose the way.

At times some children, huddled and sobbing, would not move on. Gladys wept secretly, felt very ill and blamed herself for the likely and imminent death of all her children. At such a time she would break into a hymn and the children would always join in, however dry their throats. A little village saved them with just enough food to keep them going down to the plain where the railway began again.

Two railway men helped each child hide among huge lumps of coal on open railcars because, they warned Gladys, somewhere up ahead the train would pass close to Japanese lines and the Japanese soldiers were wont to shoot at any human seen riding pillion on the coal-cars. With coal dust in her eyes and hair and feeling strangely faint, Gladys waved goodbye to the men, and the coal train headed off into the night on its long journey to Sian.

Nobody shot at the children and they did blend well with the coal, for they soon turned black from head to foot. Gladys felt increasingly light-headed and lost all track of time. At length, and not knowing how many days the journey had lasted, the train wheezed to a halt outside the walls of a great city, which Ninepence announced with joy was Sian.

The filthy column of children led by the dazed and limping foreign devil arrived at the city gates, which were closed. From high above, a watchman shouted, 'Woman, go away. We are too full of refugees. No one more enters Sian.' Gladys collapsed against the gate, her rock-like faith in her God for once definitely deserting her.

Two long and stress-filled days later another train did take the children to a refugee centre in another city, also organised by Madame Chiang Kai-shek and hosted by efficient young girls. Gladys at last allowed herself to give in to her immense tiredness and, as she later learned, she *was* seriously ill, falling rapidly into a crazed delirium. The women of the refuge contacted a Baptist hospital in Sian, where the staff managed little by little to save Gladys's life. She was diagnosed with relapsing fever, pneumonia, malnutrition, typhus and exhaustion.

Linnan found Gladys months later, but the two never married. Somewhere along her terrible journey to save her children, Gladys had changed and the certainty of her devotion to Linnan had gone away. She could explain things no more than that either to him or to herself. For the rest of her life he would remain her only accepted suitor. They parted at the gates of Sian and she never heard from him again.

After 1938 Gladys continued her missionary work, at first in Sian and its neighbourhood and later in Szechuan near the Tibetan border. She cared for lepers and prisoners, children and her groups of converts. Her health never fully recovered, but she did not allow herself any thought of retirement.

During her last years in China, after the Japanese had been defeated, she watched the Communists murdering her friends, her children and everything she had worked for. Christians were their enemies and were outlawed. Her adopted son, Less, was shot for his Christian beliefs. Eventually, under threat of execution, she and other missionaries from all over China were forced to flee, and in 1949, seventeen years after that day in 1932 when she set out from Liverpool Street with her battered suitcase and her kettle, Gladys returned to her parents in north London. She went on to give lectures in

Britain and America and, from 1957 until her death in 1970, she ran an orphanage in Taiwan (then Formosa). To me she remains the smallest, but the most resolute, of all my chosen heroes.

5

'To Kill the Beast'

'The three o'clock in the morning courage, which
Bonaparte thought was the rarest'
Henry Thoreau

The von Stauffenberg family is, in 2011, one of the oldest
aristocratic Catholic families in south Germany. Born
in their castle just east of Munich in 1907, Claus von
Stauffenberg had two older brothers, one of whom, Berthold,
would share his later fate. They both joined their traditional
family regiment where both did well. Claus, as a teenager,
watched the rise of the Austrian rabble-rouser Adolf Hitler
through the 1920s and early thirties.

When the German empire was defeated in the First World
War, its successor, the Weimar Republic, was pecked at like
a vulture-ridden corpse by the victorious Allies seeking ever
more reparations. This, plus sky-high inflation, ruined
Weimar governmental attempts to control and improve
economic conditions. Poverty and unemployment were made
worse by bitter in-fighting between violent mobs of the Left
and Right. And, just when the government was beginning to
get on top of these troubles, including even the murderous

Blackshirts of Hitler, the worst global economic catastrophe on record killed off their hopes of revival.

Communists, trades unionists and Hitler's mobs fought and murdered each other until, in 1933, the despondent and cornered Weimar's President Hindenburg appointed Hitler as chancellor exactly ten years after the latter had first tried, but failed, to mount a violent putsch against the government.

The self-styled Führer's dazzling, some said hypnotic, rhetoric was such that in the 1932 elections 37 per cent of all votes went to his National Socialist party, despite its open predilection for violence. Hitler promised to replace the poverty and the anarchy with hard work, ample food and good order. Additionally, the Nazis, good German patriots, would rid the land of the twin scourge of the Communists and the Jews.

Just a year later, after brutalising the electorate through their control of the police force and the menace of their thuggish Brownshirt Storm Troopers, they achieved 44 per cent of the vote, despite it becoming increasingly clear what Hitler's policies involved.

The Nazis' first targets were Hitler's political opponents, mainly the Communists. The hunt was swift and thorough. Within two months 25,000 were arrested and slung into concentration camps, such as the newly created Dachau.

In May 1933, with the Communists obliterated, Hitler focused his regime of oppression elsewhere. He took away all power from the individual German states, especially proud Bavaria, imprisoning or killing many popular statesmen. He abolished all trades unions and all political parties. Then he removed all civil liberties and any legal mechanism that might have served to depose him.

Claus von Stauffenberg, like millions of other Germans of all classes, watched and did nothing. Thousands of individuals who did step out of line in the slightest way were arrested and, in six years, 225,000 were imprisoned on 'political' grounds. Between 1933 and 1945 just over three million *German* citizens were imprisoned for political reasons.

The Nazis would let prisoners out from time to time to ensure that word got around as to the nature of daily existence in their prisons, including murder, rape, starvation and torture.

So what of resistance to this nightmare regime? Only the bravest of the brave would dare to conspire, let alone to act, against the all-seeing, all-knowing forces of Nazism. There were very few voices of objection during those pre-war years.

In May 1935 the so-called Markwitz Circle based in Vienna distributed forbidden documents of anti-Nazi incitement, but a Gestapo informer infiltrated the movement and nearly all were murdered. In the early 1940s a mainly Communist group with Soviet connections came together under Josef Römer and lasted over a year before they too were infiltrated by the Gestapo.

Life under Hitler involved living with fear under the permanent threat of the loss of your job, your freedom, the welfare of all your family, and the threat of torture and death in some nameless jail. Historically, Hitler can be said to be among the small group of 'all-powerful individuals', and he knew it. He boasted, 'There will never be anyone in the future with as much authority as I have.'

He had won his position of supreme power through his apparatus of terror and the ruthless efficiency of the dreaded Gestapo. His spies were everywhere, and so the bigger the ring of anti-Nazi plotters, the greater the likelihood of their detection. It followed that to act alone was the safest policy, and this was proved when an attempt to kill Hitler, which very nearly succeeded, was planned and executed by a single Nazi-hater named Elser who, knowing Hitler made an annual speech in a well-known restaurant in Munich, spent a total of thirty-five nights chipping away at the brickwork of one of the main roof support pillars to make a hidden crevice into which he stashed explosives with a timing device.

But for the fact that Hitler ended his standard speech an hour earlier than was scheduled, he would undoubtedly have been killed in Elser's explosion. Nonetheless, even though the lone wolf nature of his plot had helped Elser make his attempt undetected, the Gestapo still managed to catch him.

How much more difficult then to organise not only the assassination of Hitler but also an apparatus to take over the entire Nazi hierarchy on the day of his death. Such a proposition would need a man of extra-special courage and determination.

Claus von Stauffenberg, the archetypal German aristocrat, was intellectually inclined and an avid reader, married at twenty-six and with five children. He hated the results of the Versailles Treaty and the way that Germany was treated with contempt by her neighbours after her great defeat in the First World War, so, like many other reasonable individual Germans, he approved of Hitler's programme to restore the country's prosperity and status as a strong and influential world power. Despite this, and as early as 1934, he made it clear to brother officers in his regiment that he disapproved of Hitler's treatment of German Jewry.

All Jewish businesses were boycotted. Local newspapers

warned Germans not to buy from any Jewish shop nor to use Jewish doctors, lawyers or other services. Anti-Jew signs proliferated, warning Jews to stay away from restaurants, cinemas, swimming pools, parks and even their own gardens. Whatever the Nazis wished to do to Jews they did with impunity. Jews had nowhere to hide and nobody in authority was prepared to protect them.

A Jew in Germany was worse off than a rat, for at least rats can hide. They have the sewers all to themselves. There was no hiding place for a Jew. As enemies of the state, anybody could steal from them, rape them and beat their children to death without fear of the law. If you catch a cockroach and crush it under your heel, there is nothing that that roach can do to protect itself. It has nobody to appeal to. It is utterly vulnerable. That is how it was for a Jew in Germany through the Hitler years.

In 1935 Hitler broke Germany's terms as laid down by the Versailles Treaty, and began a huge shift to rebuild and re-equip the nation's armed forces into by far the most modern, efficient and powerful in all Europe.

Disturbed by many of the Nazi overall aims, especially the Jewish 'Solution', a number of German Army officers, including the head of the Abwehr (the Secret Intelligence Service), began to conspire and formed between 1935 and 1938 the Kreisau Circle, initially dedicated merely to preparing plans for a post-Nazi government. Many senior army officers were gradually and carefully recruited into the Circle.

In 1938 Hitler annexed Austria and marched into the German-speaking sector of Czechoslovakia. Claus von Stauffenberg was part of the occupying army and, a year later, joined his regiment for the attack on Poland which sparked Britain's declaration of war against the Nazis. He was impressed by Hitler's early military successes in the war and he turned down several invitations from close relatives in the Kreisau Circle to join their anti-Nazi movement.

From Poland, Claus was posted to the 6th Panzer Division as a general staff officer during the 1940 blitzkrieg advance into France, for which he was awarded the Iron Cross. At that point he was still clearly impressed by all that Hitler was doing for Germany's prestige and to banish memories of the shame and derision that followed the First World War.

In 1941 Claus served as a supply officer during the advance into the Soviet Union and the siege of Stalingrad. Whilst there he made new contacts with the anti-Nazi resistance movement, including its main mover at that time, Colonel Henning von Tresckow, the chief of staff of the Army Group Centre. He also listened, horrified, to increasingly widespread rumours of the nightmare Nazi policies being carried out in the Soviet Union in the name of Germany.

Claus learnt that a number of anti-Nazis in positions of high power, but watched like everybody else by the omni-present Gestapo, were leaders of the very units committing some of the most horrendous crimes on the Soviet front. Arthur Nebe was, for instance, a long-time conspirator against Hitler, yet he was also the Director of the Reich Criminal Police at the epicentre of SS atrocities. One of his units, Einsatzgruppe B, frequently conducted mass executions of Jews, partisans and their entire families which Nebe had then dutifully to report to Himmler. Although he was at the time way down the anti-Nazi conspiratorial grapevine, the tales of horror did eventually reach Claus.

Von Tresckow, the lead conspirator, heard from one witness

that, flying low over the Russian town of Borissov, he had watched Latvian SS soldiers 'murdering several thousand Jews in a most bestial manner'.

Himmler had a huge task put on his plate by Hitler – the wholesale *extermination* of Jewry. For this he needed policemen good at killing men, women and children, at close range, day after day. His duly recruited Einsatzgruppen, 80,000 of them, were mostly non-Nazi, non-SS ex-policemen who followed orders, became increasingly callous and, in many cases, enjoyed the power they wielded over their terrified prey in the ongoing series of ghetto clearances, mass executions and countryside Jew hunts conducted in the manner of pheasant shoots.

Once the army's invincible blitzkrieg had swept away initial Soviet Army resistance with its 3-million-strong force, including Claus, Himmler's clean-up men would then arrive to murder families, whole village populations and prisoner groups, sometimes a hundred, sometimes 1,200, even 30,000, in a single purge.

The toll of human suffering at that time is now hard to imagine. Many of the most brutal massacres are forgotten, as though they never happened. But week after week, month after month through three long years, the cull continued. One event in 1941 that did leak out to become general knowledge was the great Jew killing at Babi Yar, where the 'bag' was 33,860 humans shot in two days. The details helped to turn Claus and others from mere disapproval of the Nazis to active involvement in conspiracy.

Medical officers would give lectures to the Einsatzgruppen police as to correct killing methods using diagrams marked with neck and temple as best targets, and advising that bayonets should always be kept mounted since this kept the gun barrel the correct eight-inch distance from the victim, which helped avoid misfires. Nonetheless, as army gossip related, officers preferred to use their pistols, holding babies at arm's length or adults by their hair. And they made mothers hold their babies between their breasts so that one shot would pass through the baby's skull into the mother's chest, thereby saving the Reich the cost of a bullet. Death queues of many thousands, always stripped naked, would stretch back for hundreds of yards from the great death pits. A third of newly shot bodies fell onto the still writhing corpses below, amid screams for mercy or just for water; the killers were spattered with gore. And if darkness fell, those still alive must wait in their queues overnight to be killed the next day.

It was hardly surprising that details of this ongoing nightmare at length reached the ears of German Army regular officers, especially as Himmler recruited into his Jew killing units men from previously vanquished countries including Poles, Russians, Slavs and the notorious Latvians, many of whom were known to kill for pleasure, shooting women in the stomach and timing their death throes.

The corpse pits were usually dug by those whose bodies would then fill them up. In November 1941 an especially hard winter helped many Jews survive longer because the pits were too difficult to dig. The official estimate for Jews who were buried *alive* was 2 per cent. Large-scale massacres in 1941 included: Kamnets-Podolski 23,000 dead; Rovno 21,000; Minsk 19,000; Riga 25,000; and in early 1942, Kharkov 14,000. There were many thousands of lesser mass shootings all over Eastern Europe, and over 4 million prisoners died in the camps. For by the spring of 1942 Hitler realised that his dream of total extermination of the Jews was being carried out too slowly. Shooting was not an efficient method, and Germans could not be criticised for lack of efficiency. So, the custom-built death camps began to open their gates.

Sickened by all that he had heard, Claus, in August 1942, said to a close army friend, Major Joachim Kuhn, 'They are shooting Jews in masses. These crimes must not be allowed to continue.' Many other army officers at the time were thinking the same way, but how could they, Gestapo-observed as they constantly were, do anything meaningful to reduce the horror, never mind to stop it?

In the spring of 1943, Claus was sent to North Africa as Operations Officer for the 10th Panzer Division under Field Marshal Erwin Rommel and, whilst driving between front line troops, was strafed by British fighter-bombers and severely wounded, losing his left eye, his right hand and two fingers on his left hand. Sent home for rehabilitation, he had plenty of time to make contact with the main anti-Nazi conspirators in the army.

It was clear that *only* the army stood a chance against the Nazis. The previous year a group of students calling themselves the White Rose Resistance circulated anti-Hitler leaflets and dared to march in public protest through the streets of Munich. Their leaders were quickly identified and executed by guillotine.

In the Soviet Union things had, for the first time, gone badly for Hitler's war machine at the great defeat of Stalingrad. Over 500,000 German troops were killed, further adding to the determination of Claus and his brother anti-Nazi conspirators to rid the world of Hitler. Von Tresckow planted a bomb on a flight taken by the Führer, but it failed to detonate – a fine example of 'the luck of the Devil'.

Claus and his fellow officers belonged to a pre-war society that considered Germany, their Germany of Einstein and Wagner, indisputably the most civilised nation in the world. Something had to be done, and soon. A recorded comment by Claus to brother officers indicated his early intentions. 'Is there no officer over there in the Führer's headquarters capable of killing that beast?'

Hitler's policies *inside* Germany had, by the spring of 1944, convinced Claus that Hitler was mad. One Nazi programme was intent on ridding Germany of any individual that they considered to be a burden on the state. Every citizen would have to prove that they were *lebenswertig*, socially worthy, and those who could not must be prevented from passing on their genes to the next generation of the Reich. To this end they would be sterilised. The proposed new law would demand sterilisation for 'the mentally and physically defective, including alcoholics, sexual deviants, promiscuous women, anti-socials, prostitutes, backward students, and the habitually unemployed'. This sterilisation process soon proved ineffective and was switched to the euthanasia programme, which claimed 275,000 lives and was separate from the Final Solution which was to deal with Jews, Gypsies, Slavs, Communists and homosexuals. This highly successful Holocaust ended up murdering 6 million Jews, 500,000 Gypsies, over 10,000 homosexuals, 2,000 Jehovah's Witnesses, 1.5 million political prisoners, and 4 million Soviet prisoners of war.

By September 1943 Claus, though half-blind and with the use of only three fingers, had sufficiently recovered and was positioned by von Tresckow and other senior conspirators as a staff officer to the Replacement Army in Berlin. This unit's job was to arrange efficient reinforcements to front line troops and, by way of Operation Valkyrie, to assume control of the Reich should anything go wrong with Hitler's High Command structure.

The conspirators planned to man the Replacement Army's headquarters staff wherever possible with like-minded anti-Nazi officers. Then, after assassinating Hitler and his main supremos, Himmler and Goering, to take over command of all the army hierarchy through the Valkyrie structure before Himmler's Gestapo could intervene. Claus summarised their motivation with the words: 'We took this challenge before our Lord and our conscience and it must be done because this man, Hitler, is the ultimate evil.'

In October 1943 (at about the time that my own father, Ranulph, was killed by a German mine whilst commanding his tank regiment in Italy), Claus became fully involved in planning to assassinate Hitler. He organised several attempts using volunteer suicide bombers, including the war hero Axel Bussche, but all, for one reason or another, had to be aborted, usually at the last minute.

In June 1944 when the Allies landed in France on D-Day, the conspirators in Berlin could clearly see, as Hitler apparently could not, that the war was irretrievably lost. Even if a successful assassination of the Führer proved impossible, they reasoned, they owed it to Germany and to posterity to do their utmost at least to make an attempt on his life before the war ended by way of an Allied victory. They must show the world that not all Germans supported the Nazi regime. Whether or not such an assassination rationale is now considered cynical by some, it must have seemed both urgent and reasonable to the patriotic German conspirators in Berlin at the time.

That same month Claus was promoted to colonel and became Chief of Staff to Home Army Commander General Fromm, which in turn gave him direct access in person to Hitler's periodic briefing sessions. He shared this key assassination opportunity with only one other conspirator, Helmuth Stieff, Chief of Operations at Army High Command.

Stieff was already committed to attempt the assassination with a carefully developed plan. Hitler was believed to wear, when in public, a bulletproof vest and cap. Wherever he went, SS men with submachine-guns went too. He never published his schedule of public events in advance and often changed his daily programme at the last minute on a whim. His personal aides were even suspicious of Hitler's close associates. Sudden movements when in the Führer's presence were inadvisable, and one senior army officer was pounced on by the SS guards for merely trying to take his handkerchief from his pocket during a Hitler briefing.

Gestapo detectives often searched army bosses' offices and planted secretaries as office spies. The conspirators, therefore, used their wives in various roles. One, Frau von Oven, worked on conspiratorial correspondence wearing gloves to avoid leaving fingerprints on the papers. Her typewriter was always carefully hidden after use, and out-of-date drafts were destroyed with great care. Claus's wife Nina took a whole backpack of incriminating papers from his Berlin office back to their Bavarian home to destroy them, and those papers that could not leave Berlin were burnt sheet by sheet in a lavatory pan, the ashes flushed down and the blackened edges of the lavatory bowl then wiped clean. Claus's brother, Berthold, was also closely involved with all the ongoing plans.

At this time, Claus's surgeon told him that his health and state of mind clearly indicated that he should keep clear of stressful work, but Claus told his wife that he '*must* do something to save the Reich . . . I could never look the wives and children of the fallen in the eye if I did not do something to stop this senseless slaughter.'

By the late spring of 1944 a number of von Stauffenberg's assassination plans, including Stieff's, had been aborted and the conspirators' morale was at a low ebb, kept alive, according to survivors, largely by the unshakeable determination of Claus.

To kill Hitler, Claus favoured the use of an explosive device over a pistol, since an assassin was more likely to access the far side of a briefing table than a position close to Hitler, and assassin volunteers were not necessarily good pistol shots, never mind the reported bulletproof vest.

When General Stieff's best attempts at assassination during a briefing failed, even though he had smuggled his 'bomb' into close proximity to his target, Claus decided that he must do the deed himself. He said, 'It is *now* time that something be done. But he who has the courage to do it must do so in the knowledge that he will go down in German history as a traitor. If he does not do it, however, he will be a traitor to his conscience.'

The determination which Claus showed from June 1944 onwards rocketed him to the top of the conspiratorial network located in Berlin, and by early July he was at the very nerve centre of both the complex plan to use Operation Valkyrie to take over the army immediately after Hitler's death *and* to achieve the assassination himself.

Under extreme stress, Claus had to deal with a number of key issues. His direct boss, General Fromm, was only a semi-conspirator who sat on the fence and could not be relied on. The first briefing in Hitler's presence at which Claus was likely to be present as Fromm's aide was to be in the first week of June, which Claus intended to use as a reconnaissance for a later attempt at a subsequent briefing. However, on 5 July a key conspirator, Dr Julius Leber, Minister of the Interior, was arrested by the Gestapo along with other army conspirators. Claus knew that very few people, however brave, could withstand Gestapo interrogation. So, if he were to act at all then it would have to be very soon. The conspiracy was in the greatest danger and its members knew it. Without the lion-hearted von Stauffenberg, it is very likely that no assassination attempt would have gone ahead at all.

Following the initial June briefing, Claus commented to his wife, who asked if Hitler's eyes had impressed him, 'No. Not at all.' She said they were 'as if veiled.' Hitler's hands had shaken as he shuffled maps on the briefing table, constantly glancing at Claus, and Goering.

On 3 July, three days prior to the next scheduled briefing, conspirators provided Claus with an explosive device, sandwich-shaped and weighing five pounds, which fitted neatly into his briefcase alongside maps and documents.

On 6 July, and again on 7 and 15 July, Claus attended briefings a few feet away from Hitler and with his bomb at the ready in his case. But he did nothing because the conspirators had all agreed that the supreme Nazis Himmler and

Goering would, following Hitler's death, quickly use their great authority to suppress any fledgling revolt and keep the full Nazi regime going. And Himmler at least was very likely to attend those July meetings so, when he failed to appear, Claus had to repeatedly endure the stress of risking all to no avail.

He had been instructed as to how to prime the bomb which was of German manufacture but used a sophisticated British fuse device which could be set with a ten-minute delay. This pause was vital since, with only three fingers, Claus could not secretly activate the only suitable German fuse which had a four-and-a-half-second delay and, unlike the British device, hissed noisily once primed.

The plan which Claus determined to implement after his first three missed chances was to ignore the appearance of Himmler and/or Goering and, after ascertaining that Hitler himself was in the briefing bunker, set the bomb's fuse which, finger-impaired, he could only do by using a specially adapted pincer-like tool in the adjacent lavatory immediately before joining the briefing session. Despite the high state of Gestapo alert and suspicion, the very obvious and heroic injuries that Claus bore helped him to appear innocuous and clearly a loyal soldier of the Reich.

Claus was himself due to brief Hitler on the morning of 20 July, and he spent the previous evening, after visiting a church, with his brother and co-conspirator, Berthold. He had no intention of dying like some rash suicide bomber. Hitler's bunker, known as the Wolf's Lair, in Rastenburg, East Prussia was closely guarded with concentric rings of security, and Claus's plan was to fly there from Berlin, initiate the ten-minute bomb fuse and, before the explosion, escape by staff car to the airfield for a quick flight back to the Valkyrie HQ in Berlin. Once there, he would set Operation Valkyrie in motion during the immediate confusion likely after Hitler's death and before the octopus arms of the Gestapo could clamp down on the coup.

At 7 a.m. on the morning of the fateful day, Claus met his aide and fellow conspirator, Lieutenant von Haeften, at the Berlin military airfield. He had two two-pound bombs with him, both in his briefcase, and his special pincers to supplement his three remaining fingers when the time came to set the fuses.

Just after midday and immediately before Claus had to report to Hitler's current briefing room (a wooden shed containing wall maps and a long, heavy, wooden briefing table), he and von Haeften asked the briefing commandant, Field Marshal Wilhelm Keitel, where they could go for a quick brush-up and to change their shirts. They were directed to a waiting room which was empty, where Claus began the delicate task of setting and initiating the fuse mechanisms. Unfortunately, a sergeant named Vogel was sent from the briefing room to tell Claus to hurry up as Hitler would soon expect to hear his briefing.

Claus managed to set the fuse of one of his devices and, with his special tool, to squeeze its acid capsule, after which the explosion would occur in about ten minutes. Vogel stood waiting impatiently for Claus and von Haeften, so, to avoid suspicion or indeed detection, Claus decided to forget about trying to activate his second bomb and passed this to von Haeften. Claus then followed Vogel to meet Hitler whilst von Haeften went off to arrange their get-away car.

Once inside the wooden briefing shed, Claus asked to be

seated right beside Hitler at the table. As his hearing had been affected by his previous injuries, this was a reasonable request. Hitler shook Claus's hand and turned back to the current speaker. Claus placed his briefcase at his feet beneath the table, paused for a few minutes, then muttering something by way of an excuse such as having to make a sudden phone call, he went back out (as other officers were wont to do from time to time). Nobody there had anything less than top-level security clearance.

Claus was lucky, for the normally eagle-eyed Gestapo staff at the Lair who watched everybody and everything at all times, trusting no one, were unusually flustered due to the imminent arrival of the Italian Fascist supremo, Benito Mussolini, who was to meet Hitler that afternoon. So nobody noticed the inconsistency of Claus, scheduled to brief Hitler at any moment, disappearing from the room.

His car duly arrived, as arranged by von Haeften, but before his driver could open his door, a dull explosion sounded from the complex of huts. Claus started violently, but a nearby signals officer told him that there was no problem and that animals often trod on the mines laid all about the perimeters of the Wolf's Lair.

Claus and von Haeften bade their driver make haste for the local airfield, but they were stopped at the guardroom. Every minute counted, so Claus bluffed his way through, shouting that he was 'on the Führer's orders'. Browbeaten and clearly against his better judgment, the guard commander raised the barrier and the car sped on to the outer barrier fence of the Lair. Once again they were stopped, and this time the sergeant major on duty was clearly determined to let no one out. Claus stormed into the guardroom and phoned the camp commandant who, fortunately, had not yet been told of the bomb and had no reason not to trust Colonel von Stauffenberg. No doubt hugely stressed by now, Claus urged the driver on and, reaching the airfield in a mile or so, the two conspirators dismissed the driver and walked the last few hundred yards to their waiting aircraft. Within minutes they were on their way back to Berlin.

Claus was convinced that Hitler must have died in the explosion, and he arrived in Berlin believing this. Back at his Valkyrie headquarters he and his main co-conspirators attempted to rouse often lukewarm colleagues into helping them mount the pre-agreed military coup against their Nazi leaders. But word soon reached key army units that an attempt made on Hitler's life had failed, and many officers who had previously indicated that they would back the coup lost their nerve and refused to help the main conspirators.

By 9 p.m. that evening it became obvious that Hitler had indeed survived the explosion, saved by the thick bulk of the briefing table, and, of the other two dozen people in the bunker at the time, only four had been killed.

Fearing Hitler's wrath and the vengeance of the Gestapo, many conspirators, realising their game was up, committed suicide, others fled or tried to flee, but many were rounded up for execution. Claus was shot through his good arm whilst resisting arrest and then executed by firing squad alongside his three main Valkyrie colleagues. His family were arrested, his wife was sent to a concentration camp and his children to an orphanage. The Nazis also used the failed putsch as an excuse to murder a great many of their suspected opponents, at least 5,000 of whom were completely ignorant of the conspiracy. Eight of the main plotters, including Claus's brother, Berthold, were strangled slowly in a cellar hanging from meat hooks.

For years after the war, Claus was considered by many Germans merely as a traitor, but gradually they came to acknowledge that at least he had tried his utmost and risked all to show the world that not every German approved of the Nazis. If it had not been for him, Germany would not even have achieved that small claim for atonement.

The street in Berlin where he was executed, close by to the National Museum of Resistance, has been renamed Stauffenberg Street in his memory.

Forty-six million people died due to Hitler. Only one man risked everything to 'kill the beast' and nearly succeeded in doing so.

6

Daredevil Heroes

'Low arousability is thought to be shared by
participants in dangerous sports and heroes'
Michael R. Levenson

Joe Simpson, one of Britain's best-known climbers, has
escaped near-death on many occasions and scaled near-
vertical cliffs in many lands. In 2004 he described one
particular mountain face as 'seminal' and wrote that stories
about it had inspired his lifetime of mountaineering. In the
year 2000 he and a climbing friend tried to ascend that 6,000-
foot wall – the North Face of the Eiger in the Swiss Alps.

Camped for the night on some dizzy Eiger ledge, they
watched the bodies of two other climbers, with whom they
had previously chatted, fall free past their perch to cartwheel
down to the valley far below. Simpson and his friend, 'cowed
and haunted' by this incident, managed to descend in safety
and, over the next two summers, they again tried to scale the
wall, each time calling off the attempt as dangerous weather
conditions set in.

There is clearly a big difference between genuinely great
endeavours, such as the first ascent of Mount Everest, and

the athletic acrobatics involved with a mere daredevil clamber up Nelson's Column in London. Most climbs fall somewhere between the two. The epic mountain quest which to me stands out above most others is that of the early attempts, despite previous lethal failures, to summit the Eiger by its notorious North Face. Joe Simpson recommends a book written by one of the four-man team who first successfully scaled the wall, *The White Spider* by Heinrich Harrer. Simpson, reviewing the book, wrote: 'It is impossible to read this book without being awed by the single-minded determination of a small band of poorly equipped climbers struggling to survive in a world that few of us can imagine . . . Heroic in scale, legendary in the stories of the long-lost lives it recounts.'

I first looked up at the Eiger North Face on a summer's day in the 1960s when on leave from tank troop duties in Berlin. A friend lent me his binoculars and pointed up at the rock face towering, as it seemed, towards heaven. Following his directions, I picked out two tiny figures, one in blue and the other in red, climbers on that colossal wall. Later that day a black cloud enveloped the mountain and rumbles of thunder rolled down to our valley. I never learnt whether or not those climbers reached the distant summit, but I do remember my feelings of wonder as to how any human could dare even attempt such a climb.

The local guidebook in the village of Grindelwald, nestled in the valley immediately below the Eiger, described the first climb to the summit by Englishman Charles Barrington via the least challenging route, the West Flank, when two avalanches narrowly missed his climbing group. That was in 1858, and during the next seventy-seven years all other sides of the Eiger were scaled, other than that generally considered unclimbable, the North Wall, which receives most of the local bad weather, coming as it does from the north and north-west. By 1935 all the other formidable North Faces in the Alps, including the Grandes Jorasses and the Matterhorn, had fallen to the world's top climbers. Only the Eiger remained virgin. For good reason.

The lowest point of the Eiger North Wall is 6,900 feet above sea level, the highest is 13,041 feet. Heinrich Harrer, in his book *The White Spider*, wrote in 1958 of the many climbers who had tried and died on the North Face. 'Anyone who makes headway up the North Face of the Eiger and survives there for several days has achieved and overcome so much – whatever mistakes he may have committed – that his performance is well above the comprehension of the average climber.' He further noted: 'The North Wall of the Eiger remains one of the most perilous in the Alps, as every man who has ever joined battle with it knows. Other climbs may be technically more difficult, but nowhere else is there such appalling danger from the purely fortuitous hazards of avalanches, stone-falls and sudden deterioration of the weather as on the Eiger . . . The North Face demands the uttermost of skill, stamina and courage, nor can it be climbed without the most exhaustive preparations.'

Bestselling American journalist and one-time Everest tragedy chronicler, Jon Krakauer, wrote: 'The problem with climbing the North Face of the Eiger is that, in addition to getting up 6,000 vertical feet of crumbling limestone and black ice, one must climb over some formidable mythology. The trickiest moves on any climb are the mental ones, the psychological gymnastics that keep terror in check, and the Eiger's grim aura is intimidating enough to rattle anyone's poise. The very mention [of notorious landmarks on the face] is enough to make any climber's hands turn clammy. The rockfall and avalanches that rain continuously down the Nordwand are legendary . . . Needless to say, all this makes the Eiger North Face one of the most coveted climbs in the world.'

One of the team that eventually reached the summit wrote that their success involved 'common sense, patience and open-eyed courage. Haste born of fear . . . can only end in disaster.'

In mid-August 1935 the first two men ever to dare an attempt on the great rock face camped at its foot in a cowshed and checked out their carefully prepared climbing gear, their crampons and their food. They had no idea how long they would be on the face, despite the long hours they had spent observing its every feature from below. They could not learn from the mistakes of their predecessors, for nobody had yet been rash enough to tackle the face, soon to earn the sobriquet of 'Murder Wall'.

The world's top climbers rated these two men, Max Sedlmayer and Karl Mehringer, as among 'the most careful, the toughest and most penetrative of climbers, tested and tried a hundred times over on the severest of climbs'. But experience gained elsewhere was not some magic key to this face which suffered unique conditions, including ever-changing surfaces of black ice, slime, loose grit, wet and treacherous snow slides and sudden avalanches.

Max and Karl had with them the best technical gear of their day and they packed enough rations for six days and nights, so their rucksacks were heavy. When clinging by your fingertips to tiny holds, your booted toes clawing at wet rock, a heavy weight on your back can unbalance you and pull you away from the wall and into space. Your companion, always roped to you, may manage to halt your death-fall or may himself be torn off the rock and join your long, long drop down to the valley below.

Many of the summer guests of the Grindelwald hotels were out on their balconies that bright August morning hoping to watch from their grandstand viewpoint the historic first ascent of the North Wall. Through their telescopes and field glasses they noted the two climbers begin the actual climb at 6,900 feet, exactly 6,141 vertical feet below the summit. They could also spot a couple of holes like the black mouths of caves, hundreds of feet above the climbers. These were man-made windows engineered along an incredible railway which was drilled through the heart of the mountain by Swiss engineers.

I once travelled on that train and, joining other curious passengers at the mid-mountain halt, gazed out of what is called the Gallery Window at the sudden void below. I felt dizzy and sick despite the window glass, so I quickly retreated back to the train.

Max and Karl, during their study of the face, had tried to work out an exact route plan, but a vertical cliff surged up over 600 feet above the pockmarked smudge of the Gallery Window which might prove unclimbable. They could not know until they tried. One thing that was clear to both men – there were stretches far, far above the Gallery Window where exposed traverses would be necessary, where retreat would become impossible and the only route to survival would be upwards. At that point, rather like the first ever journey into space by man twenty-six years later, once the endeavour was under way, there would be no going back.

Late at night on 20 August, Max and Karl set out up the

lower slopes. Since neither of them kept diaries, there is no way of knowing their mood, but they must have known the odds against survival were high. Local guides watched the climbers' every move with critical eyes and were impressed by the speed and professionalism of both men.

On the first night Max and Karl dangled, pinned to the rock face well above the Gallery Window, their torchlights glinting like fireflies or stars in the night. On the morning of the second day, a technically difficult climb up some 300 feet of smooth rock tested both men to the limit. A single error by either of them on such a pitch could wipe them both out. Down below, the valley-watchers were getting their adrenalin quota, and then some.

As the sun's heat began to affect the ice and rock conditions high above, showers of stones whistled down but, due to the vertical pitch of the cliff, much of this bombardment fell away from the face and missed the climbers. By early afternoon Karl, then leading, broke out onto the first of the Eiger's three great Ice Fields, steep but not vertical and therefore landing grounds for every ice and stone fragment falling from above.

Time and again people sipping cocktails below with their eyes glued to binoculars exclaimed in delighted horror as the climbers could be seen crouching with their rucksacks placed above their heads as shields from some new fusillade. Every now and again the boom of a new avalanche or the staccato crack of splitting rock carried down to the valley, adding to the atmosphere of impending drama. But the good weather held.

The second night involved a cramped bivouac on an icy ledge. No room to lie nor to shelter from the cold night wind. Imperceptibly, such conditions take a toll on the body strength needed for such a climb. As the long hours of the third morning crept by, Karl and Max, by now mere black dots to their viewers, even as seen through field glasses, were clearly moving very slowly as they inched across a long traverse from the First to the Second Ice Field, ever vulnerable to the rain of detritus from above.

The buzz on the hotel balconies, gleaned by the ignorant from the overheard comments of guides, was that the climbers might have to spend their third night whilst still on the sheet-ice of the Second Ice Field, clearly a bad predicament to contemplate. But then, with typical Eiger ferocity and lack of warning, the weather changed with a vengeance, and gales lashed the cliffs, hailstones drummed against the rock and deafening peals of thunder vibrated the ice sheet to which Karl and Max had pinned themselves for the night.

All the next day, the next night and well into their fifth day on the face, the two men remained hidden from their watchers as the dense storm clouds covered the heights, avalanches roared down from the summit snowfields and the temperature, even in Grindelwald village, dropped to an August low of 8° below zero.

On the morning of the sixth day when most people had written Karl and Max off as dead, frozen and either hanging from their rope or smashed on rocks below the face, a cry went up from a stubborn watcher. 'They're alive. They're moving.'

Later in the day, as the two little dots were seen to reach the base of the rock wall, later called the Flat Iron, at the upper rim of the Third Ice Field, a new storm closed in to lash the face. Watching guides crossed themselves. They knew Max and Karl had planned for a maximum climb period of

NORTH FACE OF THE EIGER

Summit Ice-field

Exit Cracks

Spider

Traverse of the Gods

Death Bivouac

Flat Iron

Third Ice-field

Second Ice-field

First Ice-field

Swallow's Nest

Hinterstoisser
Traverse

Difficult
Crack

Gallery Window

six days. In such conditions and with no food to heat their bodies, their lives would be measured in hours.

Over the following week, Karl's brother with a group of climbing friends arrived to mount a search but, in such a place, rescue was impossible and when, weeks later, an aircraft flew along close to the central ramparts of the face, they glimpsed only one of the climbers whose body, still upright and knee-deep in snow, crouched on a ledge thereafter known as Death Bivouac.

The Eiger had seen off two of the world's best climbers with the latest equipment who had set out in good weather at the warmest time of year. Surely a clear warning to others to leave well alone or suffer the same fate.

Many thrill-seekers the world over find excitement and life-enhancement by way of daredevil activities, ranging from bungee jumping, base jumping, free climbing and all modes of speed racing to kayaking raging waterfalls or bullfighting. To me, the practitioners of such death-defying 'sports' are a very different breed compared to those individuals who pit their skills, their brains and their experience against virgin geographical challenges. An obvious example would be the team of Ed Hillary and Sherpa Tenzing, who first climbed Everest. Such men, to me, are heroes not fools. They were the first to dare to go where no man had been before.

Eleven months after the deaths of top climbers Karl and Max, with their bodies still attached to the Wall, two new climbers arrived from Munich to claim the North Face. The weather being bad, they decided to train by making a first ascent of a nearby peak. Both were good climbers, but an avalanche hit them and one died with a broken neck.

A month later in July 1936 a team from Bavaria met up in Grindelwald with an Austrian group. The latter, Edi Rainer and Angerer, were experts on extreme rock, whilst the Bavarians, both only twenty-three years old, were veterans of many great alpine ascents. The four set out on the same day, on two separate ropes.

At a place to the left and slightly above the Gallery Window, the Bavarians, Toni Kurz and Andreas Hinterstoisser, joined up with the Austrians, and all four carried on as a single team.

They came to 'an exceptionally severe crack' (today known as the Difficult Crack) which they climbed with speed and expertise. Above this obstacle, Hinterstoisser struck out on a new route involving a highly exposed traverse over a vertical face which led the team onto the First Ice Field. Not realising the critical danger that this would later cause, once all had crossed the cliff-face, the men pulled from its position the rope which they had used to help traverse along the cliff on their outward journey. If ever boats were burnt, this was the classic case, but hindsight is never any use when climbing dangerous mountain faces. After all, they needed all the rope they could carry for the unknown dangers that undoubtedly lay ahead.

Without knowing it, Hinterstoisser, by his clever traverse, had opened the way for future attempts on the North Face. Named after him as the Hinterstoisser Traverse, it would feature in many a fable of tragedy or triumph throughout the next half-century.

Their morale greatly boosted by this new route discovery, the four climbers on their two ropes sped up the First Ice Field with, to the thousands of watchers below, impressive proficiency. Then, just before the difficult rock section which led to the Second Ice Field where the late Karl and Max had been fatally slowed down, Angerer was struck on the head by a falling rock. Rainer moved cautiously down to his aid and shortly afterwards the Bavarians, by then crouched under a tiny ledge in a nest of snow, let a rope down to help the Austrians. The four men spent the night on this handy ledge (now known as Swallow's Nest) and, to the great excitement of the Grindelwald observers the following morning, all four left their bivouac, heading out across the rocks towards the Second Ice Field, not back down the way they had come. So Angerer's injury could not be too serious. Far slower than on the previous day, the team did nonetheless manage to reach the Third Ice Field, and got very nearly as far as the ledge which their predecessors, Karl and Max, had reached and died on.

On the third day the Bavarians could be seen to set out early and strongly ascended the steep ice slope towards the Death Bivouac. There was clearly nothing wrong with either Andreas Hinterstoisser or Toni Kurz. After some thirty minutes, the Bavarians stopped. The Austrians had not moved. The two teams must have shouted to each other, for the lead pair cautiously climbed back down to rejoin the Austrians. And then, climbing closer together, the four men began to descend.

Angerer's condition, it was generally opined down below, had presumably declined overnight and his head injury must have caused sufficient damage to make further ascent a bad idea. The sacrifice made by his companion, Rainer, was to be expected, but even greater must have been the frustrations felt by the two Bavarians in having to give up their summit dream, despite having done so well. But although all four men had clearly considered it worth risking their lives to be first up the Murder Wall, none of them considered it worth allowing an injured man to die if they could, by turning back, save his life.

At any rate, they managed to descend some 1,000 feet before camping for their third night on the face with only 3,000 feet to go. On the fourth morning they inched down to the upper lip of the great vertical cliff across which their wonderful new traverse had safely taken them. But now, just when it mattered most, the weather worsened and the temperature dropped, turning the wet July rock face into shiny black ice, the very worst conditions for even a relatively easy climb, let alone this highly technical super-exposed finger-and-toe recrossing of the traverse. From below, as clear patches in the clouds allowed the crowded watchers to witness this life-or-death scenario unfold, Hinterstoisser's best efforts throughout the long, cold, wet morning were met again and again with failure where the tiniest mistake could lead to instant death.

The four men now had to face the harsh fact that there was no way to go but back up or straight down over the overhanging cliff above which they were belayed. They could only hope that their ropes would enable them to drop straight down the 600-foot crag below them. With the cold, wet conditions ever weakening them, they made ready to rope down into thin air.

At that point, what must have seemed like a miracle occurred, for they heard through the wind and the rockfall the sound of somebody shouting from below.

Unbeknownst to the climbers, a Jungfrau Railway guard, patrolling his sector of the subterranean railway and having heard of the climbers' plight, decided to unlock and unbolt the heavy wooden shutters which blocked access to a porthole in the rock at Kilometre 3.8 along the railway's subterranean section.

He then positioned himself on the very lip of the porthole's outer ledge, for he was used to the immediate proximity of the yawning abyss that bordered his workplace. From this vantage point he leaned outwards and craned his neck so that he could face the sky but was yet protected by a slight overhang from the bombardment of ice shards and stones whistling by. He noted that on either side of the porthole the rock was coated in sheet-ice. At the top of his voice he shouted repeatedly, pausing to listen for replies but expecting none.

Hinterstoisser was about to lead the desperate descent down sheer iced rock with intermittent overhangs and under constant threat from rock missiles like that which had injured Angerer and caused their lethal predicament. On hearing the voice, he cried out with great joy and relief. Soon all four men, even the utterly exhausted Angerer, were screaming their exultant replies to their invisible saviour-to-be down in the dark gloaming below. They whooped and they yodelled. For them at that moment the most hellish of prospects had switched to a bright ray of hope.

The ever-careful Andreas Hinterstoisser, reckoning correctly that the miraculous voice had emanated from a railway port-hole some 400 feet directly below his previous belay, began to prepare his next dangerous move. At that point something went wrong; he lost his grip on the rock and cartwheeled into space. The rope rushed down and, fixed to it, Edi Rainer was hauled against a steel snap-link and killed. The injured Angerer plummeted down to the end of his rope-length where, caught in a loop, he was strangled to death. Toni Kurz, attached at the time to Angerer's rope and jerked violently from his belay, found himself dangling in thin air immediately below an overhang.

And so, when the railway guard again called up to see why his four expected guests were taking so long, he received in response no happy group yodel, but a single desperate cry from the suspended Kurz.

'Help. Help. The others are all dead. Only I am alive. Help me.'

The guard noted that the weather had turned with a vengeance, with thick mist above and below his porthole, avalanches cascading off overhangs and a biting cold wind scouring the plate-glass rock. Assuring Kurz that he would summon guides and rescue equipment at once, the guard rushed to the tunnel phone to beg for the help of experienced guides.

The *Grindelwald Echo*, the voice of the local populace including guides, had recently published the chief guide's edict: 'We must accept that the visitors who take part in Eiger North Face attempts are aware of the dangers they are themselves risking; but no one can expect the dispatch of guides, in unfavourable conditions, on a rescue operation, in case of any further accidents on the Eiger's North Face . . . We should find it impossible to force our guides to take a compulsory part in the kind of acrobatics which others are taking voluntarily.'

Despite this official statement, half a dozen top mountain guides immediately responded to the alarm call from the mountain station guard and caught the next train into the Eiger's heart, determined, if at all possible, to save the surviving climber's life.

On arrival at the porthole and evaluating the problem, they had to tell Kurz that even they couldn't climb the 400 feet of overhanging black ice-coated rock between their stance and his dangling body, but said that they would fetch rope-firing rockets and, since it was dusk, they'd be back to get him at dawn. At this, Kurz, one hand already dead with frostbite due to the loss of a glove, cried out in obvious terror for his life, 'No! No! No!' For his chances of surviving a night in such conditions were surely nil. Yet somehow, and from my own past experiences of exposure I find this truly amazing, Kurz survived that dreadful night. His gloveless hand had frozen solid so, should he be saved, he would suffer amputation and never climb again, a fact of which he would have been fully aware as he swung to and fro through the long, dark, bitter cold night. How he avoided hypothermia God alone knows.

Dawn finally broke, and when his unseen rescuers, on a precarious series of ledges only 300 feet below, told him that they would try to reach him, Kurz cried aloud and forcefully that the only way they could reach him was from above, since the rock between him and the guides was an impassable wall of sheet-ice. But the guides could see absolutely no way to gain enough height via any route to be able to reach him from above, so they fired up ropes attached to rockets. But these merely whizzed past Kurz, way beyond the reach of his one still active and semi-frozen claw.

After a desperate conference, the chief guide shouted to Kurz to climb down the rope between him and Angerer, cut away the latter's corpse, then climb back up to the top of his rope, belay to the rock there as firmly as possible, then untwist the three strands of the rope and join them together to produce a single 300-foot line out of the original 100-foot length. That should be long enough to reach down to the highest point that the guides could reach. They would then attach long ropes to it which he could haul up.

Kurz groaned his reluctant reply. He would try.

One-armed and weakened by his already nightmarish experience, Kurz slowly let himself down to Angerer. He then cut his rope free of the dead Austrian. The body remained where it was, literally glued with blood and ice to the vertical face.

The guides assumed that Kurz was either using the arm of his frozen hand wrapped around the ice-encrusted rope, together with his cramponed boots, in order to maintain his hold on the rope, or perhaps he had some slip-noose prusik loops that can be slipped *up* the rope, but will grip it when pulled down. With his gloved and still useable hand, as well as his teeth, Kurz was somehow slowly but surely managing to complete each move of their instructions. The guides heard the chip of Kurz's axe as he cut through the rope and later, with incredible tenacity, hauled himself back up his rope to its upper fixture point. There he belayed himself to the rock and spent the next five hours doggedly untwisting the three strands of his plaited rope.

Whilst this agonising life-or-death struggle of human will-power went on so close above them, the rescue guides narrowly missed being hit by a great falling rock, and then, to their horror, a body cartwheeled by, only inches from their perch. Kurz, they assumed, had finally given up his impossible task. But no, the body was Angerer's, knocked from the wall by another rockfall.

The end of Kurz's thin fabricated line finally appeared through the mist and as though from heaven, due to the distance away from the cliff that Kurz dangled. The guides, daring now to hope, fixed a proper 300-foot rope to Kurz's line as well as a supply of ice pitons, snap-links and a hammer. When the upper end of the new rope reached Kurz, its lower end was found still to be some thirty feet above the guides' reach. So he lowered it again, still attached to his makeshift line, and they knotted a second rope to the first. This time, once the top of the two-rope assembly was firmly belayed beside Kurz, its bottom end did reach the guides, and its knotted point was visible some thirty feet above the guides' heads.

A tense hour passed as the one-handed Kurz, his strength all but gone, readied himself to descend. Inch by inch he then did so, until that wonderful moment when the guides first saw his dangling crampons appear below the overhang. His body harness was attached to the rope by a sliding snap-link which, on descending to the point where the guides' two ropes were tied together, jammed hard against the knot.

'Push hard,' they shouted. 'Push it through. It will go.' The guides could not believe this last-minute hitch. Kurz, clearly as weak as a chicken and more dead than alive, tried every known trick from his experience as a climber, and he was without a doubt ranked among the best in the world. He even tried to use his teeth but, slowly circling in thin air as the rope twisted and untwisted, he finally slumped forward, his boots within a few body-lengths of the guides' outstretched hands, and they heard him mouth the words, 'I'm finished' through his livid frostbitten lips.

And so the three guides of the rescue attempt left Toni Kurz dangling in space just beyond their reach. One said later to the journalists down below, 'To leave him . . . It was the saddest moment of my life.'

Two years later, two Austrians, Heinrich Harrer and Fritz Kasparek, teamed up with Ludwig Vörg and Anderl Heckmair from Bavaria and, a few days after two great Italian climbers fell to their deaths off the North Face, they managed to find a way to the summit ridge. It took them just four days and three nights. The most notorious killer wall in Europe had been scaled, so all future ascents would lose the grail of priority as well as the menace of the unknown.

But not quite. There was still the attractive proposition of being the first man to climb the Murder Wall *alone*. Alone and without the key safety factor of being roped to a belayed comrade who might hold you when you fell.

And so, even though many great climbers died on the Eiger in the aftermath of the Heckmair team success, lone attempts were contemplated by many an ambitious alpine acrobat. The first to actually try this dangerous challenge was a brilliant rock climber, a young Austrian called Adolf Mayr, who reached the lofty gully of the Ramp before slipping and plummeting 4,000 feet to his death.

Eleven months later, in July 1962, a Swiss climber, Adolf Derungs, who had previously summited the Eiger with a colleague, decided to do it solo. He reached a group of icy rocks well short of the Hinterstoisser Traverse, made a mistake and died. That same week, two British climbers attempted the face, but one fell from the Second Ice Field and died of his injuries. Chris Bonington and Don Whillans abandoned their own attempt in order to rescue the survivor, Bonington going on to achieve the first successful British ascent a month later with Ian Clough.

A third solo attempt was made in the same month by Austria's most famous climber of the day, Diether Marchart.

He reached a point just above the First Ice Field before he fell. His body, when found, was so battered that it could be identified only by the frostbitten fingers on one hand.

In a world where millions die in horrific ways through war, disease, starvation and genocide, the many victims of the Murder Wall chose to dice with death, sometimes after dangling for days and nights from a frozen rope, of their own volition and fully aware of the appalling risks.

They may be classified as heroes or fools or daredevils, depending on the viewpoint of whoever makes the judgment. I have chosen to include them in this book of heroes because, as true pioneers, they did not allow themselves to be intimidated by the most menacing of mountain challenges and one with a deadly history.

7

The Family

'I want them never to forget the faces of their
relatives and friends who were killed during that
time . . . Their voices must be heard'
Dith Pran, 1997

My heroes of Cambodia are the hundreds of thousands
of family members who, out of love and loyalty, risked
their lives to save their nearest and dearest from death by
starvation, disease, torture and by execution. For sheer
murderous insanity and gratuitous brutality, the Angka, or
Khmer Rouge, regime of Cambodia leaves Hitler and Stalin
way down the global roll-call of irrational psychopaths.

During their four years in power, they murdered over a
million of their fellow Cambodians in the furtherance of
the mad quest of their crazed leader, Brother Number One,
Saloth Sar, whose nickname Pol Pot derived from the French
Politique potentielle. He was one of nine children born to a
wealthy family of Chinese descent in Cambodia's capital
city, Phnom Penh. His older sister was one of the king's
mistresses, and he often visited her at the royal palace. Aged
twenty-four, he went to Paris for four years and, whilst

studying electronics, mingled with young French and Cambodian Communists.

Between the time he returned home in 1954 as a dedicated revolutionary and the end of the 1990s, a series of fierce inter-Communist schisms, armed invasions and counter-invasions, interspersed with agreements and alliances, took place between Cambodia and their neighbours, the Vietnamese. China and the Soviet Union vied with each other for influence in the region, China sometimes supporting and supplying arms to Vietnam and sometimes to Cambodia, whether the two were fighting one another or not.

When, in the 1950s, both countries gained their independence from France, they fell prey fairly rapidly to different forms of aggressive Communism. At first the Cambodian monarch, King Sihanouk, suppressed the various native revolutionaries by way of successive alliances, first with the Vietnamese and later with Pol Pot's Khmer Rouge guerrillas and the Chinese. But his own Phnom Penh government grew fed up with his inconsistent policies and threw him out. Exiled to China, the king then exhorted Cambodians to rise up against their government and support the revolutionaries of the Khmer Rouge.

In 1972, as the USAF dropped nearly 3 million tons of bombs on the Vietnamese Army and the Vietcong deep inside Cambodia, Pol Pot recruited many thousands of Cambodian bombed-out refugees into his Khmer Rouge units, and by 1975 his men controlled most of Cambodia outside Phnom Penh.

Pol Pot and many of his Khmer Rouge colleagues who had studied in French universities possessed very different ideas as to what a Communist utopia should be, compared to that of

Vietnam or China. His plan was to turn all city folk into peasants and farmers or, where this failed, to simply eradicate them. When the Cham people, an ethnic Khmer minority, rebelled against the Khmer Rouge, Pol Pot crushed them by use of extreme torture prior to execution. Even before Pol Pot attacked Phnom Penh, American intelligence warned the White House that if he came to power he would massacre a million Cambodians. In the words of US President Gerald Ford, a takeover by Pol Pot would be 'an unbelievable horror story'.

This is strange when considering that the Pol Pot group were mostly of middle-class origin and by far the best educated of all Asian Communist leaders, many with degrees from French universities where they had joined the French Communist Party whose beliefs were strictly orthodox Marxist-Leninist. Despite this, the revolution they were to plan and carry out over a decade after their return home from Paris was the bloodiest in all Asia and poles apart in its aims from any known form of Marxism.

Contrary to Marxist doctrines, the Khmer Rouge did not treat urban factory workers as the true nerve centre of their revolution. For them the real proletariat, the genuine working class, were to be found only among peasant farming communities. And these people, they believed, especially their children, must become the new leaders of the new society and the only true Khmers. Any person with any form of urban background or any level of education was already damaged goods and must be wiped out.

If this meant eradicating three-quarters of the entire Cambodian population, so be it. In Pol Pot's words, referring to anyone not of a peasant farming background: 'To keep you is no benefit. To destroy you is no loss.'

They referred to themselves as Angka, the Organisation, and every Cambodian allowed to stay alive must at all times and in all ways be an obedient instrument of Angka. Memories of or talk about pre-Angka times were forbidden, and any sign of nostalgia (*chheu satek arom*) was a crime punishable by execution. No more bowing or other such signs of deference and the only approved salutation was to be that of 'comrade'.

Pol Pot's politics are today described by historians as agrarian socialism, but his manpower was derived from a mixture of villagers uprooted by American bombing and people who despised the corruption of Sihanouk and post-Sihanouk governments. As Pol Pot's armies advanced and burnt village after village through the 1960s, so they recruited children as young as six and taught them the twin tenets of fear and violence. A major section of all Khmer Rouge units were 'killer kids' as young as ten years old who had learnt to enjoy the power to be had through terrorising others; the power of life or death.

Angka believed that *all* parents were likely to be at least partially capitalist by inclination and thus, to purify the new order, children must be taken away from parents and given shock lessons in such things as the best way of torturing animals. This would turn them into the 'dictatorial instrument' of Angka. They were given the most active lead roles in both torture policy and executions. The horrifying results of this policy can be seen today by a visit to the Tuol Sleng Genocide Museum, through which torture centre some 17,000 victims passed, of which there were only twelve known survivors.

In civil wars, each side is related or of similar background to the other. Khmer Rouge soldiers about to kill some new victim would sometimes recognise them from their schooldays or other such prior shared experience and would occasionally help them escape.

Slowly but surely all Cambodia was taken by the Khmer Rouge until only in Phnom Penh did government forces hold out, and in April 1975 they too yielded to Pol Pot.

New Year's Day in Cambodia is 17 April, the very day in 1975 when Pol Pot's victorious army finally, after five years of civil war, swept into Phnom Penh and began a four year nightmare of torture and death, later to be chronicled by the famous Cambodian journalist Dith Pran by way of stories he collected from survivors who were children at the time of Angka. He summarised his book, *Children of Cambodia's Killing Fields*, with the words: 'I want future generations to learn about what these survivors, these heroes have gone through . . . [as seen] through the eyes of these Cambodian survivors, who lost their childhood one sunny day in April 1975.'

I went on to read a great deal about these children and the horrific trauma they suffered and yet who, in many, many cases, survived through the love and bravery of their family members.

For one of these, Arn Yan, his memories include the irony that when the long and bitter civil war ended with the Khmer Rouge taking power, his family had hoped for freedom, liberty and peace, but only fifteen days later his father was accused of having been a government soldier, although he was in reality just a cattle dealer. He was interrogated with his head in a plastic bag and a jar of water. Three days later the local Hitler, who called himself the King of Death, decided to have Arn's father killed. So he and fifteen other equally innocent people were shot. Arn's mother asked Angka where he was, but people who went on asking were themselves shot.

Arn and his brothers had to work for Angka in segregated age groups. With too little food, Arn was soon starving to death and, one day, too tired to work his quota, he was kicked senseless. His mother heard about this and managed to visit him. She obtained some medicine by exchanging the buried family valuables, and she stole time from her own Angka work, fully aware that if the soldiers had known, she would have been in deadly trouble.

Three years later, in 1978, one of Arn's cousins was killed when raking a field. He had seen a fish swimming in an irrigation channel, caught it and put it in his pocket. A soldier who saw this assaulted him. Arn saw this happen, but did not know until later that it was his cousin. The soldier beat his cousin with a stick until he died.

'The Khmer Rouge tortured and killed people in many different ways. They sometimes pushed people's heads into a barrel full of water. Sometimes they pulled out the fingernails . . . Many times they killed people by cutting out their livers with a knife . . . [They] used the livers and gall bladders to make traditional medicine . . . Often they ate the livers. Sometimes they hanged people . . . Babies were thrown up in the air and came down on bayonets.'

'I survived the Khmer Rouge,' wrote Arn, 'largely because my mother really cared about me.' His mother stole rice and vegetables (punishable by death). She said, 'I am old and I will be dead someday. I don't want you to die.' As a result, Arn survived and lost his father and brother. Arn Yan's family got off lightly. Many individuals, when Angka's rule ended, had lost most or all of their loved ones.

What follows is a description of the Angka years as remembered by twelve other survivors who, like Arn Yan, were young children at the time Phnom Penh fell to the Pol Pot killers.

On 17 April, Youkimny Chan recalled, his brothers and sisters, his mother and he were living with grandparents when the soldiers came and ordered them to leave their home at once. 'These soldiers were our countrymen . . . They weren't going to let us get hurt.' But Chan was wrong. The soldiers forced the citizens of Phnom Penh in their hundreds of thousands out into the countryside. Chan and his family trudged on with the multitude and watched in horror as pregnant women and old people died by the wayside. Murders by the soldiers, mostly in their early teens or younger, were common. The dead included many of Chan's friends and neighbours.

Told to stop in the jungle, Chan's family made a rudimentary hut. Malaria soon struck and near starvation. Two of his nieces died and their mother, Chan's sister, went crazy. After a year of hand-to-mouth survival in this new 'home', the Khmer Rouge arrested and killed Chan's grandfather. After another three months, his brother and brother-in-law were taken into the forest. Chan sneaked after them and witnessed their murder.

Two of Chan's aunts and his oldest sister starved to death. 'Whenever we got some food,' Chan remembered, '. . . my mother would always give me part of hers.' Then she died, leaving only Chan's little brother and sister. His brother died next and Chan buried him. Chan tried to provide for his remaining sister, but she died with her head in his lap. 'I never went back to our hut . . . Sometimes I crawled into the hut of another family. But most families had suffered like mine. No one had enough food. No one had hope.'

Pol Pot's plan was simple and utterly ruthless. His personal vision of Communism, unlike any other, involved a world of peasant farmers following his instructions to the letter at all times and without question. His early experiments taught him that people living in towns would always turn to market capitalism. So he moved them out of towns into the jungle and the paddy fields where they must become farmers or die.

He set the hugely ambitious production target of three tons of rice per hectare throughout the land, and woe betide all those responsible in any agricultural zone which failed to achieve this yield. Cambodia's best pre-Angka average harvest had been a single ton per hectare.

He closed all schools, factories and hospitals, outlawed all religions and all private property, cut off the entire telephone and postal systems, closed all banks, put a stop to currency exchange, allowing only barter for goods, and he separated people into three categories: Old People, who were genuine peasant farmers; New People, who were all the others; and Angka, the carefully selected killer-soldiers through whose callous and well-rewarded stewardship he maintained total power. His nebulous and ambiguous goal was to 'restart civilisation in Year Zero'.

Sarah Tun, now a social worker in California, remembers the 1975 exodus from her home in Phnom Penh when she was four years old. 'The twelve- to fourteen-year-old Khmer Rouge soldiers wearing black outfits and black shoes made of car tires forced all the people in the city to walk in two straight lines.' They left home in such a panic and 'I remember walking barefoot on the hot sidewalk. My feet were blistering.'

There were gunshots as people were killed. Babies screamed and they tripped over bodies. After two weeks they reached a town, by which time half the people who had started the exodus were gone; starved, sick, shot or appointed to stay in places they passed by. In their appointed village they 'lived under harsh rules. The villagers watched us like hawks. We were treated like criminals . . . Cooking at home was outlawed . . . Everything from work to sex to family life was tightly controlled.'

Sarah's father was imprisoned. Her mother and baby brother were sent to another camp thirty miles away. She and her sister were put in an orphanage. Some time later they made their way to their mother's camp and were caught. 'They warned my mother that if we did this again they would kill the whole family.'

Two years later they were all in the same rice fields, sick and starving. Sarah's brother stole fish for them all. Once he was chased and hid in their mother's hut. She was threatened but kept quiet. Sarah was dying of pneumonia on a mat and was saved only by her mother sneaking to help her with aspirins she had begged from an ex-nurse.

Savuth Penn, now an electrical engineer in Minnesota, was eleven years old when his family was thrown from their home. They took away his father and all others suspected of being from the Cambodian Army. 'They mass executed them,' Penn said, 'without any blindfolds, with machine-guns, rifles, and grenades . . . My father was buried underneath all the dead bodies. Fortunately, only one bullet went through his arm and two bullets stuck in his skull. The bullets that stuck in his skull lost momentum after passing through the other bodies.' That night Penn's father crawled away and returned to his family. Angka threatened anyone who hid a wanted person with all-family execution. So Penn's father's brother-in-law betrayed him to Angka, who dragged his father outside, kicked him down and knifed him to death. Then they forced Penn's mother to remarry one of their own men or die. Two of his sisters starved to death. 'We were too hungry to show any sign of hatred or revenge.'

Teeda Mam, now a computer engineer in Silicon Valley, recalled her father being taken away. But to what fate? '[Many] Cambodian widows and orphans [still] live in fear of finding out what atrocities were committed against our fathers, husbands, brothers.' They also later 'killed the wives and children of the executed men in order to avoid revenge. They encouraged children to find fault with their own parents and spy on them. They openly showed their intention to destroy the family structure that once held love, faith, comfort, happiness, and companionship.'

Teeda went on to list the numerous categories of people who the Khmer Rouge sought out for death. They included 'the intellectuals, the doctors, the lawyers, the monks, the teachers, and the civil servants. These people thought, and their memories were tainted by the evil Westerners. Students were getting education to exploit the poor. Former celebrities, the poets. These people carried bad memories of the old, corrupted Cambodia.'

'The list goes on and on. The rebellious, the kind-hearted, the brave, the clever, the individualists, the people who wore glasses, the literate, the popular, the complainers, the lazy, those with talent, those with trouble getting along with others, and those with soft hands. These people were corrupted and lived off the blood and sweat of the farmers and the poor.'

'Very few of us escaped these categories.'

The Family

Susie Hem, now living in California, was five when her family was told to move to a poor farm area. For the next four years they had to find their own food to survive. Susie wrote: 'We ate anything, including banana trees and all kinds of leaves that weren't poison. I ate snails, snakes, grasshoppers, crickets and crabs . . . If someone didn't work hard, he or she would be killed in front of other people . . . We always wanted to run away to a safe place, but all places were the same, with beatings, killings, and people dying of hunger . . . Pol Pot killed my mom's friend and her whole family after accusing them of being Chinese.'

Susie told how even friendships were controlled. 'There was a man who was friends with a woman, and they had a friendly chat under a tree. Pol Pot saw them and accused them of having an affair. Pol Pot tied them up on a cross and then told everyone to watch the couple being questioned and hit. The lady was pregnant and was hit until she lost the baby and died. The man also was beaten to death.'

Susie survived for, by good luck, she was never taken away from her mother. Her mother was separated from her father but she would sneak out to meet him so that they could talk about running away.

When Ouk Villa, now a teacher in Phnom Penh, was nine, his family was sent to a strange village where the locals despised them. 'We could speak only in a whisper or in private because we were fearful of being overheard. If they heard us, we would disappear for "re-education".' Re-education usually meant death. Ouk was sent to work. There were no schools. They were taught only about hard work and faithfulness to Angka. Also 'to call our parents "comrades" and to spy on them'.

One night Ouk went to a newly excavated pit to search for crickets to eat. He saw three militiamen lead six people to the edge of the hole. They were clubbed on their necks with a hoe and fell into the grave. They weren't dead. The militiamen covered them with soil. All this he witnessed, aged nine.

Ouk's father was taken for re-education and never came back. After that they were 'spied on all the time and if they had seen or heard any of us complain, we would have been arrested and killed. At night we couldn't talk or walk outside. We had to live in silence.' Ouk's sisters were starving. Their mother hugged them and said nothing. She shed her tears. Ouk had to do something, so he went at night to steal tapioca. His mother said, 'Don't do it again, my son. If caught they would kill you.' 'Yes, Mom,' he said. 'Never again.' He had become a thief to save his sisters.

Hong Chork was born lucky, one of a village farmer's nine children and, as such, favoured by Angka. He remembers being sent from home to be educated. The school was tough. 'The soldiers taught us about Angka and the wrongs of capitalism. Angka was great. The revolution was great. We were going to be Angka's helpers in the war against evil.' If accused of anything, Hong learnt to admit it even when it was not true. 'The Khmer Rouge weren't interested in the truth.' Later he met one of his brothers who had graduated as a full Khmer Rouge soldier, but, of the other seven siblings, five had been killed by Angka even though they were of farmer stock. Nonetheless Hong was fully aware how lucky he was. 'I was spared a lot of pain', is his summary of the Angka years.

Hong Chork's religious upbringing was wiped out by

Angka, along with other moral norms. Pol Pot suspected all forms of religion and executed every trace, including razing to the ground the magnificent Roman Catholic cathedral in Phnom Penh.

The Death List, rigorously pursued over four years, included ethnic Vietnamese, ethnic Chinese (despite Pol Pot's own Chinese blood), ethnic Thai, Cambodians, Christians and Muslims. Buddhist monks, Muslim imams and Christian clergy were dispatched with especial speed and brutality.

Even if Hong, like one of his brothers, had graduated to become a full Khmer Rouge soldier, he would never have been able to feel safe because Pol Pot, like most successful dictators, was at all times suspicious of everyone from his own family to his closest comrades. This, of course, instigated factional struggles within Angka, for leaders at every level were riddled with fear. Pol Pot's resultant purges peaked in 1977 when thousands of Khmer Rouge murderers were killed in-house, including many senior cadre captains.

Aged four, Seath Teng was separated from his parents, together with his little sister. 'The Khmer Rouge soldiers told us not to love our parents.' He worked seven days a week without a break. The only time they got off work was to see someone get killed, which served as an example. Eighteen years have passed and Seath can still vividly remember one of these killings. The whistle blew. They all had to go to see the punishment of a traitor. 'They made us sit in front near the victim . . . She was pregnant and her stomach bulged out. Before her stood a little boy who was about six years old and holding an ax. In his shrill voice, he yelled for us to look at what he was going to do. He said that if we didn't look, we would be the next to be killed . . . He used the back of his ax and slammed it hard on the poor woman's body until she dropped to the ground. He kept beating her until he was too tired to continue.'

Seath Teng added, 'If we were caught hugging or talking intimately to our parents, we would get a beating.' And any child who tried to run away and was caught was dragged to a meeting of all the children. Whoever was pointed at by the Khmer Rouge would have to beat the captured runaways, and 'if we didn't beat severely enough, we would be the next victim and also be beaten. To save ourselves from being hit, we hit hard.'

Pol Pot did his utmost to break basic family bonds. Seath wrote, 'I believed the Khmer Rouge soldiers when they told us that our families did not love us.' 'Familyism' (*kruosaa niyum*), which meant openly missing loved ones, was treated as a crime punishable by death, and spies appointed by Santebal, Angka's secret police, reported any signs of such emotional behaviour. All children no longer being breastfed were taken from their mothers and given to female members of the Khmer Rouge to be brought up without love. Later on in their four years of government, the regime realised that they had so alienated the average adult Cambodian that their cadres of brainwashed children were likely to become the only hope for the future of Angka. So they were encouraged to spy on their parents and to become the basis of a new society with no memories of the 'decadence' of pre-Angka days. Only through countless acts of great personal courage by parents to save children, and vice versa, did many family units survive the targeted Angka attacks on their cohesion.

In pre-revolutionary Khmer *kruosaa* meant family, but Angka altered its meaning to spouse because, to them, children were no longer part of their family since they belonged to Angka and not to their parents. Children were made to sing the new national children's song, 'We Children Love Angka Boundlessly'.

Charles Ok summarised his childhood memories: 'Clothes that had color were prohibited. Only black clothes were worn . . . There was no make-up, no high heels, no boots, no jewelery.' Their common diseases were diarrhoea, malaria and dysentery, but modern medicines were banned. Once when Charles visited his brother, 'they asked me to help bury bodies because they didn't have enough people to help. There were thousands of dead people everywhere.' In the winter most of the land was wet and full of water. 'There were so many bodies, they buried one body on top of the other . . . When a corpse was swollen it was hard to bury, making it easy for foxes and other animals to dig for it at night . . . Every night and day young adults, most of them men, were tied up to be killed. The army said that these people were either former soldiers, former police officers, CIA agents or KGB members . . . They were guilty before proven guilty.' Some tried to escape. 'Some committed suicide. Day by day the villages grew more empty except for widows . . . Sometimes I sit down and cry and think about the past . . . I have become a lonely person.'

Moly Li, now a computer engineer in California, was thirteen when Angka came to his town. '[Soldiers] threatened the crowds . . . They were dressed in black with red kramas wrapped around their heads and rifles slung on their shoulders . . . People were divided up into five classes: small children, bigger children, single women and men, married women and men, and elderly women and men . . . my sister

Kuyny and I were sent to work far from the village. We were called *kong chalat*, meaning mobile troops. Our duties included building dykes, digging canals, liquidating the forest by removing roots, chopping logs and branches and setting old brush on fire. We mixed up human remains with soil.' If people were accused of being lazy they were executed. 'Instead of bullets, the Khmer Rouge killed by beating people with the back of a hoe. They called this *vay choul*.' The swarming insects became nourishment to Moly and his family. 'Some people were so hungry that they dug up dead bodies and slit the flesh and fried it.' If caught doing this, they were killed.

When Moly was sick, it was a nightmare to see his weak and starving mother carrying buckets of water from a stagnant pond to take care of him. He knew that he should have been caring for her. Later he was almost beaten to death for collecting leftover potatoes when trying to help feed his mother. They then starved him for doing it. Moly dedicated the story of his survival to his beloved mother and other family 'who left this world in agony during the years of horror'.

Sarom Prak, who now lives in New Zealand, was a young teenager when Angka took over his life and butchered most of his family. Nobody could marry, or even propose marriage, without approval from Angka. They decided who would marry who. Sometimes they held a mass marriage for seventy to a hundred designated couples. That was a good way, said Sarom, 'for some of the people who had power – like soldiers, the chiefs of villages and districts – to molest young girls until they got pregnant. Flirtations, adultery and love affairs were reasons for execution.'

Sarom was based in the district of Takeo. A hundred yards from his hut was one of the many execution pits. 'I saw dead bodies appearing from the pits because wolves ate them at night.' Sarom's father was in one of them. The Khmer Rouge accused him of being a CIA agent and executed him. When in Tram Kak district, Sarom described the Angka practice of playing blaring music over loudspeakers to hide the screaming during killing or torture sessions.

Gen Lee, a teacher now, was seven when forced to work in paddy fields for fourteen hours a day. The long hours standing in water up to her knees gave her early arthritis. She remembered the terrible starvation and overwork and the many forms of disease. She had malaria, and would have died but for 'my mother's undying love and care. Risking her own life, she walked far' to find scraps, but Gen grew emaciated. Her mother made a plot to fool Angka and somehow had little Gen reassigned. She also stole fruit for Gen.

When in 1978 the Vietnamese Army eventually freed most of Cambodia from Angka, Gen Lee and her mother tried to flee to Thailand along with 45,000 other displaced Cambodians. En route they were attacked by bandits, turned back twice from the border, wandered through great minefields littered with shredded corpses and were driven mad by mosquitoes, leeches and lice. But always their courage was bolstered by their love and their togetherness. Two months after they had set out, they finally reached a Thai refugee camp, and found safety and escape from the long years of fear.

Altogether the Khmer Rouge regime caused the genocide of 3 million people (as estimated by UNICEF), but the Khmer Rouge themselves quoted a total of 2 million and blamed the Vietnamese. In terms of the number of people killed as a proportion of the population, Angka was the most lethal regime of the twentieth century.

8

We Will Die Together

'The smallest pain in our little finger gives us
more concern than the destruction of millions
of our fellow beings'
William Hazlitt

The Derbyshire village of Eyam, 150 miles north of
London, is as pretty a place today as it was in the seven-
teenth century, a community of neighbourly families and a
church. Then as now. Nothing special, apart from the remarkable story of those Eyam graveyard inmates buried in the
years 1665 and 1666 and their contemporaries whose remains
are heaped together in a nearby communal pit.

I have had a massive heart attack and, not long ago, cancer.
Neither problem caused me lasting pain, but I have been at
the bedside of my sister and, soon after, of my beloved wife
of thirty-six years when each died of cancer. Some illnesses
can kill without suffering and others are horrible to witness,
even in this age of morphine and pain relief.

To know that a nightmarish form of death approaches you,
to wish to escape from its clutches, but to stay where you are
in order to help others is to be truly brave. As was the vicar

of Eyam in 1665. He and his parishioners knew all about the terrors of the Black Death, for they had heard the lurid tales from passing merchants as the dreaded plague advanced north from London.

To this day scientists debate the exact nature and history of the Great Plague which struck Britain in 1665. A favourite theory deduced from plague records, held by many medical historians and geneticists, reaches back to China in the thirteenth century when the disease was endemic in the marmot population. During a severe famine, the plague virus hopped to humans, much as did modern swine flu in the twenty-first century. Aggressive Mongol armies then exported this plague to other parts of Asia and in 1347 they developed the practice of catapulting dead and dying plague victims over the walls of besieged cities.

The disease then spread rapidly, and terrified European traders fled back home by ship. The deadly pathogen which they hosted was recorded in Sicily, whence it spread worldwide, and in only three years killed over 25 million Europeans. Successive pandemics broke out over the next 300 years, but today's scientists dispute the causes of the various outbreaks. For many years, the most prevalent theory was that those outbreaks known as the Black Death were, in fact, bubonic plague attacks, caused by fleas that had bitten infected rodents and then bitten humans.

More recently, British researchers have come to believe that the Black Death pandemics were not flea-borne bubonic plagues at all, but were more like the dreaded African killer-virus Ebola, which in the 1980s was sensationalised by the media as a 'flesh-eating killer virus from the jungles of the Congo'. Researchers at Liverpool University believe that the liquidisation of the internal human organs, which causes so much agony in Ebola victims, matches the descriptions of historical autopsies on plague-infested corpses, which likewise describe their internal organs as having been 'dissolved and mixed with a black liquid'.

They further point out that the Black Death outbreaks like Ebola spread rapidly, over twenty miles in a day, whereas the bubonic rat-and-flea plagues advanced at a mere 100 yards a year. The human-to-human Ebola virus is airborne, like the anthrax spore, and can move at the speed of each and every infected carrier. The bacillus can also lie latent in faeces or clothing for months. Death in waiting, and relevant to the inhabitants of Eyam. The Ebola-plague theorists also point out that the Black Death occurred in Iceland, where there were no rats.

The first known outbreak in Britain in 1351 killed off half the entire population. Between then and 1665 the virus resurfaced many times to kill millions all over the world, and last struck Europe as a major epidemic in 1720. Today the plague bacterium is still alive and kicking but is kept at bay by antibiotics to which, as yet, it has not become drug-resistant.

Children of my generation in our British history syllabus learnt of the Great Plague of 1665, followed in 1666 by the Great Fire of London, which neatly followed the period during which King Charles I had his head chopped off and an experimental form of semi-republican democracy under Cromwell was tried and discarded before the executed Charles's son was brought back from exile in France and monarchy was restored. Unfortunately, in 1664, four years into Charles II's rule, another visitor from France settled in London, having picked up the plague bacillus in Holland. This Frenchman died at his house in Drury Lane four days before Christmas. His family, aware of the deadly symptoms, tried to hush up the nature of his death but, by way of servants or the doctor, news reached the authorities and soon word-of-mouth rumours were rife all over London. At the end of the month another man died in the same house and, six weeks later, a third person died at a nearby address. Although many folk concealed plague deaths in their homes for fear of being shunned, it became general knowledge that by May 1665 an epidemic had begun which was spreading from parish to parish.

As the month of May drew to a close and the weather hotted up, the outbreak reached pandemic proportions and a stampede of Londoners headed out of the city in all directions to escape. Many carried the bacillus with them in ignorance, others in full knowledge of their infection which arguably made them mass murderers. The entire royal court sped up river to Hampton Court without the need to seek a permit to do so, but everyone else required a certificate of health signed by the Mayor of London in order to stand any hope of gaining access to sanctuary, or even a passage through the barricades rapidly manned all over southern England against desperate London emigrants.

Any house suspected of harbouring a newly infected person was 'shut up', a method of attempting to slow the spread of the plague first introduced by King James I in 1603. All other occupants of the condemned house would be kept inside, whether they were infected or not. In order to avoid being shut up with an infected member of their family, desperate people would often lock the sick in an attic or a cellar, but their screams could be reported to the authorities by neighbours.

Watchmen, recruited from the poor and from those whose previous employment had ceased when their employers fled or died, were tasked with ensuring that nobody escaped from an officially shut house. Nor that anyone entered either. All downstairs doors and windows of condemned homes were boarded up or padlocked and over the front entrance a crude red cross was painted, along with the words 'Lord have mercy on us'. Whilst at least one inmate survived, he or she would lower a bucket from an upstairs window and the watchman would fill it with supplies. When the last person was dead, the watchman would be assigned to a new home. In the unlikely event that somebody survived at least forty days in such conditions and could prove it, they could apply through their watchman for a Clean Bill of Health.

Nobody trusted anyone else, for the breath of outwardly healthy individuals who carried the disease without knowing it could kill you with the greeting 'Good morning'. And there were others, including escapees from shut-up houses, who were well aware that they were infected but hid the outward signs behind gloves, scarves and hats, and were hell-bent on infecting as many others as they could. This inclination, according to psychologists, is the standard reaction of a small percentage of any population to great misfortune. They cannot bear to be more miserable than others, and so they try hard to spread their own misery to third parties. This unpleasant human trait is evident today in the many cases of HIV-positive individuals aggressively infecting as many sexual partners as possible.

So many corpses needed burial that coffins were soon unavailable, even to the wealthy. Huge burial pits were dug and quickly filled. Death carts creaked and rumbled by each and every night, for they were forbidden to work by day. Strict rules prevented mourners attending the 'burial' of their loved ones for fear of infection, but the records mention many folk who, near death, flung themselves into the pit where their family were already lying.

By the end of June the weather was hotting up, the bacillus thrived and daily death rates surged. In lemming-like panic, Londoners thought only of escape, but by then every town and village was blocked and defended against strangers, especially those arriving from the direction of London.

A few thousand, the rich or those with good contacts, found an uneasy sanctuary aboard boats moored midstream on the Thames. But even there the only way to survive was to cultivate an iron resolve to show no sympathy to the many supplicants, often whole families, who were rowed out by boatmen on desperate missions to find somewhere to avoid death. All along the Long Reach anchorage by Greenwich, over a thousand boats, large and small, provided at least a temporary sanctuary from the plague.

As the foetid heat of August settled about the squalid, crowded and narrow streets of London, people feared annihilation as the death toll mounted and many remembered hearing of the horrific total of the last pandemic in Naples, which had reached 20,000 deaths a day.

Describing behaviour patterns of the infected, Daniel Defoe in his *Journal of the Plague Year* wrote:

People in the Rage of the Distemper, or in the Torment of their Swellings, which was indeed intollerable, running out of their own Government, raving and distracted, and oftentimes laying violent Hands upon themselves, throwing themselves out at their Windows, shooting themselves, etc. Mothers murthering their own Children, in their Lunacy, some dying of meer Grief . . . some of meer Fright and Surprize, without any Infection at all; others frighted into Idiotism, and foolish Distractions, some into despair and Lunacy; others into mellancholy Madness.

The pain of the Swelling was in particular very violent, and to some intollerable; the Physicians and Surgeons may be said to have tortured many poor Creatures, even to Death. The Swellings in some grew hard, and they apply'd violent drawing Plasters, or Pultices, to break them; and if these did not do, they cut and scarified them in a terrible manner: In some . . . no Instrument could cut them, and then they burnt them with Causticks, so that many died raving mad with the Torment . . .

The uncontrolled and uncontrollable surge in the death toll by September had the effect of changing the outlook of many survivors, so that their previous apprehension when anyone approached anywhere near them gave way to a 'to hell with it all' abandon, for death was *everywhere*. There could be no escape, so why bother to try? One result of this attitude was that churches in the city were again frequented with crowds that mingled without caution: crowds of those who considered themselves the living dead. And worshippers who had, only months before, scorned Dissenters (the loose title given to those who failed to sign the Act of Uniformity to the Church of England), now shared pews with them and even listened to the sermons of Dissenter ministers when their own priests had died or fled.

Many doctors had also taken their families and escaped

London at the very first appearance of the contagion. Those who remained steadfast, even in London's two Pest Houses, must have been men of steel. Some took no precautions, whilst others, in the sweltering heat, donned the latest protective gear, not unlike Ku Klux Klan uniforms, consisting of an all-enveloping leather garment topped with a leather helmet, a protruding carrot-like nose flap and eye pieces of a thin membrane. High boots completed this ghostly image.

By September, survivors who were finally forced out of their bolt-holes by a lack of supplies were in an unenviable position because determined rings of defence were by then in place around every town, village and hamlet in the land.

In theory, individuals who could somehow prove that they were free of the plague, could obtain an official Bill of Health signed by a doctor or magistrate, but these were easily forged and so of little or no help to anybody trying to gain sanctuary outside London.

Countless refugees who were refused entry to shelter or food died by the roadside or in makeshift hovels: strangers in a hostile land.

Of those Londoners who had managed to flee the city in the spring and early summer before the surrounding towns were alerted to their peril, a goodly number of such refugees were already lethal hosts to the bacillus, and by the end of the summer had spread the Black Death far and wide in southern England.

The agonising process of death by the plague was particularly hard to witness, and this made especially courageous the decision of those individuals who stayed at their posts. The few that did, and often died as a result, included priests, magistrates, doctors and nurses, few of whom ever received

Toni Kurz, who died horribly on the Eiger in 1936.

he first successful climb of the North Wall of the Eiger was ade in 1938 when the German pair Ludwig Vörg and Anderl Heckmair pooled resources with Austrians Heinrich Harrer and Fritz Kasparek in a masterpiece of route-finding.

A modern climber attempting the first stage of the Traverse of the Gods, the drop immediately beneath him is over 5,000 feet. Harrer said, 'the North Wall of the Eiger remains one of the most perilous in the Alps as every man who's ever joined battle with it knows.'

Peter Godwin returned to Zimbabwe, the country of his birth, at great personal risk, to tell the world of the bravery of his fellow countrymen, black and white, in his book *The Fear*, 2010.

Roy Bennett prior to his arrest and torture with Morgan Tsvangirai, leader of the Movement for Democratic Change (MDC).

President Mugabe accompanied by the chiefs of his armed forces during the country's independence celebrations in Harare, 2008.

MDC supporters risk their lives by showing the party's open-palm salute at an election rally.

Suspected to have voted for the MDC, farm workers evicted by the ruling party's militia stand at the roadside with their possessions. Many others were beaten to death for their effrontery in voting against Mugabe.

British soldiers gather around the cook house at their camp during the Crimean War. From the outset the campaign was badly planned. No winter clothing or decent tentage was supplied. Of 98,000 Britons sent to the Crimea, 21,000 never returned home.

The Royal Scots Greys charge at the battle of Balaklava, October 1854.

A wounded soldier is tended in the open by a nurse after the battle. It is thought over a million men perished in the Crimea.

Turkish ambulance men help take the sick and wounded to safety.

Douglas Mawson led the Australasian Antarctic expedition which reached the South Magnetic Pole in 1912.

Dr Xavier Mertz, Swiss skiing and mountaineering expert who went mad, chewed off one of his fingers and spat it out in front of Mawson.

Mertz emerging from 'Aladdin' Cave', November 1912.

Lt Belgrave Edward Sutton Ninnis, English army officer, aged 22. Popular with all the expedition, he was chosen to be part of Mawson's group in spite of his youthfulness.

Ninnis driving his dog-team, shortly before disaster struck.

awson's three-man team set off into the
known. This is the last photograph taken of
e Far Eastern Antarctic party, November 1912.

Ice-mask. Drift snow settling
on the face would quickly
freeze into an iron-hard
mask. Facial hair, including
eyelashes, was often torn out
when the ice was removed.

awson, sole survivor of the Far
stern Antarctic expedition, is
my mind, the greatest polar
rvivor of them all.

With his companions both dead,
Mawson had to cut down every
ounce of equipment. This is
especially true of his sledge, which
he cleverly adaped in size (despite
his blistered and frozen hands)
and hauled 120 miles.

Londoners fleeing to the countryside in the often vain hope of
escaping the Great Plague of 1665.

The Riley graves in the Derbyshire village of Eyam, containing seven
members of the Hancock family. Eyam was the only village in plague-
striken Europe to voluntarily risk what amounted to suicide by
willingly isolating themselves to prevent it spreading.

recognition. Those who fled, their tails tucked firmly between their legs in a lather of fear, often returned post-plague to find abusive notices pinned to their surgery, courthouse or church door, branding them as deserters. In all England the most lasting memorial to those with the personal courage selflessly to risk the worst of deaths in their determination not to infect others can be found in the Derbyshire village of Eyam.

By mid-August 1665 much of southern England was plague-ridden, as were the Midlands, but Derbyshire was unscathed, and isolated villages like Eyam, with an enviable history of escaping many previous killer pandemics, were merrily celebrating an excellent harvest, whilst Londoners, a mere 150 miles away, died in their thousands by day and by night.

By way of some postal system from London that still functioned despite the obvious inherent dangers, an innocuous-looking parcel arrived at the house of Eyam's local tailor, George Viccars. He opened the package, and finding that the contents, a selection of woven cloths, were damp, he hung them out to dry by the kitchen fire. Invisible fumes from the steaming cloth contained spores of the plague bacillus which Viccars inhaled and, in a matter of hours, the round black signs or 'tokens' appeared on his skin as telltale plague symptoms. Panic seized the villagers of Eyam, and the wealthier ones with other homes to house them fled at once. Within a month of that first death, five others were buried, and it seemed that nothing would prevent a mass exodus from the isolated village.

Religion played an important role in the daily life of Eyam and, as elsewhere in England, the recent Civil War between Cromwell's Puritans and the Royalists had divided opinions about the best way to worship. After the Restoration Charles

II's Act of Uniformity made the Anglican Book of Common Prayer compulsory throughout the land. Dissenting clergy who refused to follow it were replaced by conforming priests. The nonconformist Eyam vicar, Thomas Stanley, when replaced by William Mompesson, stayed on at his home in Eyam, which must have been a touch awkward for his replacement.

When the plague appeared in Eyam, Mompesson was well aware that in London an unhealthily large number of Anglican priests had fled the city, whereas many Dissenting clergy had stayed on to officiate. He and Stanley agreed to put their religious differences aside and, together, to hold a meeting of the parishioners at which they would try to persuade everyone that, as Christians, they should love their neighbours and not risk killing them by spreading the infection all over Derbyshire by fleeing from Eyam.

The two priests argued that, unlike the normal reaction to a plague outbreak where the focus of village survivors is on getting rid of the infested and keeping all visitors *out*, Eyam should concentrate on keeping the infected inmates quarantined *inside* a set village boundary perimeter. This selfless course of action, which amounted to self-imposed suicide, was agreed by each and every villager, the number of whom was somewhere between 400 and 800 (the records are confusing).

Mompesson spoke to a local landowner, the Earl of Devonshire, and various other Derbyshire magnates, who agreed to provide supplies for as long as was necessary and place them at specific points along the boundary of the Eyam no-go zone. To lessen cross-infection within the village, movement from house to house was discouraged, and people were to drag their own dead into the nearest field where the two priests would hold services in the open air. Eyam did not have its own doctor, and the villagers refrained from attempting to hire one. Instead, they invented their own treatments, one of which was to tie a live hen to the victim so that its anus was directly over the worst plague bubo. The hen excrement was thought to 'draw out the bad blood'. We now know that hen-mess contains the antibiotic thromycin, so it is possible that such treatment may have worked.

Another treatment, discovered accidentally by a girl called Margaret Blackwell, whose descendants still live in the village, was to drink liquid bacon fat. Sick with the plague, young Margaret thought the jug full of fat was actually milk, and she drank it by mistake. She soon started to feel better and became one of Eyam's few survivors.

Winter came and, as in London, the death toll dipped, but in the summer of 1666, whilst much of London burnt down, the plague again ripped through the castaways of Eyam, killing at least a third of the village, including Vicar Mompesson's wife.

One of Mompesson's surviving letters included the following description:

The condition of this place has been so sad that I persuade myself it did exceed all history and example. Our town has become a Golgotha, the place of a skull. My ears have never heard such doleful lamentations – my nose never smelled such horrid smells, and my eyes never beheld such ghastly spectacles. Here have been seventy-six families visited within my parish, out of which two hundred and fifty-nine persons died. Now (blessed be God) all our fears are over, for none have died of the plague since the eleventh of October, and the pest houses have been long empty.

Mompesson, Stanley and their Eyam flock exemplify communal courage in a time of terror by increasing their own chances of death in order to save others.

* * *

Today there are some 900 parishioners in Eyam, including a number of families descended from survivors of the 1665–6 epidemic. Autopsies of those survivors have shown that they possessed a rare chromosome which protected them from the plague and which is still present in their descendants.

Through the long years when humans were hunter-gatherers, the instinctive reaction of 'fight-or-flight' was developed but became confused when we started to consider moral issues, such as saving others and not just ourselves.

The people of Eyam had every reason to flee in terror from their village of death, for they knew full well the dreadful nature of the plague. But they chose to stay, and probably to die, rather than to risk spreading the contagion.

9

The Teller of the Tale

In 2005 my wife Louise, five months pregnant at the time, joined me on an expedition to commemorate Dr Livingstone's arrival at the Victoria Falls exactly 150 years before. We paddled down the Zambezi River in dugout canoes with Zambian friends and local boatmen who knew how to avoid the many hippos and shallows, stopping exactly where the famous Scottish missionary and his men had camped on their epic journey to locate the fabled Roaring Waters of the Zambezi.

That expedition introduced us to white Zimbabweans who later invited us to stay in Zimbabwe on a lion cub rescue ranch. We enjoyed our subsequent visits there and, despite driving hundreds of miles inside Zimbabwe, we saw no evidence of people in distress. I was, at that point, convinced that occasional news reports of widespread persecution of political opponents by Zimbabwean President Robert Mugabe were exaggerated.

Then, in 2011, I happened to read *The Fear*, a book by Peter Godwin, a New York-based journalist born in Zimbabwe (then Rhodesia) in 1957. In Zimbabwe he trained as a policeman, later studying law at Cambridge in England. He then became a writer and journalist and watched over the years as his homeland descended from its status in the early 1980s as the 'jewel of Africa' to a hellhole of fear, starvation and disease in the latter half of that decade. A whole world of tyrannical injustice is revealed in Godwin's book. The bravery of Zimbabweans, black and white, who had for so long stood up to appalling barbarity by Mugabe's thugs is vividly described by Godwin, who risked torture and death time and again in order to find out and tell the world what was happening, and, indeed, is still happening inside Zimbabwe. For as I write, multiple murderer Mugabe, backed by a coterie of some 200 cronies, installed in key positions of power, continues to hold on to his dictatorship through maintaining an atmosphere of countrywide terror. Visiting journalists need to toe the line or suffer the same fate as the victims whose stories they seek to tell to the world.

Robert Mugabe, an ex-teacher and guerrilla fighter, took over as Zimbabwe's prime minister in 1980 on the ousting of Ian Smith and white power. Fellow freedom fighter Joshua Nkomo and his Ndebele tribesmen in Matabeleland, Southern Rhodesia, soon threatened Mugabe's dream of total power, so he crushed them with an army of men from his own Shona tribe trained by North Korean military instructors.

Over the next couple of decades of callous disregard for his fellow citizens, apart from his own clique and loyal fellow veterans of the war against the whites, Mugabe allowed Zimbabwe to fall into a ravaged state of neglect wherein all dissent was stamped on and only the super-brave dared to fight for their freedom.

In April 2008 Peter Godwin returned to the country of his early years really believing that Mugabe was about to be voted out of power. The president did indeed look vulnerable following elections that he had rigged by all known methods, but which still resulted in overwhelming electoral victory for the MDC, Morgan Tsvangirai's Movement for Democratic Change. This was not surprising, in that from having had the highest standard of living of all African countries when Mugabe came to power, Zimbabweans now suffered from starvation, a worthless currency, hospitals without basic facilities, regions almost barren due to ethnic cleansing, life expectancy fallen from sixty years to thirty-five, and a loss of at least one third of the population who had fled, mostly to South Africa, either because the economy had collapsed or because, politically active, they were targeted by the Mugabe regime.

Just a few weeks after Godwin's arrival, Mugabe, smarting from the election results, banned all foreign correspondents and escalated his torture campaign. Godwin (and his jour-nalist sister with whom he travelled) knew the risk they took in remaining in Harare after all Western journalists had been banned and both of them had previously been declared enemies of the state due to less-than-polite reports on Mugabe's rule that they had issued from London. Also, back in 1983 when Godwin had written for the *Sunday Times* about the Mugabe-inspired massacre of over 20,000 Nkomo supporters in Matabeleland, he had been accused of being a British spy and was forced to flee under a death threat.

Godwin's hopes that Mugabe would be so thoroughly defeated in the 2008 elections that he would concede victory to the MDC had collapsed overnight with the news that successful government rigging of the voting system, plus concerted campaigns of violence and intimidation, had reduced the MDC lead at the polls to under 50 per cent.

Thus a second 'run-off' vote was mandatory, and that would give Mugabe time to menace and murder on a truly grand scale unknown by the world beyond Zimbabwe, due to the exclusion of all journalists who valued their skin.

Godwin, deeply troubled by the continued crookery, decided to gather proof of the intimidation masterminded by the regime's secret service, the CIO (Central Intelligence Organisation). By keeping at least one step ahead of their goons, Godwin hoped to contact his many old friends and contacts in Harare and the outlying areas where he had been brought up and schooled. Most of the white farmers and their workers of his youth had long since been forcibly evicted or murdered, but some 20,000 whites still lingered on in the country of their birth. One of them, Roy Bennett, was even lined up to be a minister, should the MDC ever become the government.

Godwin was soon to discover that the overwhelming victory of the MDC at polling stations, despite the intense efforts of Mugabe's rigging methods, had so alarmed the Mugabe clique that a new and radical operation had been launched to ensure that anyone involved in any way with the MDC would be made to pay for their temerity and discouraged from any future such stupidity.

Godwin's subsequent descriptions of individual MDC members' experiences prior to and after the 2008 election in his book *The Fear* makes for grim reading but, to me, provides the brightest testament to human courage and endurance, starting with that of their leader Morgan Tsvangirai. Once a supporter of Mugabe, he had become a mining trades union leader and founded the MDC because of the 'misrule, official corruption and dictatorship' in Mugabe's Zimbabwe African National Union party, ZANU.

He was arrested a dozen times, beaten to within an inch of his life, charged with treason, escaped an assassination attempt, festered in filthy prison cells and suffered also in the knowledge that his closest associates, his bodyguards, his MDC leaders, and even his family were under constant threat of murder. In 2007 a journalist who managed to smuggle film footage of Tsvangirai in prison with a fractured skull, hugely swollen face, slashed eyelid and internal bleeding was himself abducted, beaten to pulp and left for dead on a rubbish dump.

Soon after Godwin's arrival in Harare, Tsvangirai was warned of imminent plans to assassinate him, so he fled his homeland and spent the time touring various African countries to try to persuade them to accept him, on clear electoral evidence, as Zimbabwe's new leader. When he felt it safe to return, by a sad twist of fate, he and his beloved wife Susan were involved in a road accident. He was not badly hurt, but Susan was killed and, at a very testing time, he lost his greatest supporter. A lesser man would surely have crumbled at that point.

Ninety-nine per cent of the MDC were black, but one white man, Roy Bennett, stood out in 2008 as a loved and respected MDC leader. An ex-policeman, speaking fluent Shona, he was a founder member of the party and became an especially hated target of Mugabe, who had his farm burnt down and forced him and his family into exile in South Africa.

Good friends of Bennett, soon visited by Godwin, included Shane and Birgit Kidd who rented out their local village shop to the MDC. Government thugs then took over the store and the Kidds' attempts to object made them targets of the local CIO tyrant, Joseph Mwale.

Mwale had previously attacked two MDC election agents

by driving his truck into their car, beating them up, pouring paraffin over them and leaving them on fire. An eyewitness, who then tried to help, said: 'We tried to lift them with our bare hands. They were still burning. Talent Mabika was still screaming, she was not dead yet, she had been badly burnt. Her whole body was black with smoke and soot. And their skins were peeling from their bodies.'

Godwin saw Shane Kidd's diary. Mwale had thrown him into jail where, at night, the police sprayed the cell inmates with freezing water through the bars, leaving the floor ankle-deep in water and then heaving in buckets of urine for good measure. Shane's wife, Birgit, brought in lawyers, but Mwale chased them away and had Shane thrashed all over. It was a standard Zimbabwe prison where murderers, rapists and howling mad folk were jammed together. Lice crept from body to body and weevils swam in the maize-porridge bucket which provided their only daily meal and which was left in the cell for less than a minute. When Shane was let out, he had lost one fifth of his body weight in two weeks.

The diary made clear that prison had not chastened Shane through fear of going back there. He wrote of his cellmates, 'The guys are magnificent in their fortitude. We are moulding our own hard core right here. They are now genuine political prisoners, which is turning into a badge of honour and they are no longer frightened. I am confident now of my ability to handle prison. I no longer fear its threat, and I am confident in my ability to make trouble wherever I go.'

Back at their store, Shane and Birgit hired a sign painter to draw new, bold MDC logos on the store front. But Mwale arrested the painter. Local black residents asked Shane to stand in elections as their councillor. He knew that this would mean constant police and CIO harassment and certain prison visits, but he stood anyway. Sure enough he was soon back in jail, sharing lice and a blanket with a rapist.

Mwale wouldn't tell Birgit where Shane was, so she drove from prison to prison trying to find him, knowing that he might be dead or beaten to pulp. He was let out at length, but the lawyer who arranged his bail was himself arrested, beaten and imprisoned (the fate of many lawyers who dared to represent MDC people).

Shane's post as councillor was revoked because his birth certificate was not Zimbabwean. This ignored the fact that he was a Zimbabwean citizen who had been a councillor in previous years.

Mwale later found Shane on the farm of white MDC leader Roy Bennett, so he clubbed Shane's mouth with his rifle butt and the following day had his men start a grass fire that all but destroyed the village. Shane recorded that Bennett's wife, Heather, waiting outside the police office where her family bodyguard was being tortured, 'could hear his screams of agony and saw him running out of the office with a bleeding head, only to be dragged back by Mwale and the torture continued'.

One day, when Shane was away, a mob of Mugabe's ZANU thugs surrounded his house. Birgit faced them alone. 'Why,' they shouted, 'have you given your shop to the MDC?' Another screamed, 'Go back to Britain', and ignored her reply that she was Finnish. They forced her to march down the village road holding their ZANU flag to the store which they had burnt out. She was made to clean up the blackened mess while they hooted and jeered. A ZANU truck arrived and a local MDC officer, David Mudengwe, was pushed out. The mob attacked and he was soon spouting blood. Birgit tried to help David but was pinned down. He was stripped and beaten until raw, swollen and senseless. When Birgit was allowed home, she found that the family dog had been poisoned.

Shane's diary comment was simply, 'We will reopen the MDC office again.' Mwale re-arrested him as he was painting over a ZANU sign. Six policemen beat him up, whilst three others attacked Birgit with rocks in their hands. They cut her head open. Whilst blinded by her own blood, she tried to flee, but they twisted and dislocated her shoulder. MDC locals took Birgit to a doctor who set her shoulder and sewed up her head gash with sixteen stitches. Shane limped to the local government office and dripped blood on the governor's desk. He wrote, 'I'll be buggered if I'll be told what I can and can't do in my own country.' He noted that when a local woman he knew was arrested and imprisoned, but heard that he and Birgit had yet again reclaimed the store for the MDC, 'it brought a smile to her face and a little hope'.

In the short week since the election, Mugabe's rage and his determination to crush the MDC had resulted in ten witnessed murders, 500 hospitalised and unknown hundreds arrested and tortured to ensure that they would never vote MDC again.

Godwin started his hunt for proof of torture at the private Dandaro Charity Clinic in Harare. Denias Dombo had an entire leg and both arms in plaster and several ribs broken. He had worked hard all his life, so he owned a thatched hut, seven cows and a groundnut crop. His big mistake, and that of thousands of other Dombos all over Zimbabwe, was to vote for the MDC and, in his case, to become a known party worker. Soon after the election, his house was set on fire by

ZANU locals, and everything that he and his family owned was destroyed.

As I read Godwin's description of Dombo's plight, I pictured the scene as though, on Exmoor, I had voted for some opposition party, my home was burnt down, my wife and family terrorised and everything I had possessed was gone. And there was nobody to appeal to for help. This was and, as I write, is still happening to thousands of Zimbabwean families.

Dombo walked fifteen miles to report the burning to the police. He then walked back to the shell of his home, where his wife, two daughters and four-month-old son were cowering. Soon after his arrival, thirty ZANU youths began to stone the family. To save the others Dombo rushed outside, where he was beaten by the mob and left in a pool of blood. The ZANU leader announced that they would have a celebration in town and then return to kill Dombo that night.

He tried to stand as soon as they left, but both his arms were broken and jagged bone ends protruded from one leg. His family had fled, so, in great pain and wishing only to die, he managed to tie some wire round his neck, hooking the other end round a protruding brick, and then flung himself sideways. But he did not die. At some point his nine-year-old daughter found him and fetched a neighbour who wheelbarrowed him into the bush, where he lay, trying not to groan, as the ZANU mob returned to kill him. They killed his seven cows and left to deal with other MDC suspects in the village.

Later, brave friends took Dombo in secret to a clinic, but only aspirins were available. They then took him on to a big government hospital in Harare where, likewise, there was no help. Finally, in Dandaro Charity Clinic poor Dombo received treatment. Godwin knew that hundreds with similar injuries merely died slowly and flyblown in the bush or in their trashed homes.

Dombo, holding up his broken arms, told Godwin that his wife and little children had disappeared. Maybe they were dying in the bush. He wanted to be with them to protect them. He might as well be dead. Godwin heard that the MDC people in Dombo's area had tried to help but had, as a result, been raided and arrested.

In a nearby bed to Dombo, Norest Muchochoma told Godwin that he and a dozen other villagers had been taken at random to a local school and been badly beaten by Mugabe war veterans who said that there had been exactly 210 votes for MDC in the village and they would seek out every one of them for punishment.

In another ward Godwin found Tichanzii Gandanga, his body grossly swollen and bloody and with severely crushed legs. Abducted from his office in Harare, he had been driven sixty miles to an interrogation in the bush. After an hour of questions, being lashed with whips made from tyre rubber, he was repeatedly kicked in the face. Nine men were involved. One stood on his neck. They stripped him naked and pinioned his head whilst their 4x4 vehicle drove slowly over his legs, back and forth four times. Then they left him on a track to die. Gandanga was lucky, for a passing truck driver dragged him on board and took him to Dandaro. His testament to Godwin included details of his MDC friends who, following the election, had their feet burnt with hot wires and their voting fingers cut off.

Despite the growing risk of discovery by the CIO, Godwin managed to persuade a priest, who he met at a Harare official function, to visit the ward in Dandaro. This priest was

Mugabe's personal chaplain who, Godwin felt, should see for himself the very un-Christian treatment that his evil mentor was doling out to innocent people. The priest was clearly shocked by the pitiful state of Dombo and the others, but there was nothing he could do, despite his elevated status.

Godwin visited Harare's main clearing centre for badly wounded victims of beatings. The place was crowded and buzzed with stories of terror by those who had dared to vote for freedom. A man had been pulled naked around his village by a leash of wire attached to his testicles until he fainted from the pain. Others had been beaten with barbed wire and flayed alive or dunked in puddles until they drowned.

The director of the clearing centre, the CSU, told Godwin that Mugabe's current policy to counter the MDC threat was that of politicide, whereby his thugs selectively attacked MDC individuals countrywide, killing hundreds but, more effectively, raping and torturing thousands of others who were then released as bloody advertisements of the consequences of misplaced opposition. The name given by the persecuted to Mugabe's ongoing campaign of suppression was simply *Chidudu*, meaning the Fear.

In other words, Who Dares Dies.

In the region of Mount Darwin, Godwin met folk fleeing from the ubiquitous new torture camps, where people routinely had their wrists and knuckles crushed to pulp with hammers after their homes had been burnt, their only possessions stolen and their cows' legs cut. Godwin continued to collect testaments of the tortured, keeping one jump ahead of the CIO police. He interviewed a Yugoslav orthopaedic surgeon, Mr Coric, at a hospital where once Godwin's mother had trained the nurses and where Godwin's father had died.

A private hospital, the Avenues Clinic, it is one of the remaining functioning lifelines to near-dead victims of ZANU gangs.

Godwin listed his testimonies by their bed numbers. Mr Coric explained that most of the worst smashed bone cases were 'defence injuries' where the victims had curled up into foetal positions to try to protect their genitals and heads. So their legs and arms received the full impact of repeated blows from iron bars and steel truncheons, with the beatings often lasting on and off for hours. Coric used pins and plates to join shattered bones that he had reset, but he was desperate as he had run out of supplies. He called the non-stop flow of newly arriving broken people 'PEV victims', standing for Post-Election Violence.

In Ward 15 Godwin met Reason Mashambanaka whose skull was horribly gashed. His family had all been asleep when they were attacked. 'They beat my seventy-two-year-old mother all over her body and my children, including my three-year-old.'

In Bed 15D was Jonathan Malikita, an MDC campaign manager, who along with his wife and eighteen-month-old son had all been beaten. His left arm had been machete-chopped three times, with bones left sticking out at right angles.

In Bed 15-1, twenty-nine-year-old Grace Gambeza was approached, as Godwin sat by her bed, by a nurse who placed Grace's tiny baby by her breast because both Grace's arms were shattered and lay useless by her sides, alongside the plasters that covered her suppurating whip-wounds. Coric could not fix her arms for he had no pins.

Godwin wrote of this visit: 'Bed after bed, in ward after ward, on floor after floor, are filled with Mugabe's victims.

A hospital full of those he has injured, tortured and burnt out of their homes . . . I am bearing witness (to these brave men and women) to what is happening here and to the sustained cruelty of it all. I have a responsibility to try to amplify this suffering, this sacrifice, so that it will not have happened in vain.'

Godwin's next stop after the Avenues Clinic was the Salvation Army-run Howard Mission Hospital, which he visited together with the African-American US ambassador. They found there dozens of torture victims, many from a nearby torture camp called Gum Tree Base, where a speciality was savage beatings to the soles of the feet. This was known as *falanga* and was usually followed by a standard body beating.

After seeing so many crippled people, Godwin felt it necessary to stress: 'Don't think of this as a "normal beating". Think of deep, bone-deep lacerations, of buttocks with *no* skin left on them, think of being flayed alive. Think of swollen, broken feet, of people unable to stand or sit or lie on their backs because of the blinding pain.'

On a further sortie Godwin encountered the man voted by a great majority of Harare citizens to be their mayor, one Emmanual Chiroto. He worked at the time in his own little shop printing logos on T-shirts, and his wife Abigail looked after their four-year-old son as well as selling eggs and cold drinks. Having an MDC man like Emmanual voted to be mayor of Harare was a clear affront to Mugabe, so his house was burnt down and his son kidnapped. Abigail was later found in a mortuary. She had been tortured to death and then burnt. When Tsvangirai later asked Emmanual if he still wished to be mayor of Zimbabwe's capital city, he replied,

'My wife has died while we were fighting this election, so I must continue.'

A white miner, Jeremy Sanford, had helped hide Emmanual whilst he was on the run after Abigail's murder. But Sanford lived with the ever-nagging conscience that he should be doing more for the MDC himself. His workers had shown him mobile phone images of naked MDC supporters beaten until they were mere 'slabs of meat' and of villages, some of whose inmates had dared to vote MDC, burnt to the ground. 'If I had any balls,' he told Godwin, 'I'd be sitting in jail . . . I have compromised my morality.'

MDC man Chenjerai Mangezo won a local council election in Bindura in the Mugabe heartland and soon after his victory was attacked at home in the night. He fled to save his family but was brought down by a spear. The ZANU mob closed about him with iron bars, broke both his legs and his arms and smashed in his skull. Somehow he survived, and friends dragged him to a clinic. When the ceremony to swear him in as a Bindura councillor took place, the ZANU thugs who had, only weeks before, left him for dead were amazed when the MDC locals drove him to the ceremony almost entirely encased in plaster emblazoned with MDC graffiti.

By the time he told his story to Godwin, Mangezo was a busy councillor in Bindura, sitting alongside councillors from the ZANU party. 'I see those who tried to kill me every day. They are from my village.'

Godwin wrote of Mangezo: 'He has refused to kneel, refused to prostrate himself before the dictatorship whatever the consequences.'

Gift Konjana, MDC administrator for Mashonaland West

made the mistake of leaving cards in his office printed with 'Mugabe Must Go'. ZANU men beat the soles of his feet with rods, pulled a noose of wire tight about his testicles and ducked him up and down in a water drum. Released, he went back to his MDC office and was arrested again. And tortured again. They threatened his wife and children. He still worked on, so they put him in prison. He told Godwin: 'They forced me to eat my own soiled underpants until I vomited. They tied me to a bench and beat my buttocks so severely I could neither sit nor walk and opened up raw wounds all over my back. I had no access to lawyers.'

A teacher, Henry Chimbiri, at the same school where Mugabe had once taught, stood for parliament for the MDC, was arrested and beaten several times, and he described to Godwin how he was tortured. 'They said I was mobilising other teachers against the government and arrested me together with Raymond Majongwe, the Head of the Teachers' Union. I heard Majongwe cry out as they beat him in another room.' His interrogator showed him a crochet hook attached to thread and asked who else was involved in 'the school strike'. When he refused to give names, they held his penis, inserted the hook and twisted it violently until blood spurted out and Henry screamed in agony. Later they threw him out at night, disabled for life, but Henry never gave in. His wife suggested that they flee from Zimbabwe, but Tsvangirai convinced them that they would be abandoning him. So they stayed. 'I know it's dangerous,' Henry said, 'but at least I've done my part.'

Godwin decided to visit the church where his father's funeral had been held and, by chance, ran into a stand-off between police and a group of about a hundred women in their Sunday best clothes who were being barred from entry because they supported the 'wrong' vicar, rather than the pro-Mugabe priest.

The women confronted the police who were unable to shift them with threats. So the senior inspector screamed at his men to arrest every one of them. The deputy church warden, a woman, suggested that they all link hands.

'They will beat us,' said one woman.

'Yes, very probably,' said another. So they all linked hands and walked towards their church, towards the police batons.

Godwin backed away from the women, but one of them grasped his hand. He knew his position was already highly dangerous without this, but, as he recorded: 'These black women in their best clothes prepare to confront the riot police in order to go to church. I am ashamed to walk away, ashamed to let them do this on their own. So, to my surprise, I find myself reaching for her hand.'

The women began to sing hymns as they advanced, and at first the police backed away, but their sergeant ensured that they allowed nobody through the church door. The ousted vicar then began to conduct the service on the church lawn with a conga drum standing in for the organ. The first hymn, sung in full voice, was 'Stand Up, Stand Up for Jesus'.

A truck with more police arrived and their inspector, seeing Godwin, the only white face, ordered his arrest. Quickly the vicar linked his arm with Godwin's and shouted, 'He is part of my flock. You can't arrest him.' When they then tried to arrest the priest too, the whole congregation closed in like angry mother hens. So the inspector again ordered his men, 'Arrest them all.'

A long column was formed and marched down the street

towards the nearest police station. Godwin knew he was in trouble. His backpack contained all his notes and, in his mobile, the contact details of his Zimbabwe contacts and victims who had testified. He whispered this to the vicar who, in turn, told the nearest women behind them and they, as they walked, surreptitiously removed the incriminating items and shoved them down their underclothes.

At the station the inspector interrogated Godwin and the priest separately and together. Was Godwin a journalist? No, he replied, he happened to be at the church to pay respects to his father who was buried there (by the now pro-Mugabe priest!). In the background the women sang 'Onward Christian Soldiers' in Shona. Gravestones were checked and Godwin's story verified. Nonetheless, the increasingly livid inspector tried to call in the CIO which Godwin knew would for him signify torture or worse, but luckily their phone was permanently engaged. The inspector, seething, drove off to the CIO office, having told his men that he would be back with CIO men shortly.

The priest and the women, all their names logged, were by now free to go, but they stayed behind to protect Godwin. He knew that the CIO would quickly work out his Most Wanted identity.

At this point Godwin's diary recorded the chilling thoughts and the apprehension which I have heard described by other foreign news reporters who risk their lives in lethal places, such as John Simpson of the BBC with whom I spent a week in Afghanistan. Godwin wrote of those moments awaiting the CIO: 'As I listen to the ladies singing, I can't help but spin through the parade of images of the torture victims I've seen so much of recently. Deep in my stomach I feel a hernia of panic rising – polyps of fear threatening to burst out of the abdominal wall of my calm . . . I suppose this could end with being blindfolded and driven to some wasteground outside the city to be shot in the back of the head and dumped there, doused with kerosene and burned like rubbish.'

Fate, on this occasion, smiled on Godwin, for a senior officer who clearly disliked the inspector and was getting a headache, he said, from the women singing next door, released Godwin, but added an urgent warning: 'Get out of this country. Now. It will not be safe for you to stay.'

The following morning Godwin caught a flight to South Africa where he ran into mass gangs of black locals hunting and killing poor immigrants who, they raged, were taking their jobs by working for rock-bottom wages. Most of the hunted immigrants were part of the 3 million Zimbabweans who had escaped from Mugabe's tyranny. But Godwin, like even the bravest of journalists, could only fight one battle at a time.

Back home in New York Godwin continued, in print and on the web, to spread the word of Mugabe's corruption and reign of terror. An election rerun was to take place, and Godwin's Zimbabwe contacts kept him up to date. *Chidudu*, the Fear, continued. MDC officials everywhere were arrested, burnt out of their homes and murdered. Wives were taken when their hunted husbands were not found.

MDC boss, Morgan Tsvangirai, tried to hold one last pre-election rally in Harare, but Mugabe's men, over a thousand of them armed with staves, beat up the attendees and broke up the meeting. Faced with the escalating murder of his followers, both at organisational and grass-roots levels, a desperate Tsvangirai announced his party's withdrawal from the election, describing it as a 'violent, illegitimate sham where the bullet has replaced the ballot'.

Mugabe was now the only person that a Zimbabwean citizen could vote for, but he still feared a situation where people might refrain from voting at all. So he announced all votes must be placed with the little finger dipped in indelible red dye, and that, after the election, anyone without a red finger would have it cut off.

The presidents of those African nations whose countries form the Southern African Development Coordination Conference held Mugabe in respect for his presidential longevity and his history as a freedom fighter. But even they, for the first time, ceased to be pliant to his every whim. They branded the election as 'not representing the will of the people and involving politically motivated violence, intimidation and displacement'.

Unabashed, Mugabe challenged his fellow African presidents to show that they were not themselves authoritarian. And so, with South African President Mbeki as Mugabe's main crony, the SADC Conference failed to take any action at all to protest Mugabe's latest corrupt election. The United Nations, likewise, did nothing because interested parties, caring little for the principle of democratic elections, refused to support any move against Mugabe. Those who blocked anti-Mugabe moves were the Chinese, the Russians, the Libyans and the South Africans.

Godwin worked night and day to expose to the world the horrific realities behind Mugabe's re-election. From meetings in the White House, TV chat shows, internet forums and radio broadcasts to major articles in the *New York Times*, he gave his testimonies to the amazing bravery of Zimbabwe's unarmed freedom fighters. The South African embassy simply wrote Godwin off as emotional and irrational. Nonetheless, thanks largely to the efforts of Godwin and his like, news of Zimbabwe's plight did continue to seep out to the world at large. The United Nations, the USA and the European Union angrily refused to accept Mugabe's continued rule.

Inside Zimbabwe, and after the sham election, a cholera outbreak caused by a lack of clean drinking water added to the general misery, raging inflation, unemployment, the ongoing AIDS epidemic and widespread starvation. Only the favoured elite, the original war veterans still loyal to Mugabe and those regime-recruited youths brought up on a daily dose of power by terrorising the weak, still voted for Mugabe. At this point Mbeki of South Africa put maximum pressure on Mugabe to offer an olive branch to Tsvangirai by way of agreeing to form a Government of National Unity (GNU) which would, at least, give the appearance of power-sharing between ZANU and the MDC. Mbeki was certain that the ever-deteriorating situation in Zimbabwe would otherwise, and very soon, end with Mugabe being forced out, and that would not suit Mbeki.

Tsvangirai took the bait, despite the forebodings of those MDC colleagues who saw power-sharing as a bad mistake. Godwin, likewise, feared the worst, seeing only another Mugabe ploy to gain time and favour, an impression strengthened by a Mugabe speech to his party on the topic of the coalition. 'Here we are, still in a dominant position which will enable us to gather more strength as we move into the future. We remain in the driving seat.'

Despite, or because of, his fears that Mugabe was merely

using the GNU as a cover for his ongoing reign of terror, Godwin headed back to Zimbabwe in 2009 to find the same Harare hospitals so filled with the torture-maimed on his last visit, now crammed with the dead and dying of the nation-wide cholera epidemic.

Godwin visited Roy Bennett who, following his forced exile in South Africa, had been asked back by Tsvangirai, President Mugabe's increasingly powerless prime minister in the token Government of National Unity. Whilst with Godwin, Bennett received the official request from Tsvangirai to be the Deputy Minister of Agriculture. The very notion of a white minister would, he knew, enrage Mugabe. It might, hopefully, even give him a heart attack.

Bennett asked Godwin to go with him to the official swearing-in ceremony of Tsvangirai as prime minister and his various nominees as junior ministers. On their way there, a mobile phone call from prime minister designate Tsvangirai ordered Bennett *not* to come after all as there were apparently roadblocks with CIO men waiting to arrest him en route. Back at Bennett's house, they watched on television the appointment of Tsvangirai as prime minister and his shaking the hand of his baleful nemesis, the scowling Mugabe. Not a marriage made in heaven, Godwin mused, more likely just another sleight of hand by Mugabe in his violent game of political poker.

Tsvangirai later spoke to a party rally in the suburbs, the first such public affair allowed in years, and the party faithful turned up in their optimistic thousands. Tsvangirai reminded them that nineteen years before to the day, Nelson Mandela had walked free. 'A culture of entitlement and impunity,' Tsvangirai stressed, 'has brought our nation to the brink of a dark abyss. This must end today . . . Walk with me on this promising phase of our journey to a true and lasting democracy.'

The truck that took Godwin away from the rally was full of mostly white and young Zimbabweans, and as they crept through the black crowds they were given MDC hand salutes and shouts of, 'Go back to the farms now and grow food.'

The euphoria of Tsvangirai's swearing in and the rally did not last long. The CIO renewed their terror tactics, starting with a determined hunt for their most hated target, Roy Bennett. He moved from hide to hide but was caught at an airfield on his way to spend his birthday weekend with his wife. He was immediately accused of various charges and thrown into a cell at Mutare's central police station, outside of which several hundred MDC supporters mounted a vigil with singing and dancing. Police attacked them with dogs, tear gas and live bullets.

Godwin found himself being tailed by the CIO as he met the Shona lady lawyer representing Bennett. He suggested to her that, since Mugabe was clearly using Roy Bennett's white-man status as a pretext for attacking the MDC, 'Maybe we should all leave. It might be better for all of you.' 'Nonsense,' the black lawyer replied. 'Whites have been here for 120 years. You're as much a part of this place now as anyone. If you all go, who's next? You guys have to stay involved for the sake of *all* of us.'

Godwin visited Bennett in the prison inner yard when he was briefly let out from his cell. Godwin gave him food and insect spray. Bennett instantly handed all the food, but for a banana, to his cellmates, people arrested from the vigil outside the station, and he knelt to spray their legs one by one. He told Godwin, 'It stinks so bad in there that it gives you a headache.' Godwin could see why Bennett was a real threat to Mugabe. For the white ex-policeman had a huge black provincial following, and this indisputable fact clearly undermined Mugabe's main line of anti-white rhetoric.

Later, when Bennett was taken to court to be sentenced, Godwin provided vital evidence for the defence and thereby broke his fragile cover with the CIO. Bennett was anyway taken back to prison to await a further trial and, through the bars of his cell door, he instructed Godwin, 'Leave me here as long as it takes. Don't trade me for anything.'

A while later Godwin heard that a Harare magistrate had ordered Bennett to be freed on bail, but a prison officer refused to release him and, soon after, the magistrate was himself arrested for 'exceeding his powers'. Eventually Bennett was released from prison, due to mounting pressure on Mugabe from all sides, and he was mobbed by black crowds wherever he went.

He told Godwin the details of his stay in prison. Designed for 150 inmates, there were 360 crammed in with Bennett, packed so tight that at night, when one turned over, they all did. Each man in Bennett's 'dangerous prisoner' category was strip-searched every night and made to sleep naked on the filthy concrete floor.

The mortuary in the Harare Remand Prison was designed, Godwin learnt, for twenty-five bodies but usually contained eighty. When the power was cut off, which was a frequent occurrence, the body fluids from the rotting corpses used to leak under the door and into the corridor. The stink was indescribable. The noses, eyes and lips of corpses were frequently gnawed off by rats.

Mugabe has his own Gulag and his own Auschwitz . . . and the torture goes on. Just as if the new government, back in 2009, had never been formed. Dr Frances Lovemore of the Harare Counselling Services Unit told Godwin that Chris Dhlamini, Head of MDC Security was, only the previous week, hung by his feet from a tree and near-drowned in a water drum. Eighty new cases of torture injuries Dr Lovemore had logged at the CSU that week had, for the first time, included ZANU men beaten by their own men for a lack of loyalty. Maybe that was a good sign.

The MDC leader appointed by Tsvangirai as finance minister, Tendai Biti, told Godwin that Mugabe was a prisoner of his own junta. He might die, but his nest of generals would unleash whatever terror they could in order to hold on to power. Like the junta in Burma.

Bennett added, 'Mugabe doesn't even consider Tsvangirai who, to him, is nothing. He's not even allowed an official prime minister's residence.'

As I write this chapter, based on Godwin's reports of his two visits to his old homeland, freedom fighters are in arms, or at least on the streets of many authoritarian countries. In Tunisia and Egypt they appear to have triumphed over their erstwhile dictators. In other lands, tyrants such as Mugabe, Gaddafi and Ahmadinejad still hold sway, and those courageous enough to risk all for freedom must still fight on.

At the end of his book *The Fear*, Peter Godwin writes: 'I am obliged to all the people who were brave enough, in dangerous times, to talk to me.' By the time you read this book, it could be that both Mugabe and Gaddafi may be gone, but there will be other tyrants and, one must hope, other Godwins.

10

War Makes or Breaks

'Then it's Tommy this, an' Tommy that, an'
"Tommy 'ow's yer soul?"
But it's "Thin red line of 'eroes" when the
drums begin to roll'
Rudyard Kipling, 'Tommy', 1892

My direct ancestor, a Norman crusader called Godfrey de Bouellon, became King of Jerusalem after leading the First Crusade which massacred 40,000 of that city's inhabitants in a single night. That was in the year 1099.

Another Holy War, often known as the Last Crusade, was sparked off 754 years later in 1853, just a few hundred yards away from the site of my ancestor's bad behaviour, at Jerusalem's Church of the Holy Sepulchre. At Easter Christian pilgrims arrived as usual at the sepulchre to worship on Good Friday. This great jostling crowd of Christians was mainly divided between devotees of the Roman Catholic Church and the Greek or Russian Orthodox Churches. Each denomination loathed the other.

The full-scale war that followed this holy spat is, to my mind, a showcase of the bravery which thousands of soldiers on both sides managed to summon up repeatedly, despite appalling conditions, rampant diseases and cruel discipline from officers who seldom shared their men's gross discomfort and whom they often despised. On top of all this, they were well aware of the chronic tactical mistakes made time and again by their generals, as well as the horrendous hospital conditions, amputations without anaesthetic and the high death rates of the wounded. Courage under such conditions is courage indeed.

By bad luck, Easter fell on the same date in both the Greek and the Roman calendars that year, which resulted in an unusually large crush of pilgrims at the sepulchre. The high priests of each group clashed with mutual hatred over the matter of which religious community should have the first right to carry out their very different rituals on the holy altar of Calvary.

Jerusalem was then a part of the Turkish, or Ottoman, Empire, so it fell to Jerusalem's Muslim authorities to maintain order between these fractious Christians. They clearly failed, for the pilgrims, monks and priests laid into each other with knives and pistols, and by the time that order was restored, forty would-be worshippers lay dead before the sepulchre.

The behaviour of the followers of the Orthodox Church, with their colourful symbolism and raw emotions, seemed to contemporary Catholics to be embarrassing and almost pagan when compared with the dignity of their own ceremonies. In Jerusalem's holy places they even found themselves more at ease with the local Muslims.

Most Orthodox pilgrims were Russians, whose tsar was suspected by Western countries, especially France and Britain, of plotting to throw the Turks out of the Holy Land, wanting to crush the Ottomans and then to extend the Russian Empire far to the east. There were over 11 million Orthodox Christians living within the Ottoman Empire, and Russia, by vanquishing the Turks with a Holy War, could 'liberate' all these Eastern Christians from the tyranny of Islam.

By the time of the Easter killings at the Holy Sepulchre, there had already been seven major Russo-Turkish religious wars over the previous 160 years. The tsar was determined to protect European Orthodoxy, not only from the Ottoman Muslims, but also from the ever-spreading infection of Western European ideas of revolution, liberalism and rationalism.

Britain and France had many reasons for wishing to curb the advance of Russian influence in the Holy Land and elsewhere. Britain, then the greatest trading nation in the world, feared for her own commercial interests in Turkey and India. France sought patriotic glory and revenge for defeat by the Russians at Waterloo some forty years before. So when, after the Easter troubles in Jerusalem, the Turks ruled in favour of Catholic, not Orthodox, priority at the Holy Sepulchre and Tsar Nicholas I responded by moving his Black Sea fleet from its Sebastopol base to threaten the Turkish capital of Constantinople, Britain and France declared war, not against Muslim Turkey but against Christian Russia.

Seen, as it were, from outer space, this would have bewildered a rational alien. There were, of course, as always in the complex politics of nineteenth-century Europe, many other subsidiary causes for what became known as the Crimean War, but the Easter squabble in Jerusalem is agreed by most historians to have been the spark that ignited the ensuing slaughter of Christian by Christian.

The Turkish Army that the Western Allies were about to fight alongside as brothers-in-arms was, at the time, busy in its subjugated Christian colonies subduing the locals by murdering priests, burning down churches and raping girls. In Georgia, to the east of the Black Sea and north of Turkey, another Turkish army overran the key Russian citadel of St Nicholas, systematically torturing over a thousand of the inhabitants, raping women of all ages, and shiploads of children were sent to Constantinople as slaves. Some years before, when Turkish forces put down an uprising on the Greek island of Chios, they hanged 20,000 islanders and deported as slaves the remaining 70,000 Christians. These then were the chosen allies of the British and the French in the Crimean War.

Their enemy, the Russians, fielded the biggest army in the world, over 2 million men, mostly conscripted serfs who, forty years before, had defeated the hitherto all-conquering armies of Napoleon. These Russian soldiers were accustomed to suffering, iron discipline and harsh treatment, which included floggings of 1,000 lashes. They had no medical corps and, twenty years before when fighting the Polish, 85,000 had died of sickness and wounds, whilst only 7,000 were killed in battle.

The British, for a while, kept their battle squadron in the Dardanelles, close enough to Constantinople to deter the Russian fleet. But in November 1853 the Russians destroyed the Turkish fleet at Sinope on the Anatolian coast, which caught the Royal Navy unawares.

Queen Victoria, her prime minister, Lord Aberdeen, and many Anglo-Catholics were horrified at the idea of siding with Muslims against Christians of any hue, but the War Cabinet under the fiery anti-Russian Lord Palmerston won the day, thanks to the fragile nature of the government (a Liberal-Conservative coalition) and the newly found power of public opinion and the media, who were virulently in favour of all-out war against the Russians, no matter what their religion.

'An English Minister must please the newspapers,' moaned Lord Aberdeen. One journal wrongly reported that Prince Albert, disliked by the public for his 'foreign views' and thought to be pro-Russian, had been sent as a traitor to the Tower for execution. The Queen was so upset by this that she threatened to abdicate.

The aim of the British, when the government eventually agreed to declare war, was to launch an incisive attack on Sebastopol to destroy the Russian fleet, which was based there, and for the Allied armies of Britain, France and Turkey to take the Black Sea Crimean peninsula, prior to a subsequent advance north on mainland Russia as far as St Petersburg. Palmerston's end game was the dismemberment of the Russian Empire.

At first the French and British Armies camped near Constantinople, well positioned to protect the city against a sudden Russian attack. None came, and as boredom set in, old rivalries between the Allies began to surface. The commander-in-chief of the British Army, Lord Raglan, had fought Napoleon under the Duke of Wellington, as had many of his senior officers. He had lost one of his arms at Waterloo and, famously, when it was amputated without anaesthetic, he had asked for it back so that he could retrieve his ring for his wife. He was sixty-six when he took command in the Crimea and, a touch forgetful, often referred to the French as the enemy.

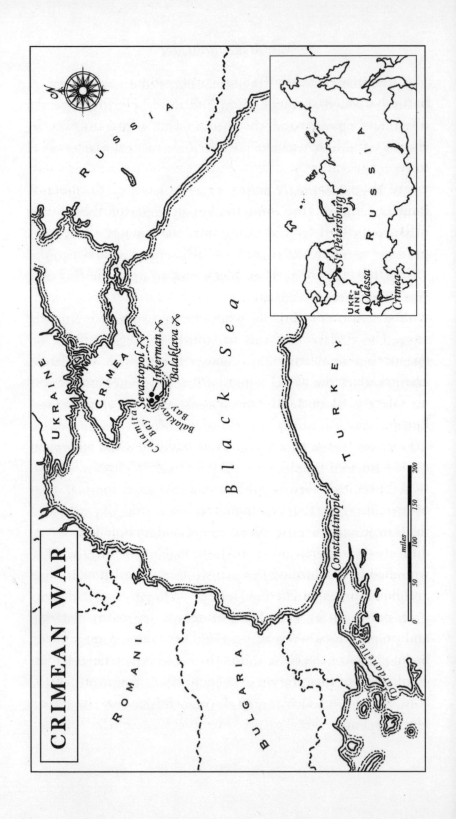

CRIMEAN WAR

A majority of the French, all professional soldiers, were battle-hardened through many years of fierce fighting in Algeria, whereas virtually none of the British had any experience of war. All were volunteers, many of whom had responded to recent recruitment drives, and a third came from Ireland where thousands were dying of hunger from the potato famine. Others came from the lowest levels of the British urban poor. Officers, who obtained their commissions by paying for them, were almost all from the aristocracy.

Spurred on by the Russian fleet's destruction of the Turkish Navy, the Allies finally launched their attack on Sebastopol, with their armies aboard some 400 ships, in mid-summer 1854. The First Lord of the Admiralty told the nation: 'The eye-tooth of the Russian Bear must be drawn. Until his fleet and naval arsenal at Sebastopol are destroyed, there will be no safety for Constantinople and no security or peace for Europe.'

Fine words, but the invasion was badly planned and what could have been speedily successful was to turn into the longest siege in military history and an episode rich with examples of raw courage by the combatants on both sides. The suffering, the horror and the misery involved was unprecedented and is difficult to comprehend or to picture. To most of the men who died in and around Sebastopol, death was an agonising and lingering experience.

From the outset, the British campaign was badly planned and preparations were negligible. Their army commanders had no maps of the Crimea nor any idea of the cruel weather conditions, of the broiling summer heat or the vicious winter cold. No winter clothing or decent tentage was supplied. Nobody knew the size or exact location of the Russian opposition. Ignorance ruled and disaster was bound to follow.

All that could be said in favour of the British was that their dogged courage had a long tradition, and their infantry's new rifle, the Minié, was vastly superior to the Russian's comparable weapon, for they could fire with accuracy at an enemy 1,200 yards away, whereas the Russian musket was prone to inaccuracy at more than 300 yards' range.

But a far greater killer than all the weapons of both sides was the ever lurking cholera bacteria ingested by way of contaminated food or water. Even before they arrived in the Crimea, soldiers were dying in their hundreds on board the invasion fleet. So the sick carried the comma-shaped bacillus in their bodies, and with no sanitary facilities available, the sickness spread like wildfire, quickly killing over half those infected with agonising cramps, vomiting and crippling diarrhoea.

Within two days of landing at the aptly named Calamita Bay, over 1,000 soldiers were taken back out to quickly prepared sick-bays on the anchored ships. Calamita Bay is some sixty kilometres to the north of Sebastopol so, when the British were eventually ready to join the more efficient and impatient French, the armies advanced in a column six and a half kilometres wide and five kilometres long.

The Russian Army was spotted in a defensive mass on high ground overlooking the Alma River, which the Allies would have to cross. Their officers brimmed with confidence and joked that the British were only capable of thrashing the savages in their colonies and, as for the French, the Russians toasted the memory of their 'great victory' at Waterloo. A carriage-borne, parasol-wielding picnic party of fine ladies from Sebastopol excitedly awaited the coming spectacle.

Heavy guns from the Allied fleet opened fire with distant thunder and little effect. Bugles and bagpipes shrilled and thrilled to the menacing backdrop of drums and the neighing of nervous horses. The armies of the French and British advanced over the wide coastal plain below, and the Russian commander, Prince Menshikov, signalled his artillery into action.

Lord Raglan, commander of the British Army, ordered his troops to halt in order to let the French make the first move to reach the enemy defences on and inland of the sea cliffs. So the British lay down within range of the Russian artillery, whilst the French attacked with speed and efficiency. They swam the river's estuary and scrambled up the broken cliffs under cover of low trees and brush.

Further inland, the British eventually received Raglan's orders to advance, and did so in thin red lines only two deep, which surprised the Russians, one of whom, an eloquent lieutenant named Chodasiewicz, wrote: 'This was extraordinary. We had never before seen troops fight in lines two deep, nor did we think it possible for men to be found with sufficient firmness of morale to be able to attack, in this apparently weak formation, our massive columns.'

The advantage of and reason for the traditional columns of massed infantry was partly that braver and more experienced men could reassure the fearful and prevent the breaking of ranks. But on the downside, a single cannonball from either flank could smash a hundred bodies in an instant, and a leaden ball from a Minié rifle could drill through three or four stomachs at a time.

The repetitive drills practised over the years by British infantry included advancing in two-deep lines which contracted on the move to cover each new gap as casualties mounted. Even under murderous fire the target was less dense than a column, and survivors, their minds preconditioned by endless practice, were able to use self-control to advance into hell.

The high degree of discipline needed to instil such self-control can be imagined, considering the horrific sights of the injuries caused by weapons developed by the time of the Crimean War, including murderous, apple-sized, close-cluster grapeshot, cannonballs that exploded on impact rather than bouncing, and bullets from lethally accurate long-range rifles which killed or maimed long before those from older models, and thus prolonged the most frightening stage of a fully frontal advance with no cover.

When the British troops reached the Alma River under heavy fire, many swam across, many were hit and drowned, and others, finding the river literally red with blood, lost their nerve and cowered by the near bank until their officers drove them across at sabre point. There they found rocky shelter from the Russians above, and for a while refused to advance. Officers on horseback managed to exhort them to renew the attack and, all order lost, they milled uphill, where superior numbers of Russians counter-charged with bayonets and drove survivors back down to the river in a disorganised mob.

At this point, a massed Russian charge advanced downhill and, against the repeated orders of their officers to advance uphill, 2,000 British Guardsmen formed themselves into long lines, their backs to the river, and fired volley after volley into the approaching Russian columns. A Russian engineer, Eduard Totleben, commented: 'Left to themselves to perform the role of sharpshooters, the British troops did not hesitate under fire and did not require orders or supervision. Our columns suffered terrible losses, found it impossible to pass through the hail of bullets and were obliged to fall back.'

Soon afterwards, the British overran the heights and, with the French in command of the flanking cliff-tops, the battle was won. The Russians fled in all directions, despite the best efforts of their captains to hold the line.

Raglan suggested to the French that an immediate advance would stand a good chance of destroying much of the fleeing Russian Army and, if followed up immediately by a massive attack on Sebastopol, could win the day. But the French were for caution, so the chance was missed.

The British dead at Alma numbered over 1,800, and the Russians over 5,000. Lord Raglan's nephew walked over the battlefield the following morning. 'It was a horrible scene,' he wrote, 'death in every shape and form. Those shot through the heart or forehead appeared to be smiling with arms and legs outspread, and those in the greatest pain were those shot through the stomach, whose faces expressed agony.'

The dead no longer suffered but, two days after the battle, hundreds of wounded still lay where they had fallen. A Russian orderly wrote: 'Those deserted by their regiments, with heart-rending cries and pleading gestures begged to be lifted into our carts. But we were already overloaded. One man could hardly drag himself along: he was without arms and his belly was shot through. Another had his leg blown off and his jaw smashed with his tongue torn out. Only the expression on his face pleaded for water. But where to get even that?'

The Allies, having landed on the coast to the north of Sebastopol, now discovered that its defences appeared far weaker on its southern flank. So they decided to skirt inland around their target and, having done so without serious incident, they made their new front line on the heights above Sebastopol's southern ramparts and their coastal supply base some five miles further south at Balaklava Inlet. The French fleet moored slightly closer to Sebastopol, with less distance between their ships and their front line troops.

As the Allies set up their camps, the Russians worked desperately to improve their southern defences. The 40,000 inmates of Sebastopol, all connected in some way with serving or servicing the Russian fleet, strove to shift great rocks and reposition their heavy cannons, in the knowledge that all hell was about to let loose. Prisoners dug trenches and prostitutes carted baskets of earth to new ramparts. Raglan wanted an immediate attack, but his own engineer advisers and the French preferred a massive bombardment and siege.

At dawn in late October, the Allies began a bombardment with over a hundred heavy guns. An inmate of Sebastopol wrote: 'For twelve hours the wild howling of the bombs was unbroken and the ground shook beneath our feet. Smoke blotted out the sun and it became dark as night.'

The Russian admiral, Vladimir Kornilov, toured the defences, and his aide wrote: 'Inside No. 4 bastion the scene was frightful and the destruction enormous, whole gun teams struck down by shellfire. The wounded and dead lay around in heaps.' Kornilov went to every gun crew with words of encouragement. He passed one gunner whose face had been plastered by the fleshy remains of a blown-up colleague. Against his subordinate's advice, Kornilov moved on to the bastion named as the redan and, as he arrived there, its commander was killed. The next five commanders who took over that day were all killed in their turn before the following dawn. Kornilov's tour of the trenches and bastions continued until a shell blew away the lower part of his body, and he died soon after.

An artillery officer in the bastion most targeted by the French artillery noted that he saw individuals, who had previously been decorated for bravery, run away in sheer panic under the constant thunderous bombardment. He also wrote of his own dilemma, for his family was living in the battered town. 'One half of me wanted to run home to save my family, but my sense of duty told me I should stay. My feelings as a man got the better of the soldier within me and I ran away to find my family.'

When the guns at last fell silent and the smoke drifted away, over a thousand Russians were dead, but every gunner had been replaced and every bastion remained effective. The Russians were as surprised at their survival as were the Allies.

With their Alma-battered confidence back in place, the Russian generals decided that, attack being the best form of defence, they would mount a major offensive to cut permanently the highly vulnerable supply route between the British siege troops and their supply base down at Balaklava Bay. Over the previous fortnight, thousands of Russian reinforcements had marched south through the Ukraine and were then ferried over to the northern tip of the Crimea from the mainland, just east of modern day Odessa. The Russians now had over 120,000 troops to attack the cholera and Alma-weary British. On their way down to the valley of Balaklava and within sight of the British fleet, they wiped out a garrison of a thousand Turks: 'Dead or fled.'

In between Balaklava and the Russians was a single infantry regiment of 500 Highlanders and the recently landed group of cavalry regiments known as the Heavy Brigade. Lord Lucan, in charge of all the cavalry, detested the overall army commander, Lord Raglan. Raglan, from the heights above Sebastopol and alerted to the sudden threat of the newly arrived Russian Army, could observe every move down below in Balaklava Valley. He had to keep enough troops in place on the heights to prevent a breakout from Sebastopol, but he immediately ordered an infantry division down to assist the Highlanders.

The Scotsman in charge of the Highlanders, Sir Colin Campbell, moved his men back from the advancing Russian mass to the point where the Heavy Brigade could threaten the enemy's flank. Then he cried out, 'Men. Remember. There is no retreat from here. You must die where you stand.'

He gave the order to fire, and his men, stretched out in their thin red line, fired volley after deadly volley into the Russian cavalry, whose thunderous charge, miraculously as it seemed to Raglan through his field glasses on the high ground, slowed, wheeled and then withdrew back towards the main mass of their army.

The Highlanders had held their line long enough for Raglan's battle orders to arrive by messenger (taking thirty minutes at the gallop). The Heavy Brigade was to attack the Russian cavalry at once.

The regiment my father would command eighty-eight years later at the key Second World War battle of El Alamein, the Royal Scots Greys, lined up in parade ground precision with the Irish horsemen of the Inniskillings and the English-Welsh mix of the Dragoon Guards and awaited orders from their brigade commander, John Scarlett.

In all, due to sickness, the Heavy Brigade fielded some 500 sabres, and the Russian cavalry they faced outnumbered them by at least eight to one. Scarlett managed, even as the massed Russian cavalry, swords waving, thundered downhill towards them, to keep the double line of his horsemen in two near perfect parallel lines.

Scarlett's opposite number could not believe that the British would remain stationary with no momentum to counter the Russians' impact. That was against all cavalry tactics and made no sense. Baffled and suspicious that this was some cunning British trap, the Russian cavalry's general ordered his trumpeters to sound the Halt at the last minute.

Scarlett had never fought before, but he was no fool. The instant the confused Russian cavalry reined to a dust-raising halt, he raised his hand and his men moved from stationary to gallop in impressive formation. The Greys and the Inniskillings had charged side by side at Waterloo and swept all before them. And so it was again. They aimed their sabre blows at the enemy's faces, for they knew the Russian greatcoats were as thick as armour and their helmets undentable. There was no room for bullets nor cannonballs now, only the slash of sabres, the battle screams of the fighters and their skill with cold steel.

Raglan, glued to his field glasses as though watching some distant chess game, saw patches of red – his men – surrounded by a sea of Russian grey. His heart must have lifted as he watched the great body of Russians begin to lose shape, to waver and, finally, to break up, as Scarlett, with perfect timing, sent in the rest of the Heavy Brigade, the Dragoons, whose bloodlust was up at the sight of their predecessors' remarkable success. The Russians were penetrated from flank to flank by the sheer ferocity of the Dragoons, and sounded the retreat.

This was a great chance for the Light Brigade, faster and more mobile than the Heavies, to mop up the fleeing Russians. But, probably due to the contrary character of their commander, Lord Cardigan, they failed to make a move.

One hundred and nine years later, when I was myself a lieutenant in the Scots Greys during the Cold War, I listened to an old major, Tarry Shaw, who had soldiered in the regiment at the time my father was killed in Italy, telling me the story of the charge of the Heavy Brigade. General Scarlett, he said, had received a message from Raglan which he read out to the tired and bloody horsemen all around him – a rare message of 'Well Done' from the Boss. There were then tears of pride in the eyes of the men of the Heavy Brigade; they had at last earned their reward for all those long hours, days and years of endless drill manoeuvres with horse and sword. Their historic charge had proved both their courage and their iron discipline.

As the Russian cavalry retreated, Raglan's reinforcements arrived from the heights, and Balaklava was saved. Unfortunately, however, Raglan spotted a group of Russians removing British guns they had captured earlier from outposts manned by Turkish units. Having served under his hero, the Duke of Wellington, at Waterloo, Raglan knew well that the Duke had *never* 'lost a gun'. Determined to prevent the Russians getting away with any of *his* guns, he ordered his best 'galloper', Captain Nolan, to order Lord Lucan, the overall cavalry commander, to send the Light Brigade under Lord Cardigan to recapture the guns. His message was ambiguous, since he failed to specify which guns, and down below in the valley neither Lucan nor Cardigan could see those guns which Raglan, from his superior vantage point, was watching. To add to this enigma, there was intense dislike between Raglan and Lucan, as well as long-term hatred between Lucan and Cardigan, who were brothers-in-law. A recipe for disaster.

Nolan reached Lucan, whom he despised as weak and lacking in the elan which Nolan believed should be the hallmark of the cavalry. The orders he passed on to Lucan were to 'follow the enemy and prevent them removing the guns'. 'Which enemy? Which guns?' Lucan rightly demanded.

'There, my lord,' Nolan replied, pointing wildly. 'There is your enemy. There are your guns.'

Unfortunately, Lucan interpreted the order to mean the enemy and the guns at the far end of the valley up which the entire Russian army were making an orderly and well-defended retreat. Not the captured British guns, which he could not see but which would have been fairly easy to reach.

So Lucan ordered the fatal charge of the Light Brigade, some 700 horsemen led by the hated Lord Cardigan. They advanced at a parade ground walk. Ahead, between them and the waiting Russian cannons at the far end of the valley, was the entire Russian Army, on both flanks of the valley – a death trap that must have been clear to every sane man present.

With 2,000 yards under intense fire still to go, the brigade broke into a trot. Nolan seemed at that point to spark. Perhaps he realised the horrific error and imminent catastrophe to which he was party, and tried to turn the brigade in the correct direction. He galloped forward waving his sabre, but a shell exploded nearby and killed him outright. The brigade then broke into a gallop. Cannonballs, grapeshot and bullets cut men and horses literally to pieces, but the survivors, including their leader Lord Cardigan, did reach the guns at the head of the valley.

A trooper in the Lancers saw one of his friends, 'hit by a round shot which cut his head clean off, but his headless body kept in the saddle for some thirty yards, his lance at the charge firmly gripped under his right arm'. Another lancer remembered the charge as, 'riding into the mouth of a volcano'.

A Russian officer, Stepan Kozhukhov, described the charge and its aftermath. 'Tired of slashing at our men, the English decided to go back. It is difficult, if not impossible, to do justice to the feat of these mad cavalry. Having lost at least a quarter of their number in the attack and apparently impervious to new dangers and losses, they quickly re-formed their squadrons to return over the same ground littered with their dead and dying. With desperate courage, those valiant lunatics set off again. It took a long time for our hussars and Cossacks to collect themselves. They were convinced that the entire enemy cavalry was pursuing them and angrily did not want to believe that they had been crushed by a relatively insignificant handful of daredevils.'

Alfred Tennyson's poem aptly sums up the charge:

Theirs not to reason why,
Theirs but to do and die,
Into the valley of Death
Rode the six hundred.

The Russians had failed to cut the supply line between Balaklava Bay and the British front line, but they nonetheless claimed partial success, having taken command of key high ground overlooking the supply line. This they followed up with an attack on nearby British positions on Mount

Inkerman. Thirty thousand Russians attacked under cover of rain and thick fog, which achieved an element of surprise but caused them to lose formation and end up in confused mobs. The battle that followed flowed back and forth, and its outcome was decided by the determination of individual soldiers fighting with bayonets and even hand to hand in the mist. The British were heavily outnumbered, often seven to one and sometimes twenty to one, but their skill, training and ferocity told against the masses of conscripted serfs who formed the core of the Russian infantry.

French forces eventually arrived, and together the Allies held the heights. The Russians retreated some four hours after their attack began, having lost 12,000 men out of the 30,000 involved. The British force of 4,000 lost 600 dead and 1,800 wounded, having held off a massively superior force for four hours largely with bayonets. The Russians never again threatened the siege troops around Sebastopol who, with winter imminent, settled down to dig in and lick their wounds.

A majority of the British injuries were caused by soft lead bullets fired at close range from Russian muskets which mushroomed on impact with human bone. Gangrene set in quickly and amputation of legs and arms was commonplace, usually without anaesthetic. There were no medical orderlies, no morphine, chloroform, nor even bandages. Cholera was rampant and scurvy soon made its dread appearance, since the standard issue of preventative lime juice, of which the nearby Royal Navy held a stock of 20,000 pounds, was never sent to the land forces.

Criminal ineptitude and muddle reigned supreme throughout the nightmare winter which followed, and the majority of the men who had survived the great killings of Alma, Balaklava and Inkerman perished in freezing misery on the windswept heights or down amidst the sickness and mud of Balaklava.

Despite the harsh conditions of the Crimean winter, British soldiers were issued with little or no winter clothing. Out of every hundred men who died that winter, over seventy died of hypothermia, frostbite, gangrene, or sheer weakness caused by diarrhoea and severe shortage of food. Britain was the richest nation in the world with the greatest fleet afloat, but you would never have thought so judging by the shameful treatment of its troops in the Crimea.

The invention of the electric telegraph and the presence of a new breed of on-the-spot war correspondents meant that British taxpayers with the vote soon learnt of the inexcusable suffering of their troops and forced their government to put things right. But not in time for that dread winter of 1854–55. Statistics are boring, but they expose the truth. Britain sent 60,000 troops to the Crimea, and of the 43,000 who died, only 7,000 were killed by the enemy in battle. Thousands died of terrible wounds, frostbite, hypothermia, gangrene or cholera. Hundreds were so desperate that they crept away from their trenches above Sebastopol and gave themselves up to the Russians.

A violent storm made things worse by sinking twenty British ships in Balaklava Bay, including *The Prince* with its newly arrived cargo of 40,000 winter uniforms and many other critical supplies. Jettisoned horse fodder coated the sea's surface for miles, and the army's precious pack animals died off in their hundreds. Putrescent animal corpses lay about in the mire, whilst weak, sick men toiled ant-like in knee-deep mud on the six-mile climb to the front line on the heights, shifting 110 tons of supplies every day.

The French conscript army, far better organised, watched all this askance. One of their captains wrote home: 'These English are men of undoubted courage, but they know only how to get themselves killed.'

Three other contemporary sources give an idea of the level of anguish suffered by wounded soldiers who, if they recovered, would be required to return to the fray. It is easier to be brave on a sudden impulse and when healthy. How much greater the courage when you know all too well that a single enemy bullet could land you in hell.

The great Russian novelist, Leo Tolstoy, was an army officer when he wrote about the Russian hospital in Sebastopol, but he could as well have been describing the British equivalent.

No sooner have you opened the door than you are assailed without warning by the sight and smell of some forty or fifty amputees and critically wounded, some of them on camp beds, but most of them lying on the floor . . . Now, if you have strong nerves, go through the doorway on the left: that is the room in which wounds are bandaged and operations performed. There you will see surgeons with pale, gloomy physiognomies, their arms soaked in blood up to the elbows, deep in concentration over a bed on which a wounded man is lying under the influence of chloroform, open-eyed as in a delirium, and uttering meaningless words which are occasionally simple and affecting. The surgeons are going about the repugnant but beneficial task of amputation. You will see the sharp, curved knife enter the white, healthy body; you will see the wounded man suddenly regain consciousness with a terrible, harrowing shrieked cursing; you will see the apothecary assistant fling the severed arm into a corner; you will see another wounded man who is lying on a stretcher in the same room and watching the operation on his companion, writhing and groaning less with physical pain than with the psychological agony of apprehension; you will see fearsome sights that will shake you to the roots of your being; you will see war not as a beautiful, orderly, and gleaming formation, with music and beaten drums, streaming banners and generals on prancing horses, but war in its authentic expression – as blood, suffering and death.

Dr O'Connor, a contemporary British surgeon, wrote:

The pluck of the soldier no one has yet truly described. They laugh at pain, and will scarcely submit to die. It is perfectly marvellous, this triumph of mind over body. If a limb were torn off or crushed at home, you would have them brought in fainting, and in a state of dreadful collapse. Here they come with a dangling arm or a riddled elbow, and it's 'Now, doctor, be quick, if you please; I'm not done for so bad, but I can get away back and see!' And many of these brave fellows, with a lump of towel wrung out in cold water, wrapped around their stumps, crawled to the rear of the fight, and, with shells bursting round them, and balls tearing up the sods at their feet, watched the progress of the battle. I tell you, as a solemn truth, that I took off the foot of an officer, a Captain, who insisted on being helped on his horse again, and declared that he could fight, now that his 'foot was dressed'.

Florence Nightingale and her twenty nuns and nurses arrived in the main hospital for Crimean sick and wounded at Scutari, near Constantinople, soon after the battle of Balaklava. Here, over 4,000 soldiers died in lice-infested filth. The nurses slowly began to improve the lot of the patients there by dint of their hard and heroic work and the iron will of their leader, the Lady with the Lamp, who, back in Britain, soon became the stuff of legends.

One battle-weary soldier said, 'If Florence Nightingale were at our head, we would take Sebastopol next week.'

The Allies did not take Sebastopol that quickly but, from the spring of 1855, thanks to improvements all round due to a chastened government back in London, life did improve immeasurably for the British soldier in the Crimea.

The Allied command agreed on their plan to defeat the Russians in Sebastopol. There would be ten days of non-stop artillery bombardment from the heights and on the seaward side from the navy, then an immediate infantry assault. The cannonade began on Easter Day, and by the end of the allotted period 160,000 shells had exploded inside the Russian base, destroying every building and killing 4,700 people. But this did not yield the expected easy follow-up. Far from it. The two armies failed to synchronise their attacks on their respective targets, and their frontal assaults were met with a murderous response. Within thirty minutes the Allies lost 7,980 men.

On the Russian side, that spring and summer 81,000 soldiers were killed or wounded, and conditions inside Sebastopol grew daily more untenable. Since the siege began, over 300,000 Russians had died in the city.

The last great battle of the siege was mounted with another marine bombardment on 8 September, which, at its crescendo, fired off over 400 shells a minute. The subsequent mass infantry assaults involved men who had managed to survive many previous desperate assaults on the Russian defences and who had observed the fearful wounds of so many of their fellow soldiers. On the eve of the battle there were many who deserted, including officers from both the French and British camps. Nevertheless, the final French attack was a veritable blitzkrieg, with 37,000 men overwhelming their sector of the Russian defences. A far smaller British force, most of whom were young reservists, failed to take their intended targets and were mown down beneath the Russian earthworks. Survivors, in panic, tried to flee despite attempts by their officers to stand firm. Hundreds died, thousands were wounded. An ignominious British end to a campaign treated to this day in France as a glorious victory.

The Russian defending force withdrew and retreated to the north of the peninsula. William Russell, a *Times* reporter, arriving in the shattered city, wrote:

> Of all the pictures of the horrors of war which have ever been presented to the world, the hospital of Sebastopol offered the most heart-rending and revolting. Entering one of these doors, I beheld such a sight as few men, thank God, have ever witnessed: . . . the rotten and festering corpses of the soldiers, who were left to die in their extreme agony, untended, uncared for, packed as close as they could be stowed . . . saturated with blood which oozed and trickled through upon the floor, mingling with the droppings of corruption. Many lay, yet alive, with maggots crawling about in their wounds. Many, nearly mad by the scene around them, or seeking escape from it in their extremest agony, had rolled away under the beds and glared out on the heart stricken spectators. Many, with legs and arms broken and twisted,

the jagged splinters sticking through the raw flesh, implored aid, water, food, or pity, or, deprived of speech by the approach of death or by dreadful injuries in the head or trunk, pointed to the lethal spot. Many seemed bent alone on making their peace with Heaven. The attitudes of some were so hideously fantastic as to root one to the ground by a sort of dreadful fascination. The bodies of numbers of men were swollen and bloated to an incredible degree; and the features, distended to a gigantic size, with eyes protruding from the sockets and the blackened tongue lolling out of the mouth, compressed tightly by the teeth which had set upon it in the death-rattle, made one shudder and reel round.

The end of the Crimean War was proclaimed on 14 April 1856. Of the 310,000 Frenchmen sent out to fight, one out of three never returned.

Leo Tolstoy's writings ensured that Russians have always viewed their Crimean campaign as an epic struggle against foreign invaders, a national triumph of brave resistance. And, in a roundabout way, they are right, since, twenty-four short years later, subsequent politics restored to the Russians all the ground that they had lost.

As for the original incident that instigated the war, the Christian in-fighting at the Holy Sepulchre in Jerusalem, within a fortnight of the official end of the war, Orthodox priests and pilgrims were once again fighting their fellow Christians of other orders and smashing up the hallowed sanctum.

Two years after the war, on a sunny day in London's Hyde Park, Queen Victoria instituted a new medal, the Victoria Cross, to recognise great gallantry in the face of the enemy by all ranks. Until that day, only officers were ever given medals. Sixty-two individuals from the Crimean campaign were awarded the modest-looking bronze medal, reputedly cast from a captured Russian cannon.

Heroism was thereafter no longer the preserve of the British officer class. The whole country, personified by the cartoon John Bull, had bravely defended a weak Turkey against the might of Russia. Britain stood for justice and fair play on the side of the vulnerable. The next 'bullies' they would oppose, to defend Belgium in 1914 and Poland in 1939, would be Kaiser Wilhelm and Adolf Hitler.

The bravery of a soldier is tested, as many a battle in the Crimea clearly proved, far more when the odds are in doubt, death is everywhere and the most sensible option is to flee. Self-preservation is, after all, a powerful human instinct.

In his book *Crimea*, Orlando Figes summarises the key to the confused combat at Inkerman. 'In this sort of fighting the small combat unit was decisive. Everything came down to whether groups of men and their line commanders could keep their discipline and unity – whether they could organise themselves and stick together through the fight without losing nerve or running away out of fear.'

Inkerman ended with the panic of some Russian troops spreading like contagion until, in the words of a French officer, 'They were petrified.' Their headlong flight led to their massacre.

On the Allied side, after the first post-winter assaults on Sebastopol's defences and their costly failure, widespread demoralisation set in. One British officer wrote: 'Many a man would gladly lose an arm to get off these heights and leave the siege.'

Lieutenant Damas, a French officer, wrote: 'This war has to stop. It is cowardly. We are all Christians. We all believe in God and religion, and without that we would not be so brave.'

Even among the bravest of all the French forces, the Zouaves, made up of professional soldiers with unparalleled fighting experience, there were those who lost their reason, ran away to the Russians or committed suicide. Later they were to define such behaviour as 'trench madness', later still to be classified as shell shock or, today, post-traumatic stress. Many of those who suffered from it had for months previously been the bravest of the brave.

To me, the battles and the appalling suffering of the Crimean War, a microcosm of wars over the centuries in so many lands and for so many reasons, produced a thousand heroes and a thousand cowards, with very often a razor-sharp dividing line between the mental processes that decided who would be brave and who would cower.

* * *

War by its nature offers opportunities for courage and the making of heroes that seldom present themselves to the person in the street.

General Sir Peter de la Billière

Combat jammed so much adrenalin through your system that fear was rarely an issue; far more indicative of real courage was how you felt before the big operations when the implications of losing your life really had a chance to sink in. My personal weakness wasn't fear so much as the anticipation of it. If I had any illusions about personal courage, they always dissolved in the days or hours before something big, dread accumulating in my blood like some kind of toxin until I felt too apathetic to even tie my boots properly.

Sebastian Junger, *War*, 2010

II

Extreme Survival

'As an exhibition of self-control this should surely rank
above feats of heroism performed in battle, where there
are thousands of comrades to give inspiration'
Richard Harding Davis

The instinct of survival is so strong that individuals
managing to survive against all odds, rather than giving
up the struggle and accepting death, might be considered
stubborn rather than brave – donkeys not lions. To some
extent I would agree with this, but not in the remarkable case
of Douglas Mawson.

During the carnage of the 1914–1918 trench warfare, the
British government helped publicise the story of Captain Scott
and his men, including Captain Oates, as examples of heroic
and patriotic deaths. This was intended to bolster the morale
of the thousands of young men being sent to their own deaths
at the front line. As a result, most English schoolchildren of
the earlier half of the twentieth century learnt of the heroic
age of the late nineteenth and early twentieth centuries when
individuals made their names and reputations by exploring
Antarctica, chief among them Scott, Amundsen and Shackleton.

All three men achieved prodigious feats of discovery and undertook struggles against an unforgiving environment, but none, in my opinion, rivalled the sheer mental and physical tenacity of the Australian explorer, Sir Douglas Mawson, the ultimate hero of survival.

Scott died of slow starvation, extensive frostbite and hypothermia in a frozen sleeping bag between the stiff corpses of two good friends. That was in 1912, the same year that Douglas Mawson led the Australian expedition which first reached the South Magnetic Pole and mapped huge chunks of hitherto unexplored coastal territory. To achieve this, Mawson had split his team into various sledging groups in order to survey different regions of Adélie Land during the short Antarctic summer. All would have to return to their coastal bases by a set date when a ship would collect them and head back to Australia. Mawson himself planned to lead a three-man team with two sledges pulled by huskies. He hoped to complete an 800-mile return journey into the unknown.

As it turned out, the very day that Mawson's ship returned home to Australia, she received the news that Amundsen and his Norwegians had reached the South Pole first, and not long afterwards banner headlines across the world screamed out the news of Scott's death. As a result, public awareness of the incredible story of Mawson's own journey was minimal, and today, even in Australia, is little known.

Mawson was born in Yorkshire in 1882, but moved with his family at the age of two to sunny Australia, at a time when a great many Britons settled in the colonies. He became a geologist, which involved many rough travels in the outback. When Scott and Shackleton advertised for geologists, he applied to both, but ended up leading his own Australiansponsored expedition to investigate Adélie Land, a part of that great quadrant of the frozen continent nearest to Australia.

Despite the trials and tragedy that this chapter describes, Mawson's teams, by the time they sailed back to Australia in 1913, had added more to the maps of Antarctica than anyone else, having mapped some 2,000 miles of the unexplored coastline on which humans had first set foot only thirteen years before.

Of the thirty or so members of Mawson's team, all but a handful were Australian. Mawson's chosen methods of polar travel involved both manhaul and dog teams. Sledges from Norway and huskies from Greenland were loaded in London onto Mawson's ship, the *Aurora*, the dogs being under the charge of English army officer Lieutenant Ninnis and Swiss skiing and mountaineering expert Dr Xavier Mertz.

From Hobart in Tasmania they set sail for Antarctica on 2 December 1911, receiving, by telegraph, messages of encouragement from the King and Queen.

Men and dogs suffered from huge seas on the voyage south, during which the drinking water tanks were contaminated by sea water, and half of the ship's bridge was completely swept away by a single wave. Long days then passed in thick fog with icebergs on all sides. Only four months later in similar conditions a single iceberg the size of a castle was to sink the *Titanic*, the largest ship in the world. The icebergs encountered by the *Aurora* measured up to forty miles long and a hundred feet high.

A site for Mawson's main base was found at Cape Denison in Commonwealth Bay but, since the ship could not safely approach the beach, she anchored in the bay and lifeboats ferried prefab hut parts and general cargo to the land. This was hazardous due to constant high winds, but the work was all done by 19 January, when the *Aurora* returned to Australia to escape the imminent onset of the Antarctic winter.

At that moment, Mawson's men were utterly cut off in an unknown land on the edge of an immense ice cap far bigger than all India and all China combined. Inland of Mawson's hut, the ice fields rise to 12,000 feet and are over a mile in depth, covering great mountain ranges. All this ice is slowly seeping outwards and downwards and will eventually reach the coast. Nobody had wintered in the Adélie Land region before, and its uniquely ferocious weather was soon apparent to Mawson's team. Plenty of seal and penguin meat was, however, available in the bay, and the dog-men, Ninnis and Mertz, cut up over a ton of meat and blubber which they stored in an ice cave.

On the rare occasions when consecutive blizzards allowed, Mawson patrolled south to mark a route up the ice slope from the hut to the high polar plateau, eventually fixing flagpole markers at points two miles and three miles inland. By March such forays would be suicidal, and all the team's efforts were concentrated on preparations in and around the hut. The dogs roamed loose but mostly slept in the lee of the hut where they curled up and were soon covered by blown snow, often to be trodden upon by passing men. Driven snow would partially thaw in their coats, then freeze again, matting their fur into plate armour. At other times they would become frozen to the ice and would have to be chipped free with ice axes.

As the sunless polar winter advanced, it became clear that Mawson had selected his base at the most windy place on earth. Spiralling 'whirlies', or wind-devils, were common and easily capable of whisking up three-hundredweight steel objects and dropping them a hundred yards away. Whirlies moving over the sea close by the hut created 1,000-foot-high waterspouts. Drift snow filled the air, caking every nook and creating nil visibility conditions, so that a man checking a scientific recording instrument fifty yards from the hut could become instantly disorientated. Drift snow settling on a man's face would quickly freeze into an iron-hard mask framed by the hood of his jacket and his beard. Attempts to clear away this ice-mask in order to see, or merely to breathe, could cause painful scratches to the cornea, because of frozen eyelids. Facial hair, including eyelashes, were often torn out when the ice was removed, because the skin underneath was frozen and insensitive.

By mid-May the average wind speed recorded over a twenty-four-hour period was 90 mph, with gusts of over 200 mph. Mawson's men nicknamed their base the Home of the Blizzard.

The weather showed slight signs of improvement in August, so Mawson, with two others, managed to reach a point five miles inland and 1,500 feet above sea level, where they dug out an ice grotto, Aladdin's Cave, which would later prove to be a life-saving sanctuary.

By September, with winds averaging 60 mph most days, another group managed to travel fifty miles up and along the plateau. They returned exhausted and frostbitten and one man had experienced an interesting new cold affliction, when one of his eyelids froze solid so that he could no longer blink with it. His eyeball then began to freeze, so he rubbed the lid vigorously, whereupon it blistered badly, giving him the look of an actor in a horror film.

By October the monthly wind speed average had dropped to 57 mph and the sun had made a welcome reappearance. Mawson held a meeting to confirm the make-up of his various sledge teams and their goals. His own team's goal would be to travel to the furthest easternmost coastal region of Adélie Land with Ninnis, Mertz and their dogs as his companions.

On 16 November they left Aladdin's Cave, heading south and east on a route that crossed the upper reaches of great coastal glaciers riven with crevasses and jumbled ice formations. To plan the best direction to advance with minimal obstacles meant careful observation into the blinding glare. So, whenever their goggles misted up, the three men had to remove them, despite the obvious risk involved. Ninnis was the first to suffer from sun blindness. The pain was crippling, and Mawson applied zinc sulphate and cocaine tablets under the eyelids to lessen the feel of grit scraping across the retina.

A husky bitch began to give birth to a litter of puppies in a crevasse field, so the team at once pitched camp. As Mertz boiled the cooker, Ninnis, walking around the back of the tent, suddenly plunged up to his neck into a hidden abyss. Mawson hauled him out, and the tent was moved as soon as possible.

There followed many other equally lethal crevasse experiences involving whole sledges or several harnessed dogs hanging over apparently bottomless voids. Crevasses in Antarctic glaciers are known to reach 200 feet in depth, and many may be deeper still. Since they occur along the upper reaches of most Antarctic glaciers, which was precisely where Mawson's projected route needed to follow if he were to survey the coastline properly, the team were in constant danger.

The dogs found the unremitting blown drift snow their major problem, for this frozen spray caked their eyes so that every few minutes a whole team would have to stop whilst one of them scraped the snow away with a paw. Nonetheless, Mawson's desired progress rate of sixteen miles a day was, for a while, achieved. December, the month containing Antarctica's Midsummer Day, brought two or three periods of hot sun, a shade temperature of 34°F and a sticky snow surface that acted like treacle on the sledge runners, and the dogs could no longer haul the loads uphill. Towards evening the sun would sink, the snow harden and the workload ease.

In many areas the team fought their jolting way over sastrugi up to four feet high, ridges of iron-hard ice stretching across their route like endless deep furrows in a ploughed field. The men had to push and pull at the sledges, for the dogs alone could not manage such obstacles. Every four minutes one or other of the sledges would capsize, and the three exhausted men would then struggle to re-right and often to re-lash the load.

Blizzards of up to three days at a time kept them, frustrated and cramped, in their tiny tent. Mawson's rule was to cut the daily ration whenever a full ration was not 'earned' by achieving the set daily mileage. Frostbite was a constant danger, for many daily tasks could only be managed glove-less. Ninnis had special trouble, doubtless due to poor circulation, and spent many nights with only minimal sleep, due to the severe throbbing of inflamed fingers.

By mid-December, in sunny weather, Mertz led the way on skis, weaving through obstacles and singing Swiss moun-tain songs. On the night of the 13th, Mawson told the others that they had travelled over 300 miles so they would soon

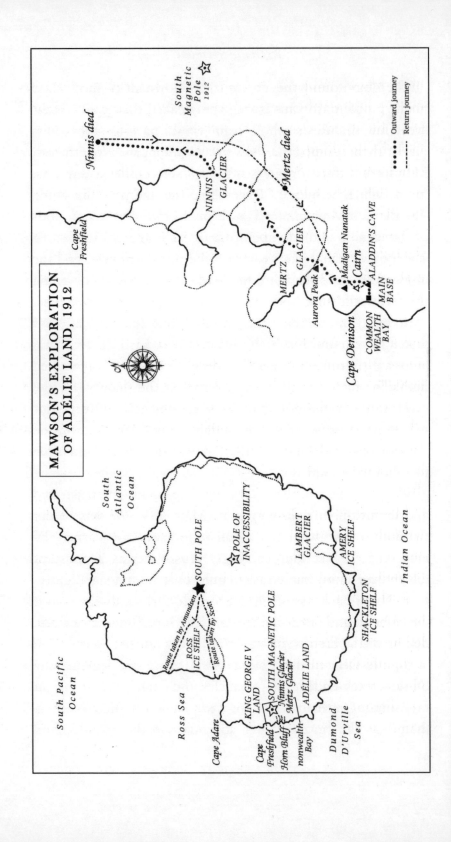

MAWSON'S EXPLORATION
OF ADÉLIE LAND, 1912

South
Magnetic
Pole
1912

Ninnis died

Mertz died

NINNIS
GLACIER

MERTZ
GLACIER

Cape
Freshfield

Madigan Nunatak

Aurora Peak

Cairn

ALADDIN'S CAVE

MAIN
BASE

Cape Denison

COMMON
WEALTH
BAY

····· Outward journey
‑ ‑ ‑ Return journey

N

South
Atlantic
Ocean

POLE OF
INACCESSIBILITY

SOUTH POLE

Route taken by Amundsen

Route taken by Scott

ROSS
ICE SHELF

LAMBERT
GLACIER

AMERY
ICE SHELF

SHACKLETON
ICE SHELF

Indian Ocean

South Pacific
Ocean

Ross Sea

Cape Adare

KING GEORGE V
LAND

SOUTH MAGNETIC POLE

Cape
Freshfield
Horn Bluff
nonwealth
Bay

Ninnis Glacier
Mertz Glacier

ADÉLIE LAND

Dumond
D'Urville
Sea

make a food dump for later retrieval and then, lightly laden, make a final dash eastwards to the planned longitude which constituted the eastern limit of their coastal survey. Then back to the dump and homeward-bound with just enough rations and time to make the base camp before the *Aurora*, on a tight schedule, called in to collect everyone. That was the plan, anyway.

Tired, thin and sore, but optimistic, the three men set out the following morning on the last leg with fully laden sledges, a clear sky and an unusually light breeze. At about noon, Mertz, out front on skis, lifted a ski stick and stopped. Then went on. This was his standard signal to Mawson to watch out for crevasses. But they were at the time in a flat smooth area away from the broken coastal slopes, so crevasses were unlikely.

However, when Mawson and his dogs reached the place where Mertz had paused, he did notice a faint indication of an old crevasse, but nothing likely to subside. Nonetheless he shouted a warning back to Ninnis, as was the normal drill.

Mertz stopped once more and this time gazed back intently without a signal. Alarmed, Mawson again halted his team and turned back. There was behind him a wide white world of endless snow, but no Ninnis, no dogs and no sledge.

Rushing back along the trail, and soon joined by Mertz, he came to a gaping hole eleven feet wide. Two sledge tracks led up to the fissure where Ninnis had made his approach on a slightly different line to Mawson's own trail. But there the Ninnis track ended.

'Cherub, Cherub.' Both men screamed out Ninnis's nick-name, as they gazed horrified into the void below, but the only response, a low yelp, came from a dog caught on an ice ledge just visible 150 feet down. It tried to crawl across the ledge, but its back was probably broken.

Mawson wrote: 'For three hours we called his name, but heard no response. The dog ceased to moan and lay unmoving. A chill draught rose out of the abyss. We felt that there was no hope.

'It was difficult to realise that Ninnis, who was a young giant in build, so jovial and so real but a few minutes before, should have vanished without even a sound. It seemed indeed so incredible that we half expected, on turning round, to find him standing there.'

They tied all their ropes together, but could not reach even as far as the dead dog's ledge.

They took stock of the situation, which did not look good. They were 2,400 feet above sea level and 315 miles from their coastal base. The slopes that descended north to the coast were hopelessly shattered by crevasse fields, and the sea ice just off the coast was mostly broken, offering no safe route back home.

Only the day before they had loaded their rear sledge with as much heavy gear as feasible, specifically because the front sledge would be more likely, in Mawson's experience, to collapse a weak crevasse. So when that rear sledge was lost, so was all the dog-food and all but one and a half week's rations of man-food. Lost, too, were the tent, complete with floor cover and poles, the shovel, the ice axe and all eating utensils. They were in dire straits and they knew it. There was no means of communication with anyone, anywhere.

Mawson wrote: 'Our dinner was thin soup made by boiling all the empty food bags. Not very sustaining, but it quenched our thirst. There was nothing for the dogs, but we tossed them some worn-out fur mitts, boot linings and spare leather straps, all of which they devoured.' As with all such groups of huskies, there were varying grades of sledging strength, and all the most powerful dogs had been attached to the heavier sledge of Ninnis.

Mawson said the words of the burial service, and the expedition set out westwards. Even by killing and eating the remaining dogs one by one, both men knew that they would need a good deal of luck and reasonable weather to make it back alive.

Mertz skied ahead through a maze of crevasses, and Mawson gave the dogs their heads. He wrote: 'In a wild race the dogs cut across crevasses, plunged over the lids of crevasses and thundered across the sunken ways. It was only our pace that saved us. We crashed into hummocks of ice and frequently capsized, rolling over and over, dogs, sledge and me, for yards at a stretch.'

That night, using the tent fly sheet which had somehow avoided stowage on the Ninnis sledge, Mertz erected a make-shift frame out of two half lengths of sledge runner and his own skis, all lashed together at the apex. This gave just enough room for the two sleeping bags laid on the snow within, but only one man could move at a time.

They killed the weakest dog, George, and fed him to the others, except for his liver which they boiled to supplement their own pathetic rations. They chewed in silence. 'We tried to concentrate our thoughts on our future, which loomed up sinister before us.'

Light snow fell for days, and clouds created total white-out. Without shadows, every ice bump became invisible, even when directly underfoot. The magnetic compass was useless, and without the sun, they relied for direction solely upon the trend of the sastrugi ridges, which the prevailing winds had chiselled into north–south channels. 'With our gaze straining for a hint as to direction, we stumbled on . . . The glare caused me bad sun-blindness and I had very little sleep due to the smarting of it, though Mertz treated both my eyes with zinc sulphate and cocaine.'

A second dog, Johnson, became too weak to walk, so he was strapped to the top of the sledge.

Unable even to see the direction of the sastrugi ridges, the men's only means of knowing which way to go was to probe with their booted feet below the ever-drifting snow in order to feel for the ridges.

That night they killed Johnson. The meat was 'tough, stringy and without a vestige of fat, but we crunched the bones and ate the skin until nothing remained'. The next day, only one dog, Ginger, could help the men haul the sledge. The bitch called Mary was so weak that her turn came to be carried on the sledge, the prelude to slaughter.

Five days of struggle in horrendous ice and weather conditions saw both men slowly starving and physically deteriorating. Their food supply totalled six ounces a day, eked out from their standard sledging rations, and ten ounces of meat from their dogs. They drank water laced with a sprinkle of Primus spirit. On the seventh day they were halted by bad visibility, coupled with a major crevasse field running across their front. To advance in such conditions would be risky in the extreme, so they camped and shot Pavlova, a bitch unable to continue.

They stewed Pavlova's sinews and gristle to make 'jelly soup . . . The paws took longest to cook, but even they proved digestible.' They cracked the long bones open with their spade to get at the marrow.

They celebrated Christmas Day with dog soup. On Boxing Day they improvised a sail from their tent cloth and two ski sticks. A 30 mph wind helped them up steep slopes which, in soft snow with only one remaining dog, would otherwise have proved a killer for the two starving men.

To stew the meat enough to render it digestible meant leaving the cooker on for long stints, and this caused the improvised tent to reach thawing temperature along the walls and, worse still, at ground level, so, since there was no rubber floor mat, the sleeping bags quickly became soaked outside and soggy inside, adding hugely to the men's misery quota. As soon as the cooker was turned off, the tent cooled, where-upon the wet walls and sleeping bags froze solid, except against the two men's bodies which remained damp.

Neither man was aware that eating husky livers could be catastrophic to their bodies. In 1971 scientists were to discover and prove that a mere four ounces of dog liver contained a lethally toxic dose of vitamin A. Mertz and Mawson, in an already weakened state, were to consume over sixty deadly doses. As the symptoms grew in each man (much more slowly with Mawson), they put them down to hunger and exhaustion.

On 28 December Ginger finally succumbed. His skull was boiled whole, and each man ate from opposite sides of it, passing it between them. 'The brain,' Mawson noted, 'was certainly the most appreciated and nutritious section.'

Mawson spent four hours at a time cracking and boiling bones in order to extract the nutriment for future use. He could only squat to do this, which gave him severe cramps, but the tent was too small to allow both the men either to lie down or to sit comfortably on a rolled-up bag.

Fifteen days after Ninnis died, they finally reached a stretch of flat snowfields, which gave them good enough going to achieve fifteen miles in a day, but that same evening a new threat surfaced. Mawson noticed that Mertz was not his normal cheerful, optimistic self. He had muttered that he *hated* the diet of dog meat, but otherwise gave no hint of any reason for his unusual mood change. Next morning atrocious conditions forced the men to make camp after stumbling about on iron-hard slippery ice for two hours. A day later at the dawn of new year with conditions of untravellable whiteout and two tent-bound days, both men suffered a 'dull, painful gnawing sensation in the abdomen', and Mertz, although technically starving, lost his appetite. Something, Mawson suspected, must be seriously wrong with him.

The night of 3 January was bitingly cold but clear. So they tried to travel, but the wind cut, knife-like, through their emaciated frames. After a mere five miles progress, they had to make camp when Mertz, with badly frostbitten fingers, suffered a severe attack of dysentery. For two more days the Swiss doctor's condition prevented travel, and the time ticked by towards the end of January, the start of the polar winter, the date when the *Aurora* would come and go, and, worst of all, valuable rations were being eaten for no mileage gained.

Scott was delayed in similar circumstances the previous year by two of his injured men, Evans and Oates. If Scott had abandoned those two, he and his other two companions would not have died. But circumstances made such a course impossible for Scott because, to summarise a complex set of events, Scott was himself unable to travel by the time his last companion was dead. Mawson, on the other hand, was still just fit enough to make it back to base if he had allowed Mertz to simply die, rather than to stay and nurse him over a period of several crucial days.

A day of good travel weather passed by, but Mertz said he still felt too ill to travel. Then, on 6 January he tried to walk beside Mawson, who towed the sledge. He soon grew weak and agreed to ride *on* the sledge. But then he became badly chilled, so they had to camp again.

'Starvation,' Mawson wrote, 'combined with surface frost-bite, caused wholesale peeling of our skin and our bodies were rubbed raw in many places. Chafing on the march had developed into large open sores and, as we never took our clothes off, the peelings of skin and hair worked their way down into our socks, from whence we would remove them.' He added, 'At night I tossed about without sleep, for our chances of reaching safety were now slipping silently and relentlessly away. I was aching to get on, but there could be no question of abandoning my companion whose condition now set the pace.'

On 7 January the two men agreed that they would set out the following morning with Mertz strapped to the sledge load in his sleeping bag. It was, therefore, a huge psychological blow to Mawson that, when dawn came, he found Mertz once again attacked by dysentery and as weak as a lamb.

One of Mawson's ears lost its outer layers of skin, which came away in a single caste, and deep sores opened up at both corners of his mouth. Movement made him disorien-tated. But he peeled away Mertz's soiled sleeping bag, did his best to rub the faeces from the doctor's peeling legs with their many open sores, and then re-inserted the patient into his stinking bag.

Mertz relapsed that evening into madness. He screamed, raged at Mawson, vomited and, at one point, rammed one frostbitten finger between his teeth and tore at it, as though at a chicken bone, until the end came away, which he then spat into the snow between the two sleeping bags.

When Mertz quietened for a while, Mawson dressed the stump of the mutilated finger as best he could, but he knew Mertz would never leave the tent alive, and that he himself had, in all likelihood, sacrificed his own thin chances of survival by lingering alongside the stricken Mertz. He had heard of the Eskimos in Canada who, faced with similar delays caused by sick, injured or simply elderly companions, sacrificed personal emotions for common sense, and abandoned the weak to cope for themselves. Mawson knew that, outside the miserable confines of the tent, good travel conditions existed, and he thought of his beloved Paquita, the woman back home that he loved and planned to marry.

That night Mertz turned violent in their fragile shelter, forcing Mawson to hold him down until he lapsed into unconsciousness. A few hours later Mawson touched his hand and found that he was dead. Dragging the skeletal corpse from the tent, Mawson constructed a snow cairn, and for the second time in a month spoke the words of the burial service. He cut their sledge down to make it more wieldy and fashioned the resulting spare runners into a crude cross, which he placed by the gaunt remains of the once sturdy doctor.

For ten hours Mawson, severely weakened by the long tent-bound days on minimal rations, fought the overwhelming temptation to give in, to gorge on the remaining rations in one great binge and then, as Oates had done the previous year, to strip off his outer clothes, leave the tent, and allow the cold to numb his senses into a merciful escape from the pain and the hunger or the desperate struggle for survival against huge odds that was the only alternative.

His diary records: 'I wondered how I would break and pitch camp single-handed. There appeared little hope of reaching the Hut, still 100 miles away. It would be so easy to sleep in the bag, and the weather was cruel outside. But inaction is hard to bear, so I braced myself, determined to put up a good fight.'

If he could not make it to the hut, then at least he would try to reach a known point or major feature where a search party the following summer might stand a chance of finding his tent, his body, and his diaries with their survey notes.

Two days of blizzard cleared on 11 January, allowing Mawson good conditions to set out, painfully aware that in four days' time his team and the others were, at the latest and on his own instructions, due back at the hut in readiness for the arrival of the *Aurora*. Many obstacles still lay between him and the hut, including a great glacier, a long steep climb, and a region as badly crevassed as any in Antarctica.

Within an hour of his leaving Mertz's burial site, Mawson's feet felt 'curiously lumpy and sore'. For over a week during Mertz's terminal illness, Mawson had kept his warm inner socks on, but now, sitting on his sledge, he removed his boots and socks and was shocked to find that 'the thickened skin of my soles had separated, in each case as a complete layer, and abundant watery fluid had escaped, saturating the socks. The new skin beneath was abraded and raw, several of my toes were black and festering near the tips, with their nails puffed and loose. I began to wonder if there was ever to be a day without some new and special disappointment.'

He smeared his damaged feet with lanolin cream and bound the old skin castes of each sole back in place with bandages. He then donned six pairs of woollen socks, fur boots and crampon over-shoes. His feet remained agonisingly tender, but he forced himself to achieve five miles before he stopped.

For thirty-six hours a blizzard kept Mawson tent-bound. He spent it caring for the various raw patches all over his body, his festering fingernails and his frostbitten nose. On 13 January a long downhill stretch of rough blue ice caused a day of intense pain to the bleeding pads of his feet. But, one by one, he counted off the torturous miles to the hut and travelled whenever weather conditions allowed.

When the sun's rare heat melted patches of surface snow, the sledge runners clogged and jammed, so precious time was wasted scraping great lumps of wet snow from their surface. When clouds hid the sun, especially in areas of crevasses, Mawson had to camp, rather than grope blindly through shadowless white-out.

On 17 January, two days after he should have been back at the hut and ready for the arrival of the *Aurora*, bad luck struck again. Hauling through deep snow up a steep incline, he plunged to the full length of his fourteen-foot manhaul rope into a crevasse and dangled there, held only by his sledge which had snagged above him on one lip of the crevasse.

Mawson's diary: 'I looked around. The crevasse was sheer-walled down to the blue depths below. My clothes were full of wet snow and I was chilled. In my weak condition the prospect of climbing out seemed very poor indeed, but a great effort brought a knot in the rope into my grasp and, after a short rest, I was able to draw myself up and reach another.' Completely exhausted and with raw, bleeding, frost-bitten fingers, he reached the lip of the crevasse and was, at last, poised to crawl to safety, when another chunk of the crevasse-lid collapsed and Mawson once again swung round and round in space.

'Exhausted and chilled, I knew I was done for. I had no more strength to try again. It was to be a miserable and slow end, but I almost looked forward to the peace of the great release . . . But then my thoughts returned to reality. I remembered how Providence had brought me so far, and I told myself, "Nothing is impossible."

'My strength was fast ebbing. In a few minutes it would be too late. New power seemed to come to me in one last tremendous effort, and I reached the surface, this time to crawl out to safety. Then reaction set in, I lost consciousness and woke sometime later covered in fresh snow and numb with cold.'

Ahead of Mawson lay one last major obstacle, an uphill stretch riven with fissures, but, his ever-active mind still far from beaten, Mawson devised a rope ladder system which, over the days to come, saved him many times from a dangling death.

By the late evening of 19 January, against all expectations, a break in the weather allowed a view just ahead of a 500-foot-high wall of crevassed crags which Mawson knew signalled the end of the great broken zone. He had now only to climb a gentler slope for a height of 3,000 feet in order to reach the final plateau that led, at length, to Aladdin's Cave. But, with his rations all but finished, a new blizzard kept him tent-bound until the 24th.

An attempt at travel on the 25th ended with a snow storm.

'I did not feel well enough to go on,' he wrote. 'In the tent, as the hours went by, the snow piled ever higher on both sides, so that the cloth pressed down on my sleeping bag. I became as buried.'

On the 26th, with only four pounds of food left, he dug himself out of his snowed-in shelter and 'struggled blindly through the whirl of seething snow'. The weather cleared on the 28th and allowed Mawson a view which flooded him with joy – the great sweep of the level plateau leading down to Commonwealth Bay and the hut. The next day, with but a pocketful of raisins and a few ounces of chocolate remaining, Mawson ran into his first and last bit of good luck; a freshly made snow cairn built but five hours earlier by a search party from the hut. Had he passed a few hundred yards to either side of the cairn, he would have missed it. A bag lashed to the cairn included a good supply of food and basic directions to Aladdin's Cave, still a distance of twenty-three miles. Captain Scott and his sledge team had died the previous winter when a blizzard held them up a mere eleven miles short of their food dump.

Various weather problems and his lack of crampons delayed the emaciated Mawson for three more days before reaching the cave, where further bad weather marooned him for seven long days only five miles up the icy slopes above the hut. Having no proper crampons, he knew that he could only safely attempt this final descent in nil wind conditions and with reasonable visibility. Finally, on 8 February, using makeshift crampons fashioned from planks studded with bent nails he had extracted from an old box in the cave, Mawson crept cautiously down the icy hill.

A group at work near the hut spotted him and rushed up with yells of joyous greeting. None could tell whether he was

Mertz, Ninnis or Mawson, so much had he changed to a shadow of his former self. The *Aurora*, they told him, had waited as long as she safely could and had finally sailed away that very day, leaving a small group of volunteers to stay for a year just in case Mawson's group still made it back. So Mawson would have to remain in the Home of the Blizzard through another wind-battered year, but what did that matter in the ecstasy of knowing that he had made what polar-men around the world later described as the greatest solo survival story of all time.

For ten months he recuperated, for he was very near to death. He recorded: 'I am an invalid. My legs have swollen very much. I am shaken to pieces by that awful journey.' He had set out, mostly muscle, at fifteen stone (ninety-five kilos) and, back at the hut, mere skin and bone, weighed less than eight stone. Like Mertz, he had unknowingly eaten enough vitamin A overload from the huskies' livers to kill most men, even without his horrendous struggle and emaciated state. His survival remains to this day a miracle of mind over matter of heroic proportions.

During the ensuing winter at the hut, the radio operator broke down and went mad under the stress of the long dark days and months. Mawson proposed marriage to Paquita by telegraph and was accepted (despite warning her that his hair had all fallen out). They lived happily together until his death by natural causes in 1958.

*   *   *

Mental attitude is like a lens to adrenalin. Optimism can focus the effects of adrenalin and produce intense energy and power. So . . .

Adrenalin + Optimism + Action = Courage and Strength

Adrenalin + Pessimism + Inaction = Fear and Lack of Resolve

Dr Patrick Tissington, 2011

Self-preservation and the will to survive will keep a person going through fearful circumstances, but usually only up to a certain point, and then the mind suggests that immediate death by giving up will be preferable to ongoing agony.

Ranulph Fiennes, 1979

Acknowledgements

M y thanks to all those who helped me research the heroes of this book, including Miles Barton, Dr Joanna Bellis, Brian Best, Tony Brown, Hugo Burnand, Alex Caldon, Rod Campbell, Peter Godwin, Philip Groom, Graham Melvin, Andrew Hoult, Fergal Keane, David Kelley, Mike Kobold, Jessica Lee, Michael Levenson, Duncan Massey, Laura Mayes, Arabella McIntyre-Brown, Graham Melvin, Dave Morris, Dave Pengelly, Andy Simpson, John Simpson, Dr Patrick Tissington, Hugh and Catherine Wright, and Robert and Nicola Wright.

Also to my long-suffering family for my frequent visits to the writing-stable and my constant requests for data and names from the wifely laptop.

My thanks also to Jill Firman for all the hard work deciphering my handwritten originals and for producing the finished results on time. Also to Rupert, Juliet, Kate and Kerry at Hodder for their key parts in the book's existence from its conception to your owning it!

And to all heroic individuals and groups past, present and future.

RF

Picture Acknowledgements

© akg-images/ullstein bild: 8. © AP Photo/U.S. Navy: 1 above left.
© Hugo Burnand: 10 above left. © Corbis: 2 Above right/Colin McPherson,
3 above/Jon Jones, 3 below/David Turnley, 6 above/Heng Sinith, 6 below/
Bettmann, 7 above/Kevin R. Morris, 7 below/Michael Freeman,
9 above right, 10 above right/Jon Hrusa, 10 below and 11 above/Howard
Burditt, 11 below/Philimon Bulawayo, 12 above/Roger Fenton.
© Getty Images: 2 above left/Abdelhak Senna/AFP, 2 below/Scott Peterson.
Douglas Mawson *The Home of The Blizzard* 1915, photographs by Douglas
Mawson and Frank Hurley: 15, 16 centre right and below right.
© Metropolitan Police, Public Affairs: 4 above left. © Mirrorpix/Andy Rosie:
4 below right. © National Army Museum London/Bridgeman Art Library:
12 below. © News International: 4 above right. © NTPL/Geoff Morgan: 16
below. © Ian Parnell: 9 below. Private collections: 5 above left and below. 9
above left, 13 above and 16 above/Bridgeman Art Library. © Reuters: 1 above
right. SOAS Library (MS291571)/photo Glenn Ratcliffe: 5 above right. State
Library of New South Wales Collection: 15 above. © TopPhoto: 4 below left.
© U.S. Navy: 1 below. © Wellcome Library London: 13 below.

Notes on Sources

1. Hunted
Extracts from *Lone Survivor* by Marcus Luttrell & Patrick Robinson, published by Little, Brown and Co. Used by permission of the publisher.
Extract from *WAR* by Sebastian Junger, © 2010. Published by 4th Estate, an imprint of HarperCollins. Reprinted by permission of HarperCollins Publishers Ltd.

2. Going Back into Hell
Extracts from David Pengelly are used by permission of the author.
Extracts from Dick Coombes are used by permission of the author.
Extracts from Constable Miles Barton are used by permission of the author.
Extract from Alan Briars is used by permission from the author.

3. Endurance in the Face of Terror
Multiple extracts from *An Ordinary Man* by Paul Rusesabagina. Published by Bloomsbury UK.
Cartoon caption taken from *Kigali journal Kangura*, 1994.

Extracts from *Rwanda: Death, Despair and Defiance*. Published by African Rights.

Extract taken from *The Bishop of Rwanda* by John Rucyahana. Published by Thomas Nelson.

Extracts from *The Rwanda Crisis: History of Genocide* by G. Prunier. Published by C. Hurst & Co. Publishers Ltd. Used by permission of the publishers.

Extract from *Shake Hands with the Devil: The Failure of Humanity in Rwanda* by Romeo Dallaire. Published by Arrow Books. Reprinted by permission of The Random House Group Ltd.

4. Small But Great
Extracts from *Gladys Aylward: The Little Woman* by Gladys Aylward © Gladys Aylward. Published by Moody Publishers. Used by permission of the publisher.

5. 'To Kill the Beast'
Extracts were taken from *The History of the German Resistance 1933–45*, written by: Claus von Stauffenberg / Peter Hoffmann. Published by McGill-Queens University Press.

6. Daredevil Heroes
Extracts taken from *Risk Taking and Personality* by Michael R. Levenson. From *Journal of Personality and Social Psychology*, Vol 58(6), June 1990, 1073–1080. Used by permission.

Extract taken from Joe Simpson's review of *The White Spider* by Heinrich Harrer.

Extracts from *The White Spider* by Heinrich Harrer, © 1958. Published by HarperCollins. Reprinted by permission of HarperCollins Publishers Ltd.

Extracts from *Eiger Dreams* by Jon Krakauer. Published by Lyons Press.
Chief Guide's edict was found in *Grindelwald Echo*.
Extracts taken from *Risk Taking and Personality* by Michael R. Levenson. From *Journal of Personality and Social Psychology*, Vol 58(6), June 1990, 1073–1080. Used by permission.

7. The Family
Extracts from *Children of Cambodia's Killing Fields* by Dith Pran. Published by Yale University Press. Used by permission of the publisher.

10. War Makes or Breaks
Article on the Crimean War by William Russell, 1850's, from the *London Times*. Used by permission of *The Times* and NI Syndication.
Extract from *WAR* by Sebastian Junger, © 2010. Published by 4th Estate, an imprint of HarperCollins. Reprinted by permission of HarperCollins Publishers Ltd.

11. Extreme Survival
Extracts from *Home of the Blizzard* by Douglas Mawson. Published by Wakefield Press, Australia.

Every reasonable effort has been made to acknowledge the ownership of the copyrighted material included in this book. Any errors that may have occurred are inadvertent, and will be corrected in subsequent editions provided notification is sent to the author and publisher.

Select Bibliography

Chapter 1
Marcus Luttrell and Patrick Robinson, *Lone Survivor*, Little
  Brown, 2009

Chapter 3
African Rights Report, *Rwanda: Death, Despair and Defiance*,
  1994
Gérard Prunier, *The Rwanda Crisis: History of a Genocide*,
  Columbia University Press, 1995
John Rucyahana, *The Bishop of Rwanda*, Thomas Nelson,
  1982
Paul Rusesabagina, *An Ordinary Man*, Bloomsbury, 2007

Chapter 4
Gladys Aylward and Christine Hunter, *Gladys Aylward: the
  Little Woman*, Moody Bible Institute, 1974
Alan Burgess, *The Small Woman*, Pan Books, 1969

Chapter 5
Peter Hoffmann, *The History of the German Resistance
  1933-45*, McGill-Queen's University Press, 1996

Chapter 6
Heinrich Harrer, *The White Spider*, Harper Perennial, 2005

Chapter 7
Dith Pran, *Children of Cambodia's Killing Fields*, Yale
    University Press, 1997

Chapter 8
Daniel Defoe, *A Journal of the Plague Year*, Penguin Classics,
    2003

Chapter 9
Peter Godwin, *The Fear*, Picador, 2010

Chapter 10
Orlando Figes, *Crimea*, Allen Lane, 2010

Chapter 11
Lennard Bickel, *Mawson's Will*, Stein & Day, 1977
Sir Douglas Mawson, *The Home of the Blizzard*, St Martin's
    Griffin, 1998

Index